Gender, School and Society

Gender, School and Society

Prof. Noushad Husain

Principal

College of Teacher Education

MANUU, Asansol

SP SHIPRA

SHIPRA

(2021, First Published in 2018)

Rs. 1400, US$ 56

ISBN: 978-93-86262-93-6

2024 Impression

Gender, School and Society

Published by:
SHIPRA PUBLICATIONS
LG 18-19, Pankaj Central Market,
I.P. Ext., Patparganj, Delhi 110092
11 47322068; 22235152/ 6152; 9650028065
info@shiprapublication.com
www.shiprapublication.com

The Author Gratefully Acknowledge His Indebtedness to

God

For His Mercy

Dedicated to My Beloved
Father Zakir Husain
And
Mother Aiysha Begum
Who Taught Me the First Word

Preface

The meaning and experience of being a boy or a girl is not the same across different social groups, regions and time-periods. A guiding note by NCTE rightly points out the need to examine how we learn and challenge these gendered roles in society, through a variety of institutions such as the family, caste, religion, culture, media, law and the state. Unequal access of education to girls is a well-documented reality. But, the concerns of gender-just education go beyond access to schools; gender identity construction is influenced by forces at home and in society.

In order to enforce gender parity, teachers need to understand and examine the role of the school, society, curriculum, textbooks and the media. Gender stereotypes need to be challenged. Gender equality is a prerequisite to social progress and sustainable development. Students will be expected to observe and study the distribution of roles and responsibilities in schools and classrooms, rituals and school routines, processes of disciplining distinctly as for girls and boys, and in classroom interaction. Teachers need to question stereotypes and help students rethink their beliefs. This book explains representation of gendered roles, relationships and ideas in textbooks and curricula, examining how schools nurture or challenge creation of young people as masculine and feminine selves.

This book is an attempt to help students and teachers comprehend various interconnected aspects regarding gender and society. The book looks at how education plays a vital role in promoting gender equity and gender equality. The book looks at how education plays a vital role in promoting gender equity and gender equality. I considered various books, online journals, blogs and different websites during the composition of this book.

The book consists of 24 chapters with long references of index. An outstanding feature of this book is that it has been written in an easily understanding and simple language.

I will be grateful to the, educationists, teachers, researchers and teacher educators, if they offer me their valuable suggestions and comments about this book.

First of all I thank a lot of my indebtedness to "God for His Mercy" because without the mercy of God, the present book could not be completed.

He gave me direction, knowledge, support and patience to write down this book.

I would like to show my gratitude towards all those thinkers, writers, authors and publishers whose works have been consulted, quoted and abstracted to make the book up-to-date and interesting.

With great pleasure, I express my grateful thanks to my beloved Father Mr. Zakir Husain, Mother Mrs. Aishya Begum, Wife Razda Khan, Sons Arsh Husain & Areeb Husain, Brother Shahab Husain and other family members for their encouragement and support.

In the end I am grateful to Shipra Publications for publishing this book within the shortest time with accuracy and style.

Lastly, I offer this book to all those academicians, scientists, researchers, teachers, teacher educators and policy makers who want to promote gender equity and gender equality in the society through education.

Prof. (Dr.) Noushad Husain

Contents

Preface vii

1. **Introduction to Gender** 1
Concept and Meaning of Sex / 1; Concept and Meaning of Gender / 2; Difference between Sex and Gender / 4; Fundamental Concepts of Gender / 4

2. **Gender, Sexuality and Sexual Development** 8
Human Sexuality / 8; Development of Sexuality / 11; Stages of Psycho-sexual Development / 13; Gender, Body Image and Role Models / 15; Sites of Conflicts: Social and Emotional / 19

3. **Masculinity and Femininity** 23
Characteristics/Traits of Masculinity/Femininity / 23; What is Masculinity? / 24; What is Femininity? / 25

4. **Patriarchy and Matriarchy** 27
What is Patriarchy? / 27; What is Matriarchy? / 28; Difference between Patriarchy and Matriarchy / 29; Patriarchal and Matriarchal Families / 30; Living Examples of Matrilineal Societies in India / 31

5. **Social Construction of Gender** 32
Social Constructionism / 32; Assumptions of Social Constructionism / 32; Social Construction of Gender / 33; Factors Responsible for the Social Construction of Gender / 35; Causes of Social Construction of Gender during Development / 36

6. **Sex Typing, Sex Roles, Gender Roles, Gender Stereotypes and Gender Based Division and Valuation of Work** 39
Sex Typing And Sex Roles / 39: Sex Typing / 39; Sex Roles / 39; Some Sex Stereotyped Behaviours for Males and Females / 40; Factors Influencing Sex Typing / 40; Problems for Working Women in Community / 42;
Gender Roles / 43: Meaning and Concept of Gender Roles / 43; Characteristics of Gender Roles / 44; Types of Gender Roles / 44; Gender Roles and Relationships Matrix / 45; Level of Analysis / 45; Category of Analysis / 46; Models of Gender Roles / 46; Gender Roles in India / 47;
Gender Stereotypes / 48: Female Gender Stereotypes / 48; Male Gender Stereotypes / 49; Four Basic Kinds of Gender Stereotypes / 50; How can we Challenge Gender Stereotypes? / 50; Influence of the Family on Gender

Typing / 50; Gender Roles in Children of Gay and Lesbian Parents / 51; Extra Familial Influences on Gender Roles / 51;
Gender Based Division and Valuation of Work / 52: Gender-based Division of Labour / 53; Exploring Attitudes towards Gender / 53

7. **Feminism** 54
Meaning and Definitions of Feminism / 54; Objectives of Feminism / 55; Approaches or Types of Feminism / 55; Waves of Feminism / 57; Feminism in India / 58; Phases of Feminism in India / 59

8. **Women Empowerment** 62
Definition and Conceptual Framework / 62; Reasons for Women Empowerment / 63; Characteristics of Women Empowerment / 64; Importance of Women Empowerment / 65; Major Issues Concerning Women Empowerment in India / 65; Ways and Means of Achieving Women Empowerment / 66; Government Initiatives for Women Empowerment in India / 67; Legislative Measures for Safeguarding Women's Interest / 67; Constitutional Provisions for Empowering Women in India / 67; Key Challenges for Women Empowerment in India / 68

9. **Gender Equality and Equity: In Relation with Caste, Class, Race, Religion, Region, Ethnicity and Disability** 69
Gender Inequality / 69; Gender Equality and Gender Equity / 72; Caste and Gender Issues / 76; Income, Class and Gender Issues / 76; Race and Gender Issues / 77; Religion and Gender Issues / 77; Region and Gender Issues / 78; Ethnicity and Gender Issues / 78; Disability and Gender Issues / 79

10. **Changing Status of Women in India** 80
Women Education in Indian History / 80; Social Reform and Muslim Women / 83; Women's Participation in the Freedom Movement / 83; Women Social Reformers of India / 85; Raja Rammohun Roy / 85; Ishwar Chandra Vidyasagar / 87; Swami Vivekananda / 88; Sir Syed Ahmad Khan / 89; Mahatma Jotiba Govindrao Phule / 91; Swami Dayanand Saraswati / 92; Gandhi and Women's Rights / 92; Nehru and Women's Rights / 93; Impact of the Reforms Movement / 94

11. **Issues and Concerns of Transgender** 95
Who are Transgender People? / 95; Problems Faced by Transgender in India / 96; Rights Granted under Indian Law to Transgender / 96; India Court Recognizes Transgender People as Third Gender / 97; Challenges for Education of Transgender / 97; Strategies or Solutions for Transgender / 98; India's First Transgender School / 98

12. **Violence against Women** 100
Meaning of Violence / 100; Violence within Home / 100; Violence Outside Home / 107

13. **Gender Equality and Constitutional Framework of India** 113
Constitutional Rights/Provisions to Ensure Dignity of Women / 113; Legal Rights to Women / 115; Parliamentary Provisions to Ensure Dignity of Women / 117; Major Crimes against Women / 117

14. **RESOLVING ISSUES RELATED TO WOMEN AND GIRL CHILD** 121
Female Foeticide and Infanticide / 121; Sex Ratio / 123; Factors Affecting Overall Sex Ratio / 123; Sexual Harassment of Women at Work Place / 123; Honour Killing / 125; Dowry / 126; Child Marriage / 128; Property Rights / 128; Divorce / 129; Widowhood / 131; Identification of Sexual Abuse/Violence and Its Verbalization / 131

15. **GENDER AND LAW** 133
Laws related to Rape / 133; Laws related to Dowry / 134; Laws related to Remarriage / 134; Laws related to Divorce / 135; Laws related to Property Inheritance / 137; Laws Related to Trafficking / 137; Indian Constitution / 138; Women's Reservation Bill / 138; The Indian Constitution and Provisions for Women / 139; Human Rights and Women's Right / 139; Legal Aspects related to Women / 139; Declining Sex Ratio / 140; Female Foeticide / 142; Violence against Women / 143; Domestic Violence Act / 143; Sexual Harassment at Work Place Act / 144; Indecent Representation of Women (Prohibition Act) / 144; Cybercrime / 145; Sexual and Reproductive Health and Rights (SRHR) / 145; Sexual and Reproductive Health and Rights (SRHR) / 148; Gender Discrimination and Sexual and Reproductive Rights / 151; SRHR and Violence against Women / 151

16. **COMMISSIONS AND COMMITTEES ON GIRLS EDUCATION** 152
University Education Commission or Radhakrishnan Commission (1948-49) / 152; National Committee on Women's Education or Durgabai Deshmukh Committee (1958-1959) / 153; National Council of Women's Education (1962) / 154; Bhaktavatsalam Committee (1963) / 154; Indian Education Commission or Kothari Commission (1964-1966) / 155; National Council for Women's Education in its meeting held in 1968 / 155; National Policy on Education (1968) / 156; Status of Women in India (1974) / 156; Setting up of National Core Group / 156; National Policy on Education (NPE) - 1986 / 157; Programme of Action (POA) - 1992 / 157; National Commission for Women (1992) / 158; National Perspective for Women's Education (1998-2000) / 158; National Curriculum Framework for School Education (2000) / 158; National Policy for the Empowerment of Women in 2001 / 159; CABE Committee on Girls Education and Common School System (2005) / 159; Sarva Shiksha Abhiyan (SSA) - 2001-02 / 161; National Programme of Education for Girls at Elementary Levels (NPEGEL) - July 2003 / 162; Kasturba Gandhi Balika Vidyalaya (KGBV) - 2004 / 163; Right to Education (RTE) Act, 2009 / 163; Policy Initiatives (Including Current Laws) for the Recognition of the Concept of Transgender and Third Gender / 163

17. **ADDRESSING SEXUAL HARASSMENT AND VIOLENCE: IN FAMILY, NEIGHBOURHOOD AND OTHER FORMAL AND INFORMAL INSTITUTIONS** 164
Sexual Harassment against Women / 164; Types of Sexual Harassment / 166; Extensity of Sexual Harassment / 166; Effects of Sexual Harassment / 167; Steps to Address Sexual Harassment / 167; Violence against Women / 168; Institutions Redressing Sexual Harassment and Abuse / 172

18. **SCHEMES FOR GIRLS EDUCATION AND DEVELOPMENT** 174
Women Welfare and Empowerment Schemes of Government of India / 174; Swadhar Greh / 179; 2. Central Government Sponsored Schemes for Child Protection and Welfare / 182

19. **GENDER AND SOCIETY** 186
History and Current Scenario of Indian Women / 186; Modern Indian Women's Problems / 187; Issues Related to Indian Women / 189; Gender Roles in Society through Variety of Institutions / 190

20. **GENDER, POWER AND EDUCATION** 194
Gender Identities and Socialization Practices / 194; Socialization / 196; Gender Socialization / 197; Family and Gender Socialization / 197; School and Gender Socialization / 199; Other Formal and Informal Organizations and Gender Socialization / 201

21. **GENDER AND SCHOOL** 203
Gender Bias / 203; Gender Bias in Education / 203; Gender Bias in School Enrollments / 204; Gender Bias in Dropouts / 205; Gender Bias in Household Responsibilities / 206; Social Attitudes towards Girl's Education / 206; Value accorded to Women's Education / 207; Issues related to Gender in School / 207; Perception of Safety at School, Home and Community Schools / 210; Adult and Non-Formal Education for Women's Development / 212; Importance of Vocational Training and Income Generation for Women / 213; Gender Equality / 213

22. **GENDER ISSUES IN CURRICULUM** 218
Curriculum and the Gender Question / 219; Role of Curriculum in Reinforcing Gender Issues / 221; Gender and the Hidden Curriculum / 223; Aspects of Hidden Curriculum / 225; Gender in Text and Context / 227; Textbooks and Gender / 227; Teacher as an Agent of Change / 230

23. **GENDER AND MASS MEDIA** 233
Women as Depicted in Mass Media / 233; Women in Cinema/Films / 234; Portrayal of Women on Television / 234; Portrayal of Women in Advertisements / 235; Portrayal of Women in Print Media / 235; Portrayal of Women on Internet / 235; Impact of Mass Media on Women / 236; Indecent Representation of Women (Prohibition) Act, 1987 / 236; Recommendations / 237

24. **GENDER SENSITIZATION** 239
Definitions of Gender Sensitization / 239; Need for Gender Sensitization / 239; Process of Gender Sensitization / 240; Gender Sensitization Strategy / 242; The Teacher as Facilitator / 243; Need for Gender Sensitization in Schools / 243; Strategies/Measures of Schools to Sensitize Gender / 243; Role of Curriculum in Gender Sensitization / 244; Role of Co-Curricular Activities in Gender Sensitization / 245; Role of Community Based Activities / 245; Role of Parents in Gender Sensitization / 245; Role of Media / 245

Bibliography 262

1

Introduction to Gender

Sociologists and most other social scientists view sex and gender as conceptually distinct. Sex denotes biological characteristics and exists along a spectrum from male to female. Gender, on the other hand, denotes social and cultural characteristics that are assigned to different sexes. Sex and gender are not always synchronous, meaning they do not always line up in an easy-to-categorize way.

Concept and Meaning of Sex

Sex refers to the biological differences between males and females. Sex is based on the reproductive function, since biological, physiological differences between males and females exist due to the process of reproduction.

These differences include hormones, chromosomes and internal and external sexual organs. For example, women's capability of giving birth to offspring is a difference in sex, not gender. The deeper voice inherent in men is also a difference based on sex.

Since sex is a biological factor, the characteristics that distinguish sex remains the same in any culture. It is sex that creates the distinction between male and female. Sex also determines the gender of a person. However, in some cases, an individual's gender and sex may not align; this happens to people of transgender.

Definitions of "Sex"

> *The term 'sex' is easy to understand. It simply refers to the natural biological differences between men and women, for example, the differences in the organs related to reproduction.*
>
> *"Sex" refers to the biological and physiological characteristics that define men and women.*

Thus, sex is determined biologically and refers to an individual's physical anatomy – genitalia, facial hair, body structure and composition. Sex refers to the biological characteristics that separate male from female.

Sex is not culturally influenced in a direct way (although certain cultures believe in certain practices or influences impact the sex of a child during pregnancy) and is normally considered to be completely biological in nature, uninfluenced by cultures, norms, values, or mores.

Concept and Meaning of Gender

Gender refers to the social and cultural differences between men and women. This takes into account features like gender roles, behaviour, expectations and attributes that are considered appropriate by the society. Gender can be mainly divided as masculine and feminine. This deals with the social role assigned to men and women. For example, women are expected to be more nurturing and gentler than men. This is not a difference based on physical differences, but a difference dictated by the society. There are also some physical differences that do not actually fall into the category of biological differences. For instance, the belief that women have longer hair and men have short hair is not actually based on sex, but gender, since the length of the hair, is not actually determined by biological factors, but social norms and customs. Unlike sex, gender is not created biologically, but socially. Therefore, gender differences can vary from one culture to another. What is considered to be feminine or masculine characteristics in one culture or time period may differ in different culture and time periods.

Definitions of "Gender"

> *"Gender refers to the cultural, socially-constructed differences between the two sexes. It refers to the way a society encourages and teaches the two sexes to behave in different ways through socialisation."*
>
> *Gender refers to cultural attitudes and behaviors that shape "feminine" and "masculine" behaviors, products, technologies, environments, and knowledges. "Femininities" and "masculinities" are multidimensional and can be practiced in different ways by biological females or males; gender does not necessarily match sex. Gendered attitudes and behaviors are not binary but slide along multiple continua.*
>
> *"Gender" refers to the socially constructed roles, behaviours, activities, and attributes that a given society considers appropriate for men and women.*
>
> *Gender Determined by Social, Cultural Affiliation, Learned Behaviours*

Gender is determined by social interaction, exchange, and absorption of peer, familial, and larger cultural values that determine gender identity and affiliation.

Gender can be considered fluid in the sense that one can challenge their own gender identity, in some instances holding it completely opposed to their sex.

For example, a woman who considers herself to be a male, possessing the same sexual desires as a male, and is contemplating undergoing surgery in order to become male is an example of sex and gender being separate as well as disparate.

Gender roles and identities are also culturally proscribed; these roles are commonly a crucial argument in the feminist theory aspect of sociology or philosophy. Boys play with toy soldiers, while girls play with Barbie dolls – this commonly held viewpoint or assumption is offensive to many feminist theorists who advocate a stripping of stereotype and gender bias.

Importance of the Concept of Gender

The concept of gender needs to be understood clearly as a cross-cutting socio-cultural variable. It is an overarching variable in the sense that gender can also be applied to all other cross-cutting variables such as race, class, age, ethnic group, etc. Gender systems are established in different socio-cultural contexts which determine what is expected, allowed and valued in a woman/man and girl/boy in these specific contexts. Gender roles are learned through socialization processes; they are not fixed but are changeable. Gender systems are institutionalized through education systems, political and economic systems, legislation, and culture and traditions. In utilizing a gender approach the focus is not on individual women and men but on the system which determines gender roles / responsibilities, access to and control over resources, and decision-making potentials.

The gender concept implies:

1. A rejection of the underlying biological distinction in the word "sex" and in the expression "sexual inequality", which appears as "an ideological alibi for maintaining domination, the alibi of nature". Women are no more part of nature and no less part of culture than men;
2. Grouping together all the differences identified between men and women, be they individual differences, differences in social roles or cultural representations, i.e., the grouping together of all that is variable and socially determined;
3. The non-homogenous nature of the category of women, which is transcended by differences of class, ethnicity and age;
4. The basic asymmetry and hierarchy between both groups, sexes and genders – one of them dominating and the other dominated - which is the basis of male power;

Difference between Sex and Gender

Difference between sex and gender is given in table 1.1 given below:

Table 1.1: Difference between Sex and Gender

Sex	Gender
Sex refers to the biological and physiological differences between men and women.	Gender refers to the social and cultural differences between men and women.
Sex is based on biological differences.	Gender is based on social and cultural differences.
Sex has two main two categories: male and female.	Gender has two main categories: masculine and feminine.
Sex remains the same regardless of time and culture.	Gender roles, expectations may differ across time and culture.
Sex is created by the reproduction needs, that is, biological features.	Gender distinctions are created by social norms.

To summaries:

'man' = male sex+ masculine social role
(a 'real man', 'masculine' or 'manly')
'woman' = female sex + feminine social role
(a 'real woman', 'feminine' or 'womanly')

Fundamental Concepts of Gender

A number of related concepts underlie the development of a clear understanding of gender:

Table 1.2: Fundamental Gender Concepts

Sl. No.	Term	Meaning
1	Gender	Gender refers to the socially constructed characteristics of women and men – such as norms, roles and relationships of and between groups of women and men. It varies from society to society and can be changed. While most people are born either male or female, they are taught appropriate norms and behaviours – including how they should interact with others of the same or opposite sex within households, communities and work places

Table 1.2 Continued

Table 1.2 Continued

Sl. No.	Term	Meaning
2	Gender Analysis	Gender analysis identifies, assesses and informs actions to address inequality that come from: 1) different gender norms, roles and relations; 2) unequal power relations between and among groups of men and women, and 3) the interaction of contextual factors with gender such as sexual orientation, ethnicity, education or employment status.
3	Gender Based Division of Labour	It means where, how and under what conditions women and men work (for or without pay) based on gender norms and roles.
4	Gender Equality	It refers to equal chances or opportunities for groups of women and men to access and control social, economic and political resources, including protection under the law (such as health services, education and voting rights). It is also known as equality of opportunity – or formal equality. Gender equality is often used interchangeably with gender equity, but the two refer to different, complementary strategies that are needed to reduce gender-based health inequities.
5	Gender Equity	More than formal equality of opportunity, gender equity refers to the different needs, preferences and interests of women and men. This may mean that different treatment is needed to ensure equality of opportunity. This is often referred to as substantive equality (or equality of results) and requires considering the realities of women's and men's lives. Gender equity is often used interchangeably with gender equality, but the two refer to different, complementary strategies that are needed to reduce gender-based health inequities.
6	Gender Mainstreaming	It is the process of assessing the implications for women and men of any planned action, including legislation, policies or programmes, in all areas and at all levels. It is a strategy for making women's as well as men's concerns and experiences an integral dimension of the design, implementation, monitoring and evaluation of policies and programmes in all political, economic and societal spheres so that women and men benefit equally and inequality is not perpetuated.

Table 1.2 Continued

Table 1.2 Continued

Sl. No.	Term	Meaning
7	Gender Norms	It refers to beliefs about women and men, boys and girls that are passed from generation to generation through the process of socialization. They change over time and differ in different cultures and populations. Gender norms lead to inequality if they reinforce: a) mistreatment of one group or sex over the other; b) differences in power and opportunities.
8	Gender Relations	It refers to social relations between and among women and men that are based on gender norms and roles. Gender relations often create to hierarchies between and among groups of men and women that can lead to unequal power relations, disadvantaging one group over another.
9	Gender Responsive	It is defined as a policy or programme that considers gender norms, roles and inequality with measures taken to actively reduce their harmful effects.
10	Gender Roles	It refers to what males and females are expected to do (in the household, community and workplace) in a given society.
11	Gender Stereotypes	It is images, beliefs, attitudes or assumptions about certain groups of women and men. Stereotypes are usually negative and based on assumed gender norms, roles and relations.
12	Gender Awareness	Understanding that there are socially determined differences between men and women, and that these influence access to and control of resources.
13	Gender Sensitivity	The ability to perceive existing gender differences and issues, and to incorporate these into strategies and actions. Contrast with gender blindness.
14	Gender Parity	A numerical concept concerned with the relative equality in terms of numbers and proportions of women, men, girls and boys. In education, this means that the same number of boys and girls receive educational services at different levels and in diverse forms.
15	Gender Discrimination	Denying opportunities and rights or giving preferential treatment to individuals on the basis of their sex.

Table 1.2 Continued

Table 1.2 Continued

Sl. No.	Term	Meaning
16	Gender Neutral	The claim some people make when they want to present themselves as not practicing gender-based discrimination. What it often masks, however, is the failure to take gender issues into consideration, and this can translate into discrimination against girls as it fails to pay attention to the distinct and special needs of girlsand boys.
17	Gender Blindness	The failure to recognize the differencesbetween males and females and thereforeleading to failure to provide for the differences.
18	Gender Awareness	Implies the ability to identifyproblems arising from gender inequality anddiscrimination, even if these are not apparent onthe surface.

2

Gender, Sexuality and Sexual Development

Human Sexuality

"Human sexuality" refers to people's sexual interest in and attraction to others, as well as their capacity to have erotic experiences and responses. People's sexual orientation is their emotional and sexual attraction to particular sexes or genders, which often shapes their sexuality. Sexuality may be experienced and expressed in a variety of ways, including thoughts, fantasies, desires, beliefs, attitudes, values, behaviors, practices, roles, and relationships. These may manifest themselves in biological, physical, emotional, social, or spiritual aspects. The *biological and physical* aspects of sexuality largely concern the human reproductive functions, including the human sexual-response cycle and the basic biological drive that exists in all species. *Emotional* aspects of sexuality include bonds between individuals that are expressed through profound feelings or physical manifestations of love, trust, and care. *Social* aspects deal with the effects of human society on one's sexuality, while *spirituality* concerns an individual's spiritual connection with others through sexuality. Sexuality also impacts and is impacted by cultural, political, legal, philosophical, moral, ethical, and religious aspects of life.

Definitions of Sexuality

According to Michel Foucault,

"Sexuality is not a product of a pre-given essence. Knowledge of sexuality is structured through the use of language".

Hollway defined Sexuality as

"directly produced by a biological drive, the function of which is to ensure reproduction of the species".

According to Rebecca,

"Sexuality is distinct from gender yet intimately linked to it. It is the social construction of a biological drive. An individual's sexuality is defined by whom one has sex with, in what ways, why, under what circumstances, and with what outcomes. It is more than sexual behaviour; it is a multidimensional and dynamic concept".

Broude defined Sexuality as

"a person's capacity for sexual feelings".

According to Wikipedia, *"Human sexuality is the capacity of humans to have erotic experiences and responses. A person's sexual orientation can influence their sexual interest and attraction for another person".*

According to New World Encyclopaedia,

"Human sexuality is the expression of sexual sensation and related intimacy between human beings. Psychologically, sexuality is the means to express the fullness of love between a man and a woman".

Significances of Sexuality

Social Significance of Sexuality: Gender is the social facet of sexuality. So, society is having a major significance on sexuality. In the ancient period, many social taboos were based on sexuality.Due to legitimate and illegitimate relationships in society like the earlier times and still now, punishments are prevalent. Hence, sexuality is very much society based.

Psychological Significance of Sexuality: All humanpossess fundamental psychological needs. If we do not meet our psychological needs, we suffer, sometimes severely. Just like we need food, shelter, and sleep to survive, we also need to fulfill our psychological needs to remain mentally healthy and stable. Psychologists have studied a number of psychological needs, but one can really narrow them down to four fundamental needs: security, self-esteem, autonomy and connection. To be happy, stable people, we need to meet all four of these needs consistently. If we are not meeting these needs, our minds will actually begin to rationalize ways to get them met, even at the expense of our physical or mental health. If one is never able to meet their needfor esteem, they will become chronically depressed and sometimes commit suicide. If one never meets their need for autonomy, they will fall into a state of co-dependence or learned helplessness. In short, it can be said that, sex is a strategy we use to meet our psychological needs and not a need itself.

Educational Significance of Sexuality: In the educational sphere sexuality education should take a positive view of sexual development as a natural part of growing up. It should encompass learning about physical development, including sexual and reproductive knowledge, gender identity, relationships, friendships and social issues. It sits within the broader area of relationship education, which also includes social and emotional learning (SEL), and violence prevention education. In this context young people learn about themselves and develop knowledge and skills that will help them to interact in positive, respectful, and supportive ways with others. Through learning about sexuality students also come to understand about the social and cultural influences that shape the way society views gender and sexuality. All young people need access to information and opportunities to think about, question, and discuss issues related to relationships, gender, sexual identities, sexual orientation, sexual behaviour, sexual and reproductive health, and societal messages. Sexuality education provides a framework in which this can happen. Sexuality education, as a part of health education, is vital for young people'sdevelopment, learning, and overall well-being. Learning in this area also contributes to academic success and positive mental, emotional, physical, and spiritual health. In this context, UNESCO has taken an initiative on 'Education about sexuality' and 'sex education'.

Types of Sexuality

Types of sexuality is given in table 2.1.

Table 2.1: Types of Sexuality

Heterosexuality	Heterosexuality is the sexual attraction between members of the opposite sexes such as man attracts to woman and woman attracts to man sexually.
Homosexuality	Homosexuality is the sexual attraction between members of the same sexes such as man to man and woman to woman sexually.
Bisexuality	Bisexuality is the sexual attraction to both the opposite and same sexes such as man to man and man to woman, woman to woman and woman to man.
Asexuality	Asexuality is also known as non-sexuality which is the lack of sexual attractionand sexual interest towardsothers.
Poly-sexuality	Poly-sexuality is the sexual attraction to more than one gender but do not wish to be known as bi-sexual as it implies that there are only two binary sexes, do not confuse this with pan-sexuality
Pan-sexuality	Pan-sexuality is the sexual attraction towards people regardless of gender also known as omni-sexuality, some pan-sexuals refer to themselves as gender blind as to them gender is insignificant in determining whether they will be sexually attracted to others

Table 2.1 Continued

Table 2.1 Continued

Transexualism	Transexualism is when a person identifies themselves with a physical sex that is different to their own biological one. A medical diagnosis can be made if a person experiences discomfort as a result of a desire to be a member of the opposite sex. For example a person may be born male, and is uncomfortable with their gender as a male and changes to a female, or a female may change to a male. It is a long process that they will go throughand an expensive one too.

Development of Sexuality

Though sexual development is typically associated with the teenyears, in reality young kids develop an emotional and physical foundation for sexuality in many subtle ways from infancy. Physical and emotional changes become more dramatic and complex with the onset of puberty and into the teen years, and kids are likely to have lots of questions.

Like all forms of human development, sexual development begins at birth. Sexual development includes not only the physicalchanges that occur as children grow, but also the sexual knowledge and beliefs they come to learn and the behaviours they show. Any given child's sexual knowledge and behaviour is strongly influenced by three factors. They are as follows:

1. The child's age
2. What the child observes (including the sexual behaviours of family and friends)
3. What the child is taught (including cultural and religious beliefs concerning sexuality and physical boundaries).

Children's sexual awareness starts in infancy and continues to strengthen throughout pre-school and school-age years. All aspects of children's development-including cognitive, language, motor, social, emotional, and sexual development-are linked to eachother.

Stages of sexual development is given in table 2.2

Freud's Theory

According to Freud, sex is the life urge or fundamental motive in life. All physical pleasure arising from any of the organs or any of the functions are ultimately sexual in nature. Sexuality is not the characteristic only of the adults. Children from very beginning have sexual desires also. This he termed as *'infantile sexuality'*.

According to Freud, the flow of libido controls the overall behaviours of every human being. Libido is a life-maintaining energy which aims to seek pleasure through sexual satisfaction. Freud's theory of psychosexual development is represented amongst five stages. According to Freud, each

Table 2.2: Stages of Sexual Development

Pre-school Children (less than 4 years)	1. Exploring and touching private parts, in public and in private
	2. Rubbing private parts (with hand or against objects)
	3. Showing private parts to others
	4. Trying to touch mother's or other women's breasts
	5. Removing clothes and wanting to be naked
	6. Attempting to see other people when they are naked or undressing (such as in the bathroom)
	7. Asking questions about their own-and others' -bodies and bodily functions
Young Children (4-6 years)	1. Purposefully touching private parts (masturbation), occasionally in the presence of others
	2. Attempting to see other people when they are naked or undressing
	3. Mimicking dating behaviour (such as kissing or holding hands)
	4. Talking about private parts and using 'naughty' words, even when they don't understand the meaning
	5. Exploring private parts with children their own age (such as 'playing doctor', "I'll show you mine if you show me yours," etc.)
School Aged Children (7-12 years)	1. Purposefully touching private parts (masturbation), usually in private
	2. Playing games with children their own age that involve sexual behaviour (such as "truth or dare", "playing family," or "boyfriend/girlfriend").
	3. Attempting to see other people naked or undressing
	4. Looking at pictures of naked or partially naked people
	5. Viewing/listening to sexual content in media (television, movies, games, the Internet, music etc.)
	6. Wanting more privacy (for example, not wanting to undress in front of other people) and being reluctant to talk to adults about sexual issues
	7. Beginnings of sexual attraction to/interest in peers
Adolescent Youth (13-19 years)	1. Increased interest in dating and sexual relationship
	2. Are physically able to become pregnant
	3. Peer pressure still important, though may begin to lessen toward end of this period

Table 2.2 Continued

	4. May engage in risky or even delinquent behaviour brains are still immature and child may not be able to make consistently healthy decisions 5. Increased interest in being independent, driving, having sex, tattoos, piercings, getting jobs to earn spending money, clothes 6. Increased interest in romantic and sexual relationships and in genital sex behaviours 7. Express their feelings within sexual relationships

stage occurs within a specific time frame of one's life. If one becomes fixated in any of the five stages, he or she will develop personality traits that coincide with a specific stage and its focus.

Stages of Psycho-sexual Development

A child passes through the following different stages with respect to his/her psycho-sexual development:

Table 2.3: Stages of Psycho-sexual Development

Stages	Age Range	Erogenous Zone	Principal Task	Descriptions
Oral Stage	Birth-1 Year	Mouth	Weaning	An infant's primary interaction with the world is through the mouth. The mouth is vital for eating and the infant derives pleasure from oral stimulation through gratifying activities such as tasting and sucking. If this need is not met, the child may develop an oral fixation later in life, examples of which include thumb-sucking, smoking, fingernail and overeating.
Anal Stage	1-3 years	Anus	Toilet Training	Freud believed that the primary focus of the libido was on controlling bladder and bowel movements. Training is a primary issue withchildren and parents. Too much pressure can result in an excessive need for order or cleanliness later in life, while too little pressure from parents can lead to messy or destructive behaviour later in life.

Table 2.3 Continued

Table 2.3 Continued

Stages	Age Range	Erogenous Zone	Principal Task	Descriptions
Phallic Stage	3-6 Years	Genitals	Sexual Identity	During the phallic stage, the primary focus of the libido is on the genitals. At this age, children also begin to discover the differences between males and females. Freud also believed that boys begin to view their fathers as a rival for the mother's affections. The *Oedipus complex* describes these feelings of wanting to possess the mother and the desire to replace the father. However, the child also fears that he will be punished by the father for these feelings, a fear Freud termed castration anxiety. The term *Electra complex* has been used to describe a similar set of feelings experienced by young girls. Freud, however, believed that girls instead experience penis envy. Eventually, the child begins to identify with the same-sex parent as a means of vicariously possessing the other parent.
Latent Stage	6-12 Years	None	Expanding Social Contacts	During the latent period, the libidointerests are suppressed. The development of the ego and superego contribute to this period of calm. The stage begins around the time that children enter into school and become more concerned with peer relationships, hobbies, and other interests. The latent period is a time of exploration in which the sexual energy is still present, but it is directed into other areas such as intellectual pursuits and social interactions. This stage is important in the development of social and communication skills and self confidence.
Genital Stage	12 Years onwards	Genitals	Genital Intercourse	During the final stage of psychosexual development, the individual develops a strong sexualinterest in the opposite sex. This stage begins during puberty but last throughout the rest of a person's life. If development has been successful to this point, the individual will continue to develop into a wellbalanced person

Gender, Body Image and Role Models

Gender

Gender is often misunderstood as being the promotion of women only. Gender issues focus on women and on the relationship between men and women, their roles, access to and control over resources, division of labour, interests and needs. Gender relations affect household security, family well-being, planning, production and many other aspects of life.

Gender and Sexuality

Gender refers to the widely shared set of expectations and norms linked to how women and men, and girls and boys, should behave. Unlike 'sex' which refers to the biological and physiological characteristics that define men and women, gender refers to the socially constructed roles, behaviours, activities, and attributes that are assigned to men and women in any given society. These expectations are not fixed but are continually being constructed and reinforced through social relationships and economic and political power dynamics.

Body Image

Body image is the perception that a person has of their physical self and the thoughts and feelings that result from that perception. These feelings can be positive, negative or both and are influenced by individual and environmental factors.

According to Davis and Cowles (1991), body image is how we perceive our physical appearance, as well as how we think others perceive us. It can also be defined as a person's subjective concept of his or her physical appearance. This internalized image, whether realistic or unrealistic, is created from self-observation, the feedback from outside sources, and a complex interaction of attitudes, emotions, memories, and experiences, both conscious and unconscious.

There are many different factors that affect body image, *"including sex, media, parental relationship, and puberty as well as weight and popularity"*. The intersectionality of these factors causes unique experiences for adolescents during this period within their lives. As their body changes, so does the environment in which they live in. Body image is closely linked to psychological during adolescence and can cause harmful effects when a child has body dissatisfaction.

Aspects of Body Image

How you see your body is your perceptual body image. This is not always a correct representation of how you actually look. For example, a person may perceive themselves as overweight when they are actually underweight.

The way you feel about your body is your affective body image. This relates to the amount of satisfaction or dissatisfaction you feel about your shape, weight and individual body parts.

The way you think about your body is your cognitive body image. This can lead to preoccupation with body shape and weight. For example, some people believe they will feel better about themselves if they are thinner or more muscular.

Behaviourism in which you engage as a result of our body image encompassesyour behavioural body image. When a person is dissatisfied with the way they look, they may isolate themselves because they feel bad about their appearance or employ destructive behaviours (e.g. excessive exercising, disordered eating) as a means to change appearance.

Positive body image occurs when a person is able to accept, appreciate and respect their body. Positive body image is importantbecause it is one of the protective factors which can make aperson more resilient to eating disorders. In fact, the most effective eating disorder prevention programmes use a health promotion approach, focusing on building self-esteem and positive body image, and a balanced approach to nutrition and physical activity. A positive body image will improve:

1. *Self-esteem*, which dictates how a person feels about themselves and can infiltrate every aspect of life, and contribute to happiness and well-being.
2. *Self-acceptance*, making a person more likely to feel comfortable and happy with the way they look and less likely to feel impacted by unrealistic images in the media and societal pressures tolook a certain way.
3. *Healthy outlook and behaviours*, as it is easier to lead a balanced lifestyle with healthier attitudes and practices relating to food. and exercise when you are in tune with, and respond to the needs of your body.

Body Image and Sexuality

Body image is how we feel about ourselves physically and how we think others see us. Some of us feel very good about our bodies, and some of us don't. Sometimes how we feel and what we actually look like are not the same. For example, someone who suffers from anorexia (starving oneself) may be very thin, but will look in the mirror and see someone much bigger than he or she actually is. Sexuality is often thought of as sexual orientation-whether you are hetero-sexual, lesbian, gay, bisexual, etc., but it is so much more than that. Sexuality is an important and positive part of our lives that includes our sexual orientation, but also things like our sexual health, the way we act in relationships; how we feel about our bodies; how we interact with both males and females; and our understanding of who we are sexually.

Our sexuality is influenced by our culture and by our ethical, spiritual, and moral values.

Body image is part of sexuality how we feel about our bodies. Whether we know it or not, the way we see our bodies has a big influence on us every day, including the decisions we make. People who feel bad about their bodies sometimes make sexually unhealthy decisions. But, the better the person feels, the better the decisions he/she can make.

Role Model

A role model is a person other people look up to in order to determine appropriate behaviours. Role models can be either positive or negative. Positive role models offer a range of helpful or useful behaviours. Negative role models, on the other hand, offer examples of harmful or disruptive behaviours. Virtually anyone can be a role model, but in almost all the cultures, publicly visible figures such as athletes, actors, musicians, and celebrities are the most common examples. Other common role models include and parents as well as teachers. Most of these people can be considered either negative or positive role models depending on their behaviours. While people of all ages may have role models, it is generally young people who are still developing their own identities who try so hard to emulate their role models.

The term *'Role Model'* comes from sociologist Robert K Merton who discovered that rather than modelling individual behaviours, people tend to model sets of behaviour. These sets of behaviour are demonstrated by people who occupy certain roles in society. Behaviour sets may contain contradictory ideas that do not necessarily work well together. Instances of a role model displaying one set of ideals and then, being caught living according to another set of ideals are not uncommon, and all this behaviour is part of the same set. This is why people are concerned about how role models live their notso-private lives.

Bandura found that individuals tend to be active observers of their environments. During these observations, people make note of the behaviours exhibited by others and imitate them. This imitation is part of a complex process of determining both the cause and consequence of the behaviour in question. While this may sound like common sense, Bandura's work was an important step in appreciating how humans actively learn from others instead of merely reacting to their environments.

Gender Role

A gender role is a set of societal norms dictating the types of behaviours which are generally considered acceptable, appropriate, or desirable for people based on their actual or perceived sex or sexuality. Gender roles are usually centred on conceptions of femininity and masculinity, although there are exceptions and variations. The specifics regarding these gendered expectation s may vary substantially among cultures, while other characteristics may be common throughout a range of cultures. The term gender role was first coined by John Money in 1955, during the course of his study of inter-sex individuals, to describe the manners in which these individuals expressed their status as a male or female in a situationwhere no clear biological assignment existed. The term gender role refers to society's concept of how men and women are expected to act and how they should behave. These roles are based on norms, or standards, created by society.

Gender roles are learned behaviours in a given society/ community or other social group that condition which activities, tasks and responsibilities are perceived as male or female. Gender roles vary considerably across settings and also change over time. The factors that can shape and change gender roles are age, class, race, ethnicity, religion and other ideologies, geographicalenvironment, economic environment and political environment.

Types of Gender Roles

Gender roles are a specific set of social and behavioural actions which are considered to be appropriate for the given gender. The concept of gender roles has been developed from the work of Caroline Moser. She classified Gender roles in various types:

Table 2.4: Types of Gender Roles

Reproductive Role	Child-bearing/rearing responsibilities and domestic tasks done by women, required to guarantee the maintenance and reproduction of the labour force. It includes not only biological reproduction but also the care and maintenance of the work force (male partner and working children) and the future work force (infants and school going children).
Productive Role	It includes both market production with anexchange-value, and subsistence/home productionwithactual use-value, and also potential exchange value. For women in agricultural production, this includes work as independent farmers; peasant wives and wage workers.
Community Managing Role	Activities undertaken primarily by women at the community level, as an extension of their reproductive role, to ensure the provision and maintenance of scarce resources of collective consumption, such as water, health care and education. This is voluntary unpaid work, undertaken in 'free' time.
Community Politics Role	Activities undertaken primarily by men at the community level, organizing at the formal political level, often within the framework of national politics. This is usually paid work, either directly or indirectly, through status or power.

Table 2.4 Continued

Table 2.4 Continued

Multiple Roles	Both men and women play multiple roles. The major difference, however, is that- *Men* typically play their roles sequentially, focusing on a single productive role. *Women* must usually play their roles simultaneously, balancing the demands of each within their limited time constraints.

Sites of Conflicts: Social and Emotional

Society is defined by a struggle for dominance among social groups that compete for scarce resources. In the context of gender, conflict theory argues that gender is best understood as men attempting to maintain power and privilege to the detriment of women. Therefore, men can be seen as the dominant group and women as the subordinate group. While certain gender roles may have been appropriate in a hunter-gatherer society, conflict theorists argue that the only reason these roles persist is because the dominant group naturally works to maintain their power and status. Accordingto conflict theory, social problems are created when dominantgroups exploit or oppress subordinate groups. Therefore, their approach is normative in that it prescribes changes to the power structure, advocating a balance of power between genders.

Definition of Conflict

The word *'conflict'* has been derived from a Latin word 'Conflicts' which means *'strike two things at the same time'*. Conflict is an opposition or a tug-of-war between contradictory impulses.

According to Colman,

> *"A conflict is the anticipated frustration entailed in the choice of either alternative". Conflicts occur in the individual when more than one, equally powerful desires or motives present at the same time and pressurize for immediate satisfaction".*

Gillin and Gillin (1948) stated conflict as the

> *"social process in which individuals or groups seek their ends by directly challenging the antagonist by violence or threat of violence".*

A W Green (1956) defined conflict as the

> *"deliberate attempt to oppose, resist or coerce the will of another or others".*

Characteristics of Conflict

1. It is a universal process found in every society.
2. It is the result of deliberate and conscious efforts of individuals or the groups.
3. The nature of the conflict is personal and direct.
4. It is basically an individual's process.
5. Conflict is of brief duration, temporary and intermittent in character.
6. It is a process loaded with impulsiveness of human emotions and violent passions.
7. It is cumulative; each act of aggression usually promotes a more aggressive rebuttal. Thus, termination of conflict is not easy.
8. It tends to be more intense when individuals and groups who have close relationships with one another are involved.

Causes of Conflicts

- Individual Differences
- Cultural Differences
- Clash of Interests
- Social Change

Nature of Conflict

Intra-personal Conflict: These are the conflicts caused within the individual andarise as a result of two or more motives or goals to be achieved at a time. Hence, these are called goal conflicts. It is a type of conflict that is psychological involving the individual's thoughts, values, principles and emotions. Lewin has described three types of intrapersonal conflicts. They are as follows:

Table 2.5: Types of Intra-personal Conflicts

Approach-Approach Conflict	An approach-approachconflict is one of three possible conflicts that accompany decision-making situations. "Approach-approach' conflict describes the situation where a person is trying to make a choice between two desirable options. For example, a person has two attractive job (approach) offers and he has to choose any one of themtension arises
Avoidance-Avoidance Conflict	The avoidance-avoidance conflict is one of the three possible conflicts that accompany a decision making situation. The avoidance-avoidance conflictrefers to making a decision between two equally undesirable choices. This type of conflict would normally be settled by an assessment of the relative importance of the two tasks. An example of this type of conflict would be a situation where you have to decide between doing unwanted homework (avoidance) ordoing unwanted house chores (avoidance).

Table 2.5 Continued

Table 2.5 Continued

Approach-Avoidance Conflict	The approach-avoidance conflict is one of the threepossible conflicts that accompany a decision making situation. The approach-avoidance conflict involves making decisions about situations thathave both positive and negative ramifications. For example, Purba has been with Company for 12 years. She is offered a job promotion as vice-president of the company. It would pay her muchmore than she is currently making (approach). However, if she isto accept this position, she would have to move to another city that is far away from her extended family (avoidance) and where the weather is much colder (avoidance).

Inter-personal Conflict: Interpersonal conflict is caused between individuals. This can be resolved through some strategies such as avoiding, smoothing, forcing, confronting and compromising. Assertive behaviour and I am ok, you are ok interpersonal orientation help to resolve such conflicts easily. This occurs typically due to how people are different from one another. We have varied personalities which usually results to incompatible choices and opinions. Apparently, it is a natural occurrence which can eventually help in personal growth or developing one's relationships with others. In addition, coming up with adjustments is necessary for managing this type of conflict. However, when interpersonal conflict gets too destructive, calling in a mediator would help so as to have it resolved. There are three types of Interpersonal Conflicts, as under.

Table 2.6: Types of Inter-personal Conflicts

Relationship Conflict	It exists when there are interpersonal incompatibilities among individuals, including irritation about personal taste, interpersonal style, different personal values, or other non-work-related preferences.
Task Conflict	It exists when there are disagreements about the content of tasks being performed.
Process Conflict	It focuses on disagreements about how to accomplish a task, which is responsible for a task or the delegation of duties and resource.

Besides those above-mentioned natures of conflict, there is another conflict named as Unconscious Conflict. The mental conflict below the level of conscious awareness is called Unconscious Conflict. The conflicts in conscious level, when repressed, shift to unconscious. Here the desires which cannot be satisfied at conscious level are repressed to unconscious level as a mechanism of escaping. Many of our wants raised by *Id* may not be socially acceptable. Such wants are objected by the *Ego* and the *Super-ego*. Hence, these are repressed to unconscious.

Forms of Conflicts

Social Conflict: Social conflict, by definition, is intentionally taking into accountother selves, power is a capability to produce effects, and social power is an intentionally directed capability to produce effects through another person. Social conflict is then the confrontation of social powers. Social conflict is exclusively an aspect of social power. To understand such conflict we must deal at the level of social powers and their dialectics, as power or conflict social theorists have done. Social conflict is not limited to hostile or antagonistic opposition; it is not wholly a clash of coercive powers as often is implied, but of any opposing social powers.

Cultural Conflict: Cultural conflict is a type of conflict that occurs when different cultural values and beliefs clash. It has been used to explain violence and crime. *Jonathan H Turner* defines it as a conflict caused by *"differences in cultural values and beliefs that place people at odds with one another"*.

Emotional Conflict: Emotional conflict is the presence of different and opposing emotions relating to a situation that has recently taken place or isin the process of being unfolded. They may be accompanied at times by a physical discomfort, especially when a functional disturbancehas become associated with an emotional conflict in childhood, and in particular by tension headaches expressing a state of inner tension caused by an unconscious conflict. Freud's concept of emotional conflict as amplified by Anna Freud, Erikson and others is central in contemporarytheories of mental disorder in children, particularly withrespect to the development ofpsychoneurosis.

3

Masculinity and Femininity

The terms masculinity and femininity refer to traits or characteristics typically associated with being male or female, respectively. Traditionally, masculinity and femininity have been conceptualized as opposite ends of a single dimension, with masculinity at one extreme and femininity at the other. By this definition, high masculinity implies the absence of femininity, and vice versa. In other words, people can be classified as either masculine or feminine. Contemporary definitions propose that masculinity and femininity are separate dimensions, allowing for the possibility that individuals may simultaneously possess both masculine and feminine attributes.

Characteristics/Traits of Masculinity/Femininity

Some characteristics or traits of masculinity/femininity are given in table 3.1

Table 3.1: Traits of Masculinity/Femininity

Characteristics	*High Masculine*	*Low Masculine (Feminine)*
Social Norms	ego oriented	relationship oriented
	money and things are important	quality of life and people are important
	live in order to work	work in order to live
Politics and Economics	economic growth high priority	environment protection high priority
	conflict solved through force	conflict solved through negotiation
Religion	most important in life	less important in life
	only men can be priests	both men and women as priests
Work	larger gender wage gap	smaller gender wage gap
	fewer women in management	more women in management
	preference for higher pay	preference for fewer working hours

Table 3.1 Continued

Table 3.1 Continued

Characteristics	*High Masculine*	*Low Masculine (Feminine)*
Family and School	traditional family structure	flexible family structure
	girls cry, boys don't; boys fight, girls don't	both boys and girls cry; neither fight
	failing is a disaster	failing a minor accident

What is Masculinity?

In Greek mythology, Heracles is synonymous with Apollonian masculinity. Masculinity (also called boyhood, manliness, or manhood) is a set of attributes, behaviors and roles generally associated with boys and men. Masculinity is socially constructed, but made up of both socially-defined and biologically-created factors, distinct from the definition of the male biological sex. Both males and females can exhibit masculine traits and behavior. Those exhibiting both masculine and feminine characteristics are considered androgynous, and feminist philosophers have argued that gender ambiguity may blur gender classification.

Masculinity is manly character. It specifically describes men and boys that is personal and human, unlike male which can also be used to describe animals, or masculine which can also be used to describe noun classes. When masculine is used to describe men, it can have degrees of comparison—more masculine, most masculine. The opposite can be expressed by terms such as unmanly, epicene or effeminate. A typical near-synonym of masculinity is virility (from Latin vir, man); and the usual complement is femininity.

Definition of Masculinity

According to Hoftstede, *"Masculinity stands for a society in which social gender roles are clearly distinct: Men are supposed to be assertive, tough, and focused on material success; women are supposed to be more modest, tender, and concerned with the quality of life."*

Masculine Characteristics

1. Present – Being in the moment and completely attentive to the person he is with or the event he is at.
2. Grounded – In touch with reality and able to resist pressure and events around him.
3. Contained – Able to provide all his own needs and able to provide the needs of others, allowing them to feel safe.

4. Focused – Completely absorbed by the task in hand and not distracted by what else is happening.
5. Potent – Being strong and powerful and fully in charge of his sexuality.
6. Dynamic – Able keep going, to endure and to be full of energy.

Traits of Masculinity

Masculine traits are ways of behaving that our culture usually associates with being a boy or man. Common traits related to masculinity are—Independent; Non-emotional; Aggressive; Tough-skinned; Competitive; Clumsy; Experienced; Strong; Active; Self-confident; Hard; Sexually aggressive; Rebellious

Positive Masculine Traits

Purposefulness, independence, self-confidence, self-reliance, adventurous, assertiveness, self-discipline, determination, endurance, leadership skills, courage, loyalty, persistence, decisiveness, rationality, inventiveness, ambitious, dependability, provider, worldly view.

Negative Masculine Traits

Arrogance, aggression, egotistical, risky behaviour, callousness, non-communicative, explosiveness, excessive pride, insensitivity, domineering, cold-heartedness, lack of emotion, overly competitive, closed mindedness, crudeness, coarseness, messiness, violent, life taking, indifferent, sexual promiscuity.

What is Femininity?

In Egyptian mythology, the goddess is synonymous with femininity. Femininity (also called girlishness, womanliness or womanhood) is a set of attributes, behaviors, and roles generally associated with girls and women. Femininity is socially constructed, but made up of both socially-defined and biologically-created factors. This makes it distinct from the definition of the biological female sex, as both males and females can exhibit feminine traits. People who exhibit a combination of both masculine and feminine characteristics are considered androgynous, and feminist philosophers have argued that gender ambiguity may blur gender classification. Modern conceptualizations of femininity also rely not just upon social constructions, but upon the individualized choices made by women.

Definition of Femininity

According to Hoftstede, *"Femininity stands for a society in which social gender roles overlap: Both men and women are supposed to be modest, tender, and concerned with the quality of life."*

Feminine Characteristics

1. Free – Open and unrestricted, able to be involved in anything and seeking everything.
2. Spontaneous – Reacts from the emotion of a situation and makes quick assessments.
3. Intuitive- Acts on an innate sense of what's happening and able to know beyond the senses.
4. Sceptical – Questioning others, particularly those closest to her, looking to be shown certainty.
5. Accepting – Will accept circumstances once trust is established, able to conciliate.
6. Nurturing – Caring for others as well as herself, finding compassion in any situation.

Traits of Femininity

Feminine traits are ways of behaving that our culture usually associates with being a girl or woman. The following are the traits of femininity:

Dependent; emotional; passive; sensitive; quiet; graceful; innocent; weak; flirtatious; nurturing; self-critical; soft; sexually submissive;accepting.

Positive Feminine Traits

Compassion, empathy, intuitiveness, cooperation, communication, kindness, calmness, thoughtfulness, graciousness, warmheartedness, emotionally expressive, able to be happy for others, sustainer, peacemaker, gentleness, patience, nurturing, helpfulness, open mindedness, empathetic, neatness, attentive to detail, creativeness, life giving, sexual fidelity.

Negative Feminine Traits

Frivolousness, neediness, vanity, naivety, overly sensitive, squeamishness, prudishness, clingyness, helplessness, dependency, excessively emotional, obsessed with personal appearance, primping, lacking self-confidence, indecisiveness, excessive passivity, insecurity.

Clearly, society's categories for what is masculine and feminine are unrealistic. They may not capture how we truly feel, how we behave, or how we define ourselves. All men have some so-called feminine traits, and all women have some so-called masculine traits. And we may show different traits at different times. Our cultures teach women and men to be the opposite of each other in many ways. The truth is that we are more alike than different.

4

Patriarchy and Matriarchy

Patriarchy and Matriarchy are two forms of social systems between which a key difference can be identified—in patriarchal system father is the head of the household while in matriarchal system mother is the head of the household.

What is Patriarchy?

The term patriarchy comes from the Latin 'pater' (father) and 'arch' (rule). Historically, *"rule of the father"* was the more appropriate definition of patriarchy. Valentine Moghadam has written that under classic patriarchy, *"the senior man has authority over everyone else in the family, including younger men, and women are subject to distinct forms of control and subordination"*.

Patriarchy is a social structural phenomenon in which males has the privilege of dominance over females, both visibly and subliminally. This phenomenon is manifested in the values, attitudes, customs, expectations, and institutions of the society, and it is maintained through the process of socialization. Some societies are more patriarchal than others, but virtually all are characterized by the phenomenon in one form or another. Patriarchy is a function of male physical, social, economic, and political power.

Patriarchy is also found in family traditions like women not taking the name of their husbands and children always carrying the father's last name. More women are choosing to keep their maiden names or hyphenate with their married name so they can retain their own identity. With reference of Mr. and Mrs. so-and-so, the man assumes the dominant role again and women lose.

Characteristics of Patriarchy System

The main characteristics of patriarchy system are given below:

1. Patriarchy is a social system in which the father or eldest male is head of the household, having authority over women and children.
2. Patriarchy also refers to a system of government by males, and to the dominance of men in social or cultural systems.

3. It may also include title being traced through the male line.
4. Patriarchy is a social system in which males hold primary power and predominate in roles of political leadership, moral authority, social privilege, and control of property.
5. In the domain of the family, fathers hold authority over the women and children.
6. A patriarchal system is a social system in which the father is the head of the household. This, however, is not confined to the household alone. It can be extended to the entire society where males dominate in all social, political, economic, legal and cultural roles. For instance, in most patriarchal societies women were very much confined to the domestic sphere, where they were completely cut off from the realities of the society.
7. In the patriarchal society, even philosophers such as Aristotle believed that women were inferior to men in all aspects. This emphasized the idea that the inferiority of women was not limited to biological differences but went as further as intellectual differences. However, feminist theories on patriarchy highlight that this is merely another social system that has been created to oppress women.
8. Patriarchy is best defined as control by men. The opposite is matriarchy which means women are in charge and the head of families. Obviously, the culture of the United States and most other countries is patriarchal. Men have the power and control the women. If you don't believe that consider the basics of how our society functions. Women constantly must fight for their rights and sometimes they struggle just to survive without the power and domination of men threatening them. Whether an individual woman wants to conquer patriarchy will come from her desire to be independent and defined outside the context of men.

What is Matriarchy?

Matriarchy is a social system in which females hold primary power, predominate in roles of political leadership, moral authority, social privilege and control of property at the specific exclusion of men, at least to a large degree.

In a matriarchal society, the mother is the head of the household and the governance of the society is also in the hands of women. When examining the human history, there is very little evidence of matriarchal societies, because most confuse an egalitarian (equal rights) society or matrilineal society (kinship system in which ancestral descent is traced through maternal lines) to a matriarchal society. The Mosuo culture in China can be considered as a matriarchal society. In this society, females are the head of the household and women dominate the economic activities. Also, in the Mosuo culture, inheritance is through the female line.

However, myths of the Amazon society (women-only society) can be considered as a clear matriarchal society. This is because in the Amazon societies women ruled the society. To be more explicit, Amazon queens were elected to rule over the people. They also acted as warriors and hunters as well.

Characteristics of Matriarchy System

1. Descent is reckoned through the mother.
2. The husband is marely a easual visitor or stays with his wife at her residence.
3. The children are brought up in the home of the wife's relatives.
4. Property is transferred through the mothers and only females succed to it.

Difference between Patriarchy and Matriarchy

Although the two concepts seem to stand in complete opposition with each other, it should be noted that they are not actually as contrasting as they seem. However, there are a number of obvious differences between the two social systems. Let us make an attempt to differentiate between the two social systems by placing them in parallel with each other.

Table 4.1: Difference between Patriarchy and Matriarchy

Characters	Patriarchy	Matriarchy
Definition	A patriarchal system is a social system in which the father is the head of the household.	A matriarchal system is a social system in which the mother is the head of the household.
Meaning	Patriarchy, on the other hand, is a social system, wherein males enjoy all the powers, control, and authority, and women are given subordinate roles.	Matriarchy is essentially a woman-oriented society, wherein all the leadership and authority rest in the hands of women.
Views about Nature	The patriarchal system is consumer-oriented. The patriarchs believe that nature has immense resources, which can be used by humans, in order to make profits.	The matriarchal system is nature-oriented. The matriarchs regard nature as an organic whole and lay emphasis on maintaining its balance at all times.
Philosophy and World View	The patriarchs place different entities of the universe in parallel with each other, such that the two separate entities can never meet, like they do in the matriarchal system. Therefore, God is separate from man, body from the spirit, and so on.	The matriarchs look at the world as a harmonious whole. They believe in the idea of several entities coming together in harmony, and facilitating the smooth functioning of the universe.

Table 4.1 Continued

Table 4.1 Continued

Characters	Patriarchy	Matriarchy
Head of the Household	Father is the head of the household.	Mother is the head of the household.
Power	In a patriarchal system, the father has more power and control over others.	In a matriarchal system, the mother has more power and control over others.
Sexual Orientation	A patriarchal society is often sexually repressive. This is because sex here is considered to be of two kindsone that is for procreation, in which case it is considered to be sacred, while the other one is lustful love, which is regarded to be sinful, and brings shame. Moreover, a patriarchal society essentially accepts only heterosexual relationships and is largely homophobic.	A matriarchal society is often sexually open, and sex is regarded as a religious expression. Owing to this, all kinds of relationshipsheterosexual, bisexual, homosexual, etc. are acceptable to the matriarchal society.
Property Ownership	The ownership of property goes to males.	The ownership of property goes to females.
Governance	The society is governed by males.	The society is governed by females.

Patriarchal and Matriarchal Families

Many societies, in the past and present, have patriarchies as their guiding force in social, legal, political, and economic matters. In a society that favors patriarchies, we may be able to see these factors at play:

1. Women lack the ability to control property.
2. Men rule the families and in all kinship contexts.
3. The lives of men are valued above the lives of the women.
4. Men usually are the ones who are making the major decisions in the community.
5. The work of men is considered more important than the work of women.
6. Women do not have domestic authority in the family.
7. There is a lack of male-female joint participation in warfare, work, and community decision making.

Matriarchies are not limited to families. Like patriarchy-centered societies, a matriarchal society means that women can be the big decision makers in the community.

Living Examples of Matrilineal Societies in India

Khasi Tribe

The majority of this tribe resides in the state of Meghalaya. Given the hilly terrain and dense forests of the region, it is relatively isolated from the societies residing in the plains. Though women of the tribe still lack any representation in the political arena of the state, the affairs of the tribe as well as domestic affairs are controlled by the women of the house. Following the matrilineal law of inheritance, the youngest daughter of the house will stay with the parents and inherit the house that is named after her mother. The husband is expected to leave his house and live with his wife in his mother-in-laws house.

Garo Tribe

Neighbours to Khasi, this tribe have a similar social formation and also follows the matrilineal methodology to trace property. A Garo family is headed by the mother of the house but the father is responsible for providing sustenance. The tribe is divided into sub tribes and clans, with marriage outside the tribe highly discouraged. The daughter of the family carries the clan name throughout her life, whereas the son takes up his wife's clan name after marriage. If the marriage doesn't work out, the couple can get separated without any social stigma. Similar to the Khasi tradition, the youngest daughter in a Garo family will inherit the property and if there is no female inheritor within the immediate family, the property passes to the daughter of the mother's sister.

Matrilineal Societies of Kerala

Kerala has the best sex ratio of the country, a fact which is not only to be credited to the high literacy rate, but also to the fading culture of a matrilineal society. Officially, the state has banned the matrilineal/matrilocal family structure through the Joint Family System (Abolition) Act, 1975. The act was passed by the Kerala State Legislature. Compared to the previous two social formations, Kerala is surrounded with states that have a strong culture of patriarchy, resulting in the fading of matrilineal families. On the other hand, women in Kerala enjoy a higher political stature compared to most women across the country, as well as the two aforementioned tribes. A few families still follow the matrilineal tradition of carrying the mothers name throughout their life.

5

Social Construction of Gender

The idea '*gender difference*' is '*socially constructed*' is a view present in many philosophical and sociological theories about gender. According to this view, society and culture create gender roles and these roles are prescribed as ideal or appropriate behavior for a person of that specific gender. Some argue that the differences in behavior between men and women are entirely social conventions, whereas others believe that behavior is influenced by universal biological factors to some extent, with social conventions having a major effect on gendered behavior.

Social Constructionism

The roots of the social constructionist movement in psychology are related to the criticism of the objectivism assumed by positivist/empiricist concepts of knowledge. Among the most popular variations of the social constructionist theories is the gender role theory, considered by Alsop, Fitzsimons and Lennon (2002) as an early form of social constructionism.

Social constructionism is the concept that there are many things that people "know" or take to be "reality" that are at least partially, if not completely, socially situated. For example, Harvard psychologist Steven Pinker writes that some categories really are social constructions: they exist only because people tacitly agree to act as if they exist.

Assumptions of Social Constructionism

The basic assumptions of social constructionism, as described by Marecek, Crawford and Popp are:

Social Constructionism is a Theory of Knowledge: Social constructionism focuses on how meaning is created. Emerging from the criticism of objectivity, social constructionism challenges concepts of knowledge put forward by positivism, which postulates the externality of reality and that empirically-proved truths are mind-independent.

Knowledge is a Social Product: According to Marecek, Crawford and Popp knowledge is an "account of reality produced collaboratively by a community of knowers". Thus, social constructionists focus on how meaning is created and suggest that knowledge is not only a social product, but a product of a specifically situated society; various accounts of reality depend on place and time – in order to study knowledge as a social product, one has to historicize and contextual the given description of reality.

Power and Hierarchy Underlie Social Construction: This focus results in showing how individuals differ in status, entitlement, efficacy, self-respect and other traits based on the kind of interactions one is involved in and subjected to.

Language is at the Core of Knowledge: Language is considered the building block of culture; it conveys meaning and creates the system of knowledge humans participate in. Ultimately, language has a huge influence on how humans perceive reality and, as a result, is the creator of this reality.

Social Construction is a Dynamic Process: Social constructionists emphasize the complexity of how knowledge is created in social interactions. Knowledge and meanings are not stable or constant; they are co-constructed in interactions with others, negotiated, modified and shifted. People are active in their perception, understanding and sharing of knowledge acquired from their social milieu.

The Individual and Society are Indissoluble: Social constructionists question the Western idea of an autonomous individual who can draw a clear line between the self and the society. According to social constructionism, individuals can create meaning only in relation to what they are exposed to in their environment. Paradoxically, the same individuals co-create the meanings that are available in this environment.

Social Construction of Gender

Gender is socially constructed and a result of socio-cultural influences throughout an individual's development. Gender identity can be affected by and is different from one society to another depending on the way the members of society evaluate the role of females and males. Our gender identity can be influenced from the ethnicity of the group, their historical and cultural background, family values and religion.

Often people confuse or misuse the terms gender and sex. The term sex refers to the biological distinction of being male and female. To make the distinction clearer one could consider that we inherit the sex but we learn our gender. Gender is a structural feature of society and the sociological significance of gender is that it is a devise by which society controls its members.

Gender like social class and race can be used to socially categorize people and even lead to prejudice and discrimination. Prejudice is a set of attitudes, more likely unfavorable, towards members of a group. Discrimination is overt negative behaviors towards a person based on his or her membership in a group.

When there is differential treatment of people based on their sex the term sexism defines this behavior. Sexism refers to any bias against an individual or group based on the individual's or group's sex. Gender discrimination is another way one could define sexism and in particular this is associated with discrimination and stereotyped beliefs against women.

Stereotypes are beliefs about the characteristics, attributes and behaviors of members of certain groups and most of them are socio-culturally based. Stereotype ideas and beliefs regarding women, although they have been changed and improved, are still evident in our country and in other modern cultures.

The idea of social construction of gender sees society, not biological sex differences, as the basis for gender identity. There are many different processes by which the expectations associated with being a boy or a girl is passed on through society. For instance, one could see this from the moment a child comes into the world and from the fact that he/she has to face a "blue" or "pink" reality.

The social construction of gender could be further been seen by the way parents behave to their children, by their expectations about how their children should behave and act, and by the toys they buy for them. For example, girls are supposed to play with dolls and be sweet and emotional and boys are supposed to play with action figures and be aggressive and rational. Therefore clothes, toys, and even the language used with young children follow the trend of stereotyping gender. Children learn by modeling and the messages they receive and act accordingly. An example similar to the dress code we having for children can also be seen with adults, particularly in the colors, fabrics and designs specific to each gender. Another example is the situation of a female working in the business field that is expected to dress in masculine way in order to be considered successful and to be taken more seriously. This could demonstrate again how social influences affect gender expectations and shape behaviors and norm regarding gender.

Apart from the family, which is the first agent of socialization and learning gender identity, children learn from other sources such as school. Starting from the first years of school, including day care center years, children learn their gender identity from playing and interacting with other children and care providers. By visiting a child care programme one may notice that the environment is arranged in ways to promote gender identity. Most likely there will be an area staged as the housekeeping corner where girls the play and there will be another area with building blocks and tool kit items where the boys play. However, it is believed by several that the kind of toys and roles children play affect their future and the skills they learn. Playing with blocks is considered giving experience in spatial relations and in mathematical concepts, where playing with dolls and dramatic role playing is associated with learning to be a nurturer. As children grow more stereotype ideas are involved regarding favorable and suitable subjects for each gender.

Furthermore, the media also affects and influences gender identity. For instance, children are constantly bombarded with shows depicting gender stereotype models from toys marketed as for boys or girls, to children's TV programmes and shows.

However, the social construction of gender does not happen only once and does not stop with children. It continues throughout the rest of our lives and influences our perspective and the way we view things and situations.

Additionally cultural and religious beliefs and attitudes have a serious impact on gender identity and in many cases promote stereotype beliefs against women and lead to gender discrimination. When it comes to culture and religious influences in a society regarding the view of gender, the concept of institutionalized sexism is appropriate to describe this situation. Institutionalized sexism is the sexist attitudes that are held by the vast majority of people living in a society where stereotypes and discrimination are the norm. When a society has specific norms, people living within the society adapt to them and they will do the same even for discriminatory norms. For instance when a society, due to religious and cultural reasons, view women as weak or inferior people living within the society will develop the same views and will act accordingly. One can see this for example in many Muslim countries and also with different religious groups, even in our own country. People tend to conform to their group and will do the same even when they engage in discriminatory behaviors as they want to fit in and be accepted by their group which is known as normative conformity.

Society constructs our gender and categorizes its members similar as it does with age, ethnicity, race, social class and status. However, the categorization according to gender is another way of manipulating members of a society and to promote inequalities. There are obvious biological and anthropological differences between the two sexes, but we cannot use these differences to infer conclusions and provide stereotyped models about gender. As mentioned in the beginning, sexism is the term that accounts for gender discrimination and has different forms. One of them already mentioned is benevolent sexism characterized by positive but stereotyped views of women. Contrarily another form is hostile sexism which is characterized by negative stereotypical views towards women. Lastly another form of sexism is ambivalent sexism which holds views of both hostile and benevolent sexist attitudes simultaneously. However, no matter the form, sexism has overall negative consequences and results in stereotyping women, and even prejudice and discrimination.

Factors Responsible for the Social Construction of Gender

Gender is a social construct that is manifested at various levels and reinforced by various structures:

Household: Girls and boys are assigned different roles, rights and benefits. This begins when they are small, and persists through issues of succession and inheritance.

Community: Socially constructed roles are reinforced through differential allocation of roles, rights and privileges. Women and girls cook and serve at community meetings, while men deliberate on issues and make decisions.

School: Teachers treat girls and boys differently, by reinforcing stereotyped gender roles and using texts, curricula and management styles that reinforce gender stereotypes.

Religion: Religion is used to reinforce gender inequalities in society by positioning women in a subordinate status to men. Text in the Christian Bible, for example, saying that wives should submit to their husbands is often used to dominate or even abuse women.

Government: Gender insensitive policies and plans, as well as the absence of women in decision making processes and positions, reinforce gender stereotyped roles, rights and privileges.

Media: The media play a big role in portraying stereotypical images of women and men that reinforce gender inequalities.

All these forces position women in a lower social status compared with men – socially, economically, politically and culturally.

Causes of Social Construction of Gender during Development

The following are the some of the causes of social constructions of gender:

Gender-based Harassment: Gender-based harassment serves as a form of gender boundary policing. Girls are expected to conform to stereotypical gendered appearances, as are boys. Both male and female students regularly take part in policing gender boundaries through bullying. Male students frequently harass male and female students, while female students generally only harass other female students. The practice of male students bullying other male students is explicitly linked to machismo that boys are expected to subscribe to in order to be constructed and related to as 'normal' boys. Many girls report that boys tease and ridicule them on the basis of their appearance, which is linked to boys asserting masculine power through sexist practices of denigrating girls. This also serves to perpetuate the idea that appearance is a female's most important asset. The way in which girls harass other girls is through gossiping, instead of confronting the other girls directly. Unique appearances and attempts to stand out among girls are regarded very negatively. This type of female on female bullying sets the standard for appearance norms and the importance of appearance for females. Overall, gender-based harassment serves to define and enforce gender boundaries of high school students by high school students.

Adolescent View of Adulthood: Gender is a cultural construction which creates an environment where an adolescent's performance in school is related to their life goals and expectations. Because, most young women know they want to be mothers and wives, the choice of professions and future goals can be inherently flawed by the gender constraints. Because, a girl may want to be a mother later, her academics in high school can create clear gender differences because *"higher occupational expectations, educational expectations, and academic grades were more strongly associated with the expected age of parenthood for girls than for boys"*. With *"young women recognizing potential conflicts between the demands of work and family"*, they will not try as hard in high school allowing males to achieve higher academic achievement then girls. Crocket and Beal in their article "The Life Course in the Making: Gender and the Development of Adolescents", *"gender differences in the anticipated timing of future role transitions, the impact of expectations and values on these expected timings, and the extent to which expectations foreshadow actual behavior"*. The actions of a youth in school greatly impact the choices the individual will have over a lifetime. Women especially are constrained in the way they view their adulthood even at a young age because of motherhood.

Adolescents view on adulthood is also determined by their employment in high school. Many boys work during school and *"unlike young women, young men who had not worked during high school did not quite match their peers"*. Because, many other boys are working, those who don't work may not be as successful after graduation.

Depression: High school continues to become a more high-pressure environment with academic and social triggers increasing the expectations of adolescents. High school is a large transitional period for teenagers causing them to *"cope with these various transitions in different ways; some negotiate the passages easily whereas others develop serious behavioral and psychological problems"*. One of these psychological problems is depression. While the environment of high school can be stressful biological functions also play a large role is psychological well-being. Negriff and Susman explain in their article *"Pubertal Timing, Depression, and Externalizing Problems"* that *"the same hormones that increase during puberty are also related to depression and aggressive tendencies. Higher levels of testosterone are associated with increased aggression in boys and girls, whereas higher estrogen for girls is associated with increased depressive symptoms"*. The gender differences observed may not just be due to the cultural expectations, but rather a biological function of the sex the individuals are born with. Self-esteem has also been linked to depression in high school students. One study done by James Battle in 1980 took 26 student ages 15–18 showed a correlation between depression and self-esteem. In the 80s, research had not looked past adults and Battle's research was some of the first of its kind which showed a direct correlation between self-esteem and depression. Self-esteem is not a product of our biology but rather is culturally constructed. Girls in high school also tend to have lower self-esteem due to body image. With depression and self-esteem being so closely linked the potential for having the disease can result in an educational experience which can be compromised. Depression can be isolating, and without proper academics and societal support, high school can be challenging. Along with higher rates of self-esteem issues in adolescents, this can adversely affect girls' academics and social life in high school.

Body Image: High school is a major transitional period for girls and boys as their bodies transition into men and women. The end of high school is usually marked by the 18th birthday, a major milestone in an individual's life. Boys and girls go through this transformation within high school where each gender faces body satisfaction differently. There are many different factors that affect body image, *"including sex, media, parental relationship, and puberty as well as weight and popularity"*. The intersectionality of these factors causes unique experiences for adolescents during this period within their lives. As their body changes, so does the environment in which they live in. Body image is closely linked to psychological well-being during adolescence and can cause harmful effects when a child has body dissatisfaction. Helen Winfield in her article *"Body Image and Psychological Well-Being in Adolescents: The Relationship between Gender and School Type"* explains an adolescences high school experience is closely linked to their perceived body image. She analyzed over 336 teenagers and found "ratings of physical attractiveness and body image remain relatively stable across the early teenage years, but become increasingly negative around age 15–18 years because of pubertal changes". This shift during the high school years can cause serious psychological problems for adolescence. These psychological problems can manifest as bulimia and anorexia causing serious lifelong problems. These body image issues are especially prevalent in girls but as boys enterpuberty expectations of height and muscle mass change as well. Geoffrey H. Cohane, Harrison G. Pope Jr. in their article *"Body image in boys: A review of the literature"* argue *"girls typically wanted to be thinner, boys frequently wanted to be bigger"*. This clearly shows the gender difference in body image cause different beauty ideals. An adolescent's gender affects their body image and their high school experience.

Education: Due to the amount of time that children spend in school, *"teachers are influential role models for many aspects of children's educational experiences, including gender socialization"*. Teachers who endorse the culturally dominant gender-role stereotype regarding the distribution of talent between males and females distort their perception of their students' mathematical abilities and effort resources in mathematics, in a manner that is consistent with their gender-role stereotype and to a greater extent than teachers who do not endorse the stereotype.

6

Sex Typing, Sex Roles, Gender Roles, Gender Stereotypes and Gender Based Division and Valuation of Work

SEX TYPING AND SEX ROLES

Sex Typing

Sex-typing is process of categorizing men and women on the bases of some traits. Despite of cultural differences, we find some similarities in traits. For example women are thought to be sensitive, weak, dependent and men are associated with the traits of adventurous and determined in most of the cultures. The term gender and sex are used interchangeably. The word sex gives biological affect whereas social scientists prefer to use term gender because of its socio-psychological connotation.

Development of Sex Typing: Development of sex-typing starts with sex-identity that is sense of being male or female, mostly children acquire this identity at the age of 3 years. Researchers have found that sex-identity changes with the age and experiences; according to socio-psychological phenomenon development of sex-typing takes place during late childhood. In early childhood differences in hair styles, clothes and toys aid in child's concept of sex-identity, whereas in later childhood sex stereotypes are learned through imitation and observational learning; what other people act, feel, behave or think. Mostly at the age of five children can associate certain traits like brave or weak with man and women or they are able to separate tools or things used by both sexes.

Sex Roles

Sex-roles are expected set of thinking and behavior patterns for males and females. A group of social scientists take development of gender-roles as positive factor for socialization and adjustment process of individual. Others opine that gender-identity minimize the use of individual potential and abilities considering not suitable for their sex. They view that sex-typing stereotypes also affect the process of self-exploration, especially in case of women.

Theorists concerned with women issues consider same sex-type stereotypes for females throughout the world and consider gender-roles natural and inflexible. In 1930's Mead studied three cultures in New Guinea and found out different sex-typed behaviors for women and supported hypothesis that human nature is flexible and changeable. But, biological bases of behavior cannot be ignored.

Some Sex Stereotyped Behaviours for Males and Females

Males

- Aggressive
- Brave
- Autocrat
- Dominant
- Independent

Females

- Emotional
- Sentimental
- Fragile
- Dependent
- Submissive

Factors Influencing Sex Typing

Sex-typing occurs at both intentional and unintentional level. At unintentional level biological determinants play role and intentional level is affected by psycho-social determinants.

Biological Determinant of Sex Typing

The first determinant of being male or female is biological. Chromosomes are structural units of heredity and carry genetic information. In human beings there are 23 pairs of chromosomes. 23rd pair of chromosome is called sex chromosome in females it is XX and in males it is XY. Only females can bear child, and these biological differences lead towards different sex-type stereotypes.

Psycho-social Determinants of Sex Typing

Socialization: Socialization is a process of learning sex-roles from different agents of society. Firstly parents and family are important agents that guide child in sex-typing and identification with same sex. Their different behavior with girl and boy develops gender identity. Secondly cultural sex-stereotypes also aid in identifying process. Gender role can vary according to the social group to which a person belongs or he/she identifies. For example in all over the world women share the stereotype of being coward and weepy. Sex-typing is very rigid in first 5 years of individual because girls and boys receive different treatments from the society. Sex-typing is flexible and with the passage of time when child acquire cognitive development sex-roles are learnt and changed.

Family: Family is most important of agent of socialization and sex-typing. Family members are responsible for fulfilling physical and psychological needs. Child receives inheritance from family and it guides for social, emotional development. Family provides basic knowledge of sex-typing and teaches cultural sex-stereotypes. In extended family, members (grandparents, uncle & aunts) also influence the process of sex-typing.

Parents: Parents are responsible for transmitting their own sex-roles and stereotypes to their child. Parents' verbal and non-verbal gestures and selection of toys, colors and play activities for by and girl develop concept of sex- typing. Positive encouragement or extra support from parents can develop opposite sex stereotype in girl or boy, for example girl can be more assertive or boy can take more interest in cooking or household activities.

Schools: Schools are significant institutions for sex-typing especially early perceptions about individuals and things influence the decisions of later life. Teacher's behavior, style of punishment and different play activities with boys and girls facilitates sex-typing. Schooling is threat for the child at beginning as he/she has to leave mother. So, in most of the countries nursery teaching is associated with females that provides substitute of mother to the students.

Childhood Play: Childhood play activities star in pre-school years and share stereotypes and sex-typing, socialized by parents and family. Role of childhood play in ex-typing depends on the school environments. Schools where boys are girls are stressed sex stereotypes, sex-typing is developed earlier but institutions where child are allowed to play according to their interest and cognitive abilities boys or girls can enjoy any kind of play (dolls house or boxing).

Peers: Peer groups develop at the age of six or seven when schooling starts and generally same sex groups are formed. Peer influences style of conversation, play activities, ideas and religious activities. Peer approval force child to adopt sex-biased behaviors in case of same sex peer group.

Social Discrimination: In socialization process of Indian culture females are generally victim of sex discrimination. Socialization is affected by Lullabies and marriage practices. Lullabies are practices that promote cultural norms and values. In Indian culture these lullabies promote negative or weaker position of females than males. Women are given inferior status and males are considered symbol of pride and power for the family. These practices promote sex-discrimination, negative stereotypes and inferior concept of gender-identity. When girl or boy sees his/her mother and father singing these lullabies, negative sex-identities for females are developed.

Mass Media: Media is not only source of communication or entertainment; it also plays a vital role in projecting cultural norms and values, and sex-typed behavior. Media has been depicted women concerning about family matters or house hold cores. After and during 90'smedia has started projecting women in positive way showing their educational concerns and progress, female health issues and role of women in economic development. Media transmit sex-typed behaviors via novels, stories, and cartoon movies. Children learn sex biased roles and values.

Community: Community greatly influences the decision making, achievement of goals or taking responsibilities. In the same way when an individual try to violate norms values or prevailing sex-type behaviors community oppose his/her and force him/her to follow traditional patterns. When women get some higher status than prevailing sex- biased stereotypes, because of her personal effort and individual abilities, she has to face certain obligations from community and keep herself on the way of success. The community's reaction to individual's action influences his/her sex-type behavior.

Work Environment: In choosing an occupation sex-typed behavior is very important. Male and female both think while selecting an occupation that it is according to his/her sex-role or not. Sex-typing also affect the *behavior* at working environment. When a woman wants to enter in professional life she has to take into consideration her sex- typed behavior and needs of profession. Generally the same nature of work done by male and female worker is given different weightage and males are given privilege for promotion. Theories before feminism were based on physiological differences; believe that female personality characteristics are dependent, low in mechanical abilities and resultantly cause low achievement level of women in professional life. Feminist theories have influenced the sex-typing. In case when a woman wants to achieve higher professional status relying on her individual abilities she has to sacrifice her sex-role.

Problems for Working Women in Community

Harassment at workplace, Discriminative behavior of male colleagues, Obstacles in the way of progress etc. these are all due to negative sex-biased stereotypes prevailing in the society.

Sex-roles are important for the development of any society, but these roles should give equal opportunities of development for both sexes. Specific sex-roles should not be perceived superior or inferior as it causes rigidity in behavior patterns and affect the process of social development.

GENDER ROLES

Gender roles are learned behaviours in a given society/community or other social group that condition which activities, tasks and responsibilities are perceived as male or female. Gender roles vary considerably across settings and also change over time. The following factors can shape and change gender roles:

- age
- class
- race
- ethnicity
- religion and other ideologies
- geographical environment
- economic environment
- political environment

Meaning and Concept of Gender Roles

The term *'gender role'* was first coined by John Money in 1955, during the course of his study of inter-sex individuals, to describe the manners in which these individuals expressed their status as a male or female in a situation where no clear biological assignment existed.

The concept of gender roles has been developed from the work of Caroline Moser. She explains this concept as follows: *Gender planning recognises that in most societies low-income women have a triple role: women undertake reproductive, productive, and community managing activities, while men primarily undertake productive and community politics activities."*

The World Health Organization (WHO) defines gender roles as *"socially constructed roles, behaviors, activities and attributes that a given society considers appropriate for men and women"*

A gender role is a set of societal norms dictating the types of behaviors which are generally considered acceptable, appropriate, or desirable for people based on their actual or perceived sex or sexuality. Gender roles are usually centered on conceptions of femininity and masculinity, although there are exceptions and variations. The specifics regarding these gendered expectations may vary substantially among cultures, while other characteristics may be common throughout a range of cultures. There is ongoing debate as to what extent gender roles and their variations are biologically determined, and to what extent they are socially constructed.

Gender roles are the way people act, what they do and say, to express being a girl or a boy, a woman or a man. These characteristics are shaped by society. Gender roles vary greatly from one culture to the next, from one ethnic group to the next, and from one social class to another. But every culture has gender roles — they all have expectations for the way women and men, girls and boys, should dress, behave, and look.

Children learn gender roles from an early age — from their parents and family, their religion, and their culture, as well as the outside world, including television, magazines, and other media. As children grow, they adopt behaviors that are rewarded by love and praise. They stop or hide behaviors that are ridiculed, shamed, or punished. This happens early in life. By age three, children have usually learned to prefer toys and clothes that are "appropriate" to their gender.

As we grow, we learn how to behave from those around us. In this socialization process, children are introduced to certain roles that are typically linked to their biological sex. The term *'gender role'* refers to society's concept of how men and women are expected to act and how they should behave. These roles are based on norms or standards, created by society.

Characteristics of Gender Roles

1. A Gender Role is a part that an individual plays as a social actor, including the patterns of feeling and behavior deemed appropriate or inappropriate by others because of the individual's assigned sex.
2. Gender roles are generally neither positive nor negative; they are simply inaccurate generalizations of the male and female attributes.
3. Gender roles are based on norms, or standards, created by society.
4. The term "gender role" refers to society's concept of how men and women are expected to act.
5. The term "gender role" refers to society's concept of how men and women are expected to act and behave.
6. Gender roles are based on norms, or standards, created by society.
7. In many culture, masculine roles have traditionally been associated with strength, aggression, and dominance, while feminine roles have traditionally been associated with passivity, nurturing, and subordination.
8. Gender Roles are the behaviors required by persons occupying the Male or Female Status

Types of Gender Roles

Gender roles are a specific set of social and behavioral actions which are considered to be appropriate for the given gender. Some gender roles are given below:

Reproductive Role: Childbearing/rearing responsibilities, and domestic tasks done by women, required to guarantee the maintenance and reproduction of the labour force. It includes not only biological reproduction but also the care and maintenance of the work force (male partner and working children) and the future work force (infants and school-going children).

Productive Role: Work done by both men and women for pay in cash or kind. It includes both market production with an exchange-value, and subsistence/home production with actual use-value, and also potential exchange-value. For women in agricultural production, this includes work as independent farmers, peasant wives and wage workers.

Community Managing Role: Activities undertaken primarily by women at the community level, as an extension of their reproductive role, to ensure the provision and maintenance of scarce resources of collective consumption, such as water, health care and education. This is voluntary unpaid work, undertaken in 'free' time.

Community Politics Role: Activities undertaken primarily by men at the community level, organizing at the formal political level, often within the framework of national politics. This is usually paid work, either directly or indirectly, through status or power.

Multiple Roles: Both men and women play multiple roles. The major difference, however, is that:

Men typically play their roles sequentially, focusing on a single productive role While *women* must usually play their roles simultaneously, balancing the demands of each within their limited time constraints.

Gender Roles and Relationships Matrix

The Gender Relationship Matrix is an analytical tool that uses participatory methodology to facilitate the definition and analysis of gender issues by the communities that are affected by them. Using the Gender Relationship Matrix will provide a unique articulation of issues as well as develop gender analysis capacity from the grassroots level up. The main aims of the Gender Relationship Matrix are as follows:

1. Helps determine the differing impacts of development interventions on women and men.
2. Provides a community based technique for identification and analysis.
3. Initiates a process of analysis that identifies and challenges gender roles within the community in a constructive manner.

The Gender Relationship Matrix is consisting of two parts of analysis namely level of analysis and category of analysis.

Level of Analysis

1. *Women:* All ages in the community
2. *Men:* All ages in the community
3. *Household:* All men, women, children residing together extended, nuclear family.
4. *Community:* Everyone in the project area as a whole.

Category of Analysis

1. *Labour:* This refers to Changes in tasks, level of skill required (skilled versus unskilled, formal education, training) and labour capacity (how many people and how much then can do; do people need to be hired or can members of the household do it.)
2. *Time:* This refers to changes in the amount of time (3 hours, 4 days, and so on) it takes to carry out the task associated with the project or activity.
3. *Resource:* This refers to the changes in access to capital (income, land, etc) as a consequence of the project, and the extended control over changes in resources (more or less) for each level of analysis.
4. *Cultural:* Cultural factors refer to changes in social aspects of the participants lives (changes in gender roles or status) as the result of the project.

Table 6.1: Gender Roles and Relationships Matrix Format

	Categories of Analysis			
Levels ofAnalysis	Labour	Time	Resource	Culture
Women				
Men				
Household				
Community				

Models of Gender Roles

Talcott Parsons' View

Working in the United States, Talcott Parsons developed a model of the nuclear family in 1955, which at that place and time was the prevalent family structure. It compared a strictly traditional view of gender roles (from an industrial-age American perspective) with a more liberal view. The Parsons model was used to contrast and illustrate extreme positions on gender roles.

Model A describes total separation of male and female roles, while Model B describes the complete dissolution of gender roles. (The examples are based on the context of the culture and infrastructure of the United States.)

However, these structured positions become less a liberal-individualist society and the actual behavior of individuals is usually somewhere between these poles. According to the interactionist approach, roles (including gender roles) are not fixed but are constantly negotiated between individuals. In North America and southern South America, this is the most common approach among families whose business is agriculture. Gender roles can

Table 6.2: Models of Gender Roles

	Model A Total Role Segregation	Model B Total Integration of Roles
Education	Gender-specific education; high professional qualification is important only for the man	Co-educative schools, same content of classes for girls and boys, same qualification for men and women.
Profession	The workplace is not the primary area of women; career and professional advancement is deemed unimportant for women	For women, career is just as important as for men; equal professional opportunities for men and women are necessary.
Housework	Housekeeping and child care are the primary functions of the woman; participation of the man in these functions is only partially wanted.	All housework is done by both parties to the marriage in equal shares.
Decision making	In case of conflict, man has the last say, for example in choosing the place to live, choice of school for children, buying decisions	Neither partner dominates; solutions do not always follow the principle of finding a concerted decision; status quo is maintained if disagreement occurs.
Child care and education	Woman takes care of the largest part of these functions; she educates children and cares for them in every way	Man and woman share these functions equally.

influence all kinds of behaviors, such as choice of clothing, choice of work and personal relationships, e.g., parental status.

Gender Roles in India

In India, gender roles are determined largely by sex, religion, oppressive tradition and culture. Dating back to 200 B.C., Indian tradition dictates that a woman's sole purpose in life should revolve around her husband, children and home. Though some women work alongside men in society, their efforts are expected and unappreciated. A wife is subject to her husband's authority and is required to honor him and bring him happiness. However, mothers are disciplinarians and demand obedience from their children. A son's birth is celebrated, while the birth of a daughter is considered painful to the family. Boys are lavished with love and respect and are provided better food and health care than girls. About 120 million of the country's women live in poverty, because they are considered of no value. Males generally receive better education opportunities than females. Girls are often removed from classes to perform chores and well-educated women may suffer social stigma.

Since 1993, however, women have been overcoming gender bias and filling positions in local governance. A national policy in India was drafted in 2001 in an effort to bring about advancement and empowerment of women.

GENDER STEREOTYPES

A stereotype is a widely accepted judgment or bias regarding a person or group — even though it is overly simplified. Stereotypes about gender can cause unequal and unfair treatment because of a person's gender. This is called sexism.

Gender stereotypes are generalizations about the roles of each gender. Gender roles are generally neither positive nor negative; they are simply inaccurate generalizations of the male and female attributes. Since each person has individual desires, thoughts, and feelings, regardless of their gender, these stereotypes are incredibly simplistic and do not at all describe the attributes of every person of each gender.

While most people realize that stereotypes are untrue, many still make assumptions based on gender. There are many stereotypes we may all be guilty of, such as assuming that all women want to marry and have children, or that all men love sports. The following is a list of some of the most common gender stereotypes as they pertain to either men or women.

Female Gender Stereotypes

Gender stereotypes begin the second a baby's gender is found out. As soon as we find out it's a girl, we immediately begin decorating a pink nursery filled with soft décor and butterflies and flowers. We assume that our daughter will be very "girly" and fill her closet with frilly dresses and her toy box with tea sets and dolls. What this is essentially doing, even though many parents don't realize it, is setting our child up to be the "perfect lady," and teaching her how to be the stereotypical woman. We are teaching her that girls are supposed to wear dresses, serve food, and take care of babies; the biggest and most common stereotype put on women.

The following is a list of some of the most common gender stereotypes as they pertain to women:

- Women are supposed to have "clean jobs" such as secretaries, teachers, and librarians
- Women are nurses, not doctors
- Women are not as strong as men
- Women are supposed to make less money than men
- The best women are stay at home moms
- Women don't need to go to college
- Women don't play sports
- Women are not politicians
- Women are quieter than men and not meant to speak out

- Women are supposed to be submissive and do as they are told
- Women are supposed to cook and do housework
- Women are responsible for raising children
- Women do not have technical skills and are not good at "hands on" projects such as car repairs
- Women are meant to be the damsel in distress; never the hero
- Women are supposed to look pretty and be looked at
- Women love to sing and dance
- Women do not play video games
- Women are flirts
- Women are never in charge

Male Gender Stereotypes

Stereotyping is no different when it's found out that a boy is on the way. The nursery is decked out in blue, his closet is filled with tiny jeans, polo shirts, and boots, and the theme is usually something like jungle animals or dinosaurs; something tough. Boys' toys consist of trucks, dinosaurs, action figures, and video games. From the beginning boys are taught to be tough, to be protective, and to defend themselves. Boys are taught that daddy's go to work and mommy's stay at home; from their point of view, boys have fun and girls do all the work.

Are you surprised to hear that most parents admit that they do not teach their sons how to do chores such as washing dishes or folding laundry? Instead, they teach them to take out the trash and mow the lawn; from the get-go boys are made to think that certain household chores are "women's work." This is a major stereotype, but the majority of American households today would prove this to be true. Men are supposed to do the dirty jobs and anything that requires muscle, they are also supposed to go to work and provide for the family. Little boys see this and the stereotype continues.

The following is a list of some of the most common gender stereotypes as they pertain tomen:

- All men enjoy working on cars
- Men are not nurses, they are doctors
- Men do "dirty jobs" such as construction and mechanics; they are not secretaries, teachers, or cosmetologists
- Men do not do housework and they are not responsible for taking care of children
- Men play video games
- Men play sports
- Men enjoy outdoor activities such as camping, fishing, and hiking
- Men are in charge; they are always at the top
- As husbands, men tell their wives what to do

- Men are lazy and/or messy
- Men are good at math
- It is always men who work in science, engineering, and other technical fields
- Men do not cook, sew, or do crafts

Four Basic Kinds of Gender Stereotypes

Personality Traits: For example, women are often expected to be passive and submissive, while men are usually expected to be self-confident and aggressive.

Domestic Behaviors: For example, caring for children is often considered best done by women, while household repairs are often considered best done by men.

Occupations: For example, until very recently most nurses and secretaries were usually women, and most doctors and construction workers were usually men.

Physical Appearance: For example, women are expected to be small and graceful, while men are expected to be tall and broad-shouldered.

How can we Challenge Gender Stereotypes?

We see gender stereotypes all around us. We also may see sexism. There are ways to challenge these stereotypes to help everyone, no matter their gender or gender identity, feel equal:

Point It Out: From magazines and television to film and the Internet, the media is filled with negative gender stereotypes. Sometimes these stereotypes are hard to see. Talk with friends and family members about the stereotypes you see and help others recognize how sexism and gender stereotypes can hurt all of us.

Walk the Talk: Be a role model for your friends and family. Respect people regardless of their gender.

Speak Up: If someone is making sexist jokes, challenge them.

Give It a Try: If you want to do something that is not normally associated with your gender, think about whether you'll be safe doing it. If you think you will, give it a try. People will learn from your example.

If you have been struggling with gender or gender identity, you're not alone. It may help you to talk to a trusted parent, friend, family member, teacher, or professional counselor.

Influence of the Family on Gender Typing

Parents' Influence on Children's Gender-Typed Choices: Families actively play a role in gender-role socialization by the ways in which they organize the environment for the child. Boys and girls are dressed differently, receive different toys to play with, and sleep in bedrooms that are furnished differently.

Parental Behavior toward Girls and Boys: In addition, girls and boys are viewed and treated differently by their parents, particularly their fathers. Boys are thought to be stronger and are treated more roughly and played with more actively than girls as early as birth. As children get older, girls are protected more and allowed less autonomy than boys, and girls are not expected to achieve as much in the areas of mathematics and careers as are boys.

Modeling Parents' Characteristics: As predicted by cognitive social learning theory, parental characteristics influence gender typing in terms of the role models that are available for the child to imitate. Parental power has a great impact on sex typing in boys, but not in girls; femininity in girls is related to the father's masculinity, his approval of the mother as a role model, and his reinforcement of participation in feminine activities.

Parental Absence or Unavailability: Because the father plays such a critical role in the development of children's gender roles, his absence has been related to disruptions in gender typing in preadolescent boys and to problems in relationships with peers of the opposite sex for adolescent females. Studies show that the effects of a father's absence on his daughter's interactions with men are long-lasting, extending to marital choices.

Gender Roles in Children of Gay and Lesbian Parents

There is no evidence of differences in the gender roles of boys and girls raised in gay or lesbian families. Most children of such families grow up to have heterosexual sexual orientations.

Extra Familial Influences on Gender Roles

Books and Television: Many extra familial influences affect gender-role typing. Male and female roles are portrayed in gender-stereotypic ways in television and many children's books. Males are more likely than females to be portrayed as aggressive, competent, rational, and powerful in the workforce. Females are more often portrayed as involved primarily in housework or caring for children.

Females are less likely to be leading characters on TV, and male characters are over represented in children's books-although some change toward more equal treatment has occurred in recent years. Children who are heavy TV viewers hold more stereotyped views; however, this may be due to their interpretations of what they see based on previously held stereotypes. A few attempts to use television to change gender stereotypes have been successful, but the effects typically have been modest and short-lived.

Peers, Gender Roles, and Self-Esteem: Peers also serve as an important source of gender-role standards. Children who have masculine or androgynous characteristics are likely to have higher self-esteem than those who have traditionally feminine characteristics.

Children are likely to react when other children violate gender-typical behaviors, and boys' cross-gender behaviors are more likely to meet with negative reactions from peers. Reactions from peers typically result in changes in behavior, particularly if the feedback is from a child of the same sex. This pattern of responsiveness may lead to gender segregation, which, in turn, provides opportunities to learn gender-typical roles. In *self-socialization*, children often spontaneously adopt gender-appropriate behavior.

Schools and Teachers: Teachers also treat girls and boys differently. Due to the emphasis in school on typically feminine characteristics such as quietness, obedience, and passivity, girls tend to like school better and perform better than boys in the early grades. Even in preschool, boys receive more criticism from teachers, who often react to children in gender-stereotypic ways. The implication of young boys' perceptions of school as gender-inappropriate may be lowered motivation and interest in school activities, leading to the higher rate of learning problems found in boys during the early grades.

The kinds of conforming and dependent behaviors encouraged in girls may be detrimental for their later academic success. The lack of public awareness of research findings, such as that in most areas of math girls do as well as boys, may prevent parents and others from encouraging girls to excel in these areas.

GENDER BASED DIVISION AND VALUATION OF WORK

Families provide love and support to adults and children, but homes are also workplaces, and households are important parts of the larger economy. Even when families do not directly produce or market goods and services, they keep the economy running by supporting and maintaining adult workers, buying and consuming products, and reproducing the workforce by having babies and socializing children. These domestic activities require labor. The total amount of time and effort put into feeding, clothing, and caring for family members rivals that spent in all other forms of work.

Every home is a combination of hotel, restaurant, laundry, and often childcare and entertainment center. The mundane work that goes into these activities is usually invisible to the people who benefit from it, especially children and husbands, who are the equivalent of nonpaying customers. Cleaning and cooking obviously require work, but even fun activities like parties or holiday gatherings require planning, preparation, service, clean-up, and other behind-the-scenes effort. Women perform most of this family labor, even though men do the same sorts of things outside the home for pay as chefs, waiters, or janitors. Although people tend to think of domestic activities as "naturally" being women's work, there is enormous variation in who does what both inside and outside the home. Every society has restrictions on what kinds of work men and women do, but there is no global content to these roles, and studies show that divisions of labor are influenced by specific environmental and social conditions. Activities often associated with women, such as nurturance, domestic chores, and childcare, are sometimes performed by men, and activities often associated with men, such as warfare, hunting, and politics, are sometimes performed by women.

Thus, although gender is often used to divide labor, there is no universal set of tasks that can be defined as "women's work" or "men's work."

Gender-based Division of Labour

The gender-based division of labour ascribed in a given socio-economic setting determines the roles that men and women actually perform. Since men and women play different roles, they often face very different cultural, institutional, physical and economic constraints, many of which are rooted in systematic biases and discrimination.

Definition

The gender division of labour refers to the allocation of different jobs or types of work to women and men. In feminist economics, the institutional rules, norms and practices that govern the allocation of tasks between women and men and girls and boys also constitute the gender division of labour, which is seen as variable over time and space and constantly under negotiation. The most prevalent form is the division of paid and unpaid work between women and men in private and public life.

Exploring Attitudes towards Gender

Attitudes towards Gender (also referred to as sex role attitudes) have been defined as"an individual's beliefs about appropriate behavior for men and women". One's gender role attitudes are likely to indicate her or his adherence to socially accepted and culturally based norms that dictate behavioral standards in cross-sex relationships. Gender role attitude sindicate the degree to which a person accepts or rejects socially accepted and culturally based norms that dictate appropriate behavior that is gender specific. Social attitudes surveys have included attitudinal questions asking about the roles of men and women within the family, in particular around providing an income from work versus playing a caring rolein the home.

Examples of gender role attitudes include such statements as "men should open the door for women," "fathers and mothers should participate equally in nurturing and caring for their children," "men are primarily responsible for earning money and providing for their family," and "women should adopt their husband's surname upon marriage."

Gender role attitudes and ideas about traits or tasks that are specific or inherent to a particular gender encourage us to stereotype or pigeonhole individuals according to their gender. Obviously, this practice has negative implications for both males and females. However, gender biases in language, traditions, and the work place have tended to historically favor men and produce undesirable consequences for women.

7

Feminism

There are two words one is feminism and other is feminist. Feminism refers to approach theory while feminist is a person to believes in and act according to feminist theory or theories. According to feminist thinkers, feminist is a person who believes in Equality and justice for women. Feminist may be activists, social scientist, academic, poet, social worker who express their feminism in different way. Feminism is an ideology, philosophy an attitude of mind, a way of looking at anything. It is not one unitary concept but instead of decrease and multi faced grouping of ideas and action. Feminism is mainly concern with women's inferior position in a society and with discrimination encountered by women because of their sex. Hence, all feminists call for change in social, cultural, religious, political and economic fields. They work to reduce in equality and eventually to overcome it.

Meaning and Definitions of Feminism

Feminism a doctrine that advocates equal rights for women or the movement aimed at equal rights for women. Feminism is a collection of movements and ideologies aimed at defining, establishing, and defending equal political, economic, and social rights for women. This includes seeking to establish equal opportunities for women in education and employment.

A simple meaning of the term feminism is "looking at world from women's point of view" It implies women's point of view's is relevant and effective for women, their perception and participation in social life. Feminism is a collection of movements and ideologies aimed at defining, establishing, and defending equal political, economic, and social rights for women. Feminism is defined as

> "Feminism is an awareness of women's oppression and exploitation in society at the place of work and with the family and the conscious action to change this situation."

> "Feminism is an awareness of patrician control, Exploitation and oppression of material and ideological levels of women's labour fertility and sexuality in the

family, at the place of work, and in society in general and conscious action by women and men to transfer the present situation."

Objectives of Feminism

The goals of feminism are to get women equal rights under the law and equal stature in society. It is the movement towards the social, political and economic equality of all people. A feminist advocates or supports the rights and equality of women.

The main objectives of feminism are:

1. To understand the nature of gender inequality.
2. To examine women's social roles and subjection of women in society.
3. To find out the causes of subordination status of women.
4. To analyze the origin of subordinate status of women.
5. To identify different forms of discrimination against women.
6. To identify the existing power relationships in specific spheres- family, economy, political, and other areas of social and cultural.
7. To examine social construction of sex and gender
8. To focus on Women's rights-law, wage property, voting and reproductive rights.
9. To protect women and girls from domestic violence, sexual harassment, and sexual assault.

Approaches or Types of Feminism

Some approaches or types of feminism are given below:

Liberal Feminism: Liberal feminism primarily focuses on women's ability to show and maintain their equality through their own actions and choices. It argues that our society holds the false belief that women are, by nature, less intellectually and physically capable than men, it tends to discriminate against women in the academy, the forum, and the marketplace.

Ecofeminism: Ecofeminism connects the exploitation and domination of women with that of the environment; ecofeminism argues that there is a connection between women and nature that comes from their shared history of oppression by a patriarchal Western society.

Transfeminism: Transfeminism is a category of feminism, most often known for the application of transgender discourses to feminist discourses, and of feminist beliefs to transgender discourse. It often criticizes the ideas of a universal sisterhood - instead, transfeminists view gender as a multifaceted set of diverse intrinsic and social qualities.

Anarcha-feminism: Anarcha-feminism views patriarchy as a manifestation of involuntary coercive hierarchy that should be replaced by decentralized voluntary association. Anarcha-feminists believe that the struggle against patriarchy is an essential part of class struggle, and the anarchist struggle against the state.

Black Feminism: Black Feminism argues that sexism, class oppression, and racism are inextricably bound together. The way these relate to each other is called intersectionality. Black feminist theory has argued that black women are positioned with in structures of power in fundamentally different ways than white women.

Postcolonial Feminism: Through analysis of entrenched power structures in formerly colonized nations, postcolonial feminism explains how economic and political institutions and social practices in those nations often oppress and marginalize women. In addition, it demonstrates how women around the globe struggle for equality and independence for themselves, their families, and their nations.

Multiracial Feminism: Multiracial feminism refers to the activist and scholarly work conducted by women of color and anti-racist white allies to promote race, class, and gender equality. In comparison to the highly documented second-wave white, middle-class feminism, which centered on abolishing patriarchy and privileged patriarchy as an oppression over all others, women of color feminism resists separating oppression and insists on recognizing the intersectionality of race, class, and gender oppression.

Radical Feminism: Radical feminism focuses on the theory of patriarchy as a system of power that organizes society into a complex of relationships based on the assertion that male supremacy oppresses women. Radical feminism aims to challenge and overthrow patriarchy by opposing standard gender roles and oppression of women and calls for a radical reordering of society.

Socialist Feminism: Socialist feminism argues that liberation can only be achieved by working to end both the economic and cultural sources of women's oppression.

Postmodern Feminism: Postmodern feminism incorporates postmodern and post-structuralist theory, and thus sees itself as moving beyond the modernist polarities of liberal feminism and radical feminism It has been described as the ultimate acceptor of diversity: "multiple truths, multiple roles, multiple realities are part of its focus.

Marxist Feminism: Marxist Feminism focuses on the social institutions of private property and capitalism to explain and criticize gender inequality and oppression. It posits that private property gives rise to economic inequality, dependence, political and domestic struggle between the sexes, and is the root of women's oppression in the current social context.

Chicana Feminism: Chicana Feminism analyzes the historical, social, political, and economic roles of Mexican American, Chicana, and Hispanic women in the United States

Post-structural Feminism: Post-structural Feminism emphasizes "the contingent and discursive nature of all identities", and in particular the social construction of gendered subjectivities. It resists universalist or normalizing conceptions of women as a group or altogether dismiss the category "woman".

French Feminism: French Feminism is distinguished by an approach which is more philosophical and literary. Its writings tend to be effusive and metaphorical being less concerned with political doctrine and generally focused on theories of "the body".

Transnational Feminism: Transnational Feminism is attentive to intersections among nationhood, race, gender, sexuality and economic exploitation on a world scale, in the context of emergent global capitalism. It inquires in to the social, political and economic conditions comprising imperialism; their connections to colonialism and nationalism; the role of gender, the state, race, class, and sexuality in the organization of resistance to hegemonies in the making and unmaking of nation and nation-state.

Atheist Feminism: Atheist Feminism is a movement that advocates the Feminism within atheism. Atheist feminists also oppose religion as a main source of female oppression and inequality, believing that the majority of the religions are sexist and oppressive to women.

Feminist Theology: Feminist Theology is a movement found in several religions, including Buddhism, Christianity, Judaism, and New Thought, to reconsider the traditions, practices, scriptures, and theologies of those religions from a feminist perspective. Some of the goals of feminist theology include increasing the role of women among the clergy and religious authorities, reinterpreting male-dominated imagery and language about God, determining women's place in relation to career and motherhood, and studying images of women in the religion's sacred texts.

Waves of Feminism

The three waves of feminism are discussed below.

First-wave Feminism: The term first-wave was coined in March 1968 by Martha Lear writing in T*he New York Times Magazine*, who at the same time also used the term "second-wave feminism". At that time, the women's movement was focused on de facto (unofficial) inequalities, which it wished to distinguish from the objectives of the earlier feminists. First-wave feminism was a period of feminist activity and thought that occurred within the time period of the 19th and early 20th century throughout the world. It focused on legal issues, primarily on gaining women's suffrage (the right to vote).

Second-wave Feminism: Second-wave feminism is a period of feminist activity and thought that first began in the early 1960s in the United States, and eventually spread throughout the Western world and beyond. In the United States the movement lasted through the early 1980s. It later became a worldwide movement that was strong in Europe and parts of Asia, such asTurkey and Israel, where it began in the 1980s, and it began at other times in other countries.

Whereas first-wave feminism focused mainly on suffrage and overturning legal obstacles to gender equality (e.g., voting rights, property rights), second-wave feminism broadened the debate to a wide range of issues: sexuality, family, the workplace, reproductive rights, de facto inequalities, and official legal inequalities. Second-wave feminism also drew attention to domestic violence and marital rape issues, establishment of rape crisis and battered women's shelters, and changes in custody and divorce law. Its major effort was the attempted passage of the Equal Rights Amendment (ERA) to the United States Constitution, in which they were defeated by anti-feminists led by Phyllis Schlafly, who argued as an anti-ERA view that the ERA meant women would be drafted into the military.

Third-wave Feminism: Rebecca Walker coined the term "Third Wave" to highlight the focus on queer and non-white women. Third-wave feminism encompasses several diverse strains of feminist activity and study. Though exact boundaries are a subject of debate, it is generally marked as beginning in the early 1990s and continuing to the present. It is an "individual movement" in the sense that its purpose includes redefining what it is to be a feminist.

The third wave arose partially as a response to the perceived failures of second-wave feminism, and the backlash against initiatives and movements created during the 1960s, '70s and '80s. It attempts to expand feminism to include women with a diverse set of identities recognizing that women are of "many colors, ethnicities, nationalities, religions and cultural backgrounds". Thus it can be seen as a reaction to or continuation of second-wave feminism, and constitutes a partial destabilization of constructs from the second wave.

Feminism in India

Feminism in India is a set of movements aimed at defining, establishing, and defending equal political, economic, and social rights and equal opportunities for Indian women. It is the pursuit of women's rights within the society of India. Like their feminist counterparts all over the world, feminists in India seek gender equality: the right to work for equal wages, the right to equal access to health and education, and equal political rights. Indian feminists also have fought against culture-specific issues within India's patriarchal society, such as inheritance laws and the practice of widow immolation known as Sati.

Definition of Feminism in Indian Context

Women's role in Pre-colonial social structures reveals that feminism was theorized differently in India than in the West. In India, women's issues first began to be addressed when the state commissioned a report on the status of women to a group of feminist researchers and activists. The report recognized the fact that in India, women were oppressed under a system of structural hierarchies and injustices. During this period, Indian feminists were influenced by the Western debates being conducted about violence against women. However, due to the difference in the historical and social culture of India, the debate in favour of Indian women had to be conducted creatively and certain Western ideas had to be rejected. Women's issues began to gain an international prominence when the decade of 1975–1985 was declared the United Nations Decade for Women.

Indian women negotiate survival through an array of oppressive patriarchal family structures: age, ordinal status, relationship to men through family of origin, marriage and procreation as well as patriarchal attributes. Examples of patriarchal attributes include: dowry, siring sons etc., kinship, caste, community, village, market and the state. It should however be noted that several communities in India, such as the Nairs of Kerala, Shettys of Mangalore, certain Maratha clans and Bengali families exhibit matriarchal tendencies.

The heterogeneity of the Indian experience reveals that there are multiple patriarchies, contributing to the existence of multiple feminisms. Hence, feminism in India is not a singular theoretical orientation; it has changed over time in relation to historical and cultural realities, levels of consciousness, perceptions and actions of individual women, and women as a group. The widely used definition is "An awareness of women's oppression and exploitation in society, at work and within the family, and conscious action by women and men to change this situation." Acknowledging sexism in daily life and attempting to challenge and eliminate it through deconstructing mutually exclusive notions of femininity and masculinity as biologically determined categories opens the way towards an equitable society for both men and women.

The male and female dichotomy of polar opposites with the former oppressing the latter at all times is refuted in the Indian context because it was men who initiated social reform movements against various social evils. Patriarchy is just one of the hierarchies. Relational hierarchies between women within the same family are more adverse. Here women are pitted against one another. Not all women are powerless at all times.

Phases of Feminism in India

The three phases of feminism in India are discussed below:

First Phase: 1850–1915

Kamini Roy (poet and suffragette) became the first woman Honors Graduate in India in 1886. The colonial venture into modernity brought concepts of democracy, equality and individual rights. The rise of the concept of nationalism and introspection of discriminatory practices brought about social reform movements related to caste and gender relations. This first phase of feminism in India was initiated by men to uproot the social evils of *sati* (widow immolation), to allow widow remarriage, to forbid child marriage, and to reduce illiteracy, as well as to regulate the age of consent and to ensure property rights through legal intervention.

In addition to this, some upper caste Hindu women rejected constraints they faced under Brahminical traditions. However, efforts for improving the status of women in Indian society were somewhat thwarted by the late nineteenth century, as nationalist movements emerged in India. These movements resisted 'colonial interventions in gender relations' particularly in the areas of family relations. In the mid to late nineteenth century, there was a national form of resistance to any colonial efforts made to 'modernise' the Hindu family. This included the Age of Consent controversy that erupted after the government tried to raise the age of marriage for women. Several Indian states were ruled by women during British colonial advance including Jhansi (Rani Laxmibai), Kittur (Rani Chennama), Bhopal (Quidisa Begum) and Punjab (Jind Kaur).

Second Phase: 1915–1947

During this period the struggle against colonial rule intensified. Nationalism became the pre-eminent cause. Claiming Indian superiority became the tool of cultural revivalism resulting in an essentialising model of Indian womanhood similar to that of Victorian womanhood: special yet separated from public space. Gandhi legitimized and expanded Indian women's public activities by initiating them into the non-violent civil disobedience movement against the British Raj. He exalted their feminine roles of caring, self-abnegation, sacrifice and tolerance; and carved a niche for those in the public arena. Peasant women played an important role in the rural satyagrahas of Borsad and Bardoli.

The 1920s was a new era for Indian women and is defined as 'feminism' that was responsible for the creation of localized women's associations. These associations emphasized women's education issues, developed livelihood strategies for working-class women, and also organized national level women's associations such as the All India Women's Conference. Under the leadership of Mahatma Gandhi, it worked within the nationalist and anti-colonialist freedom movements. This made the mass mobilization of women an integral part of Indian nationalism. Women therefore were a very important part of various nationalist and anti-colonial efforts, including the civil disobedience movements in the 1930s.

Women's participation in the struggle for freedom developed their critical consciousness about their role and rights in independent India. This resulted in the introduction of the franchise and civic rights of women in the Indian Constitution.

Third Phase: Post-1947

Post-independence feminists began to redefine the extent to which women were allowed to engage in the workforce. Indira Gandhi was the first and only woman Prime Minister of India and the second-longest-serving Prime Minister. Prior to independence, most feminists accepted the sexual divide within the labour force. However, feminists in the 1970s challenged the inequalities that had been established and fought to reverse them. These inequalities included unequal wages for women, relegation of women to 'unskilled' spheres of work, and restricting women as a reserve army for labour.

Feminist class-consciousness also came into focus in the 1970s, with feminists recognizing the inequalities not just between men and women but also within power structures such as caste, tribe, language, religion, region, class etc. This also posed as a challenge for feminists while shaping their over-reaching campaigns as there had to be a focus within efforts to ensure that fulfilling the demands of one group would not create further inequalities for another. Now, in the early twenty-first century, the focus of the Indian feminist movement has gone beyond treating women as useful members of society and a right to parity, but also having the power to decide the course of their personal lives and the right of self-determination.

8

Women Empowerment

"If you educate a man you educate an individual; however, if you educate a woman you educate a whole family. Women empowered means mother India empowered." Jawaharlal Nehru

The status of women in the Indian society has been a complicated one. It passed through fluctuations through the ages. While it was high during the Vedic period, it slumped in the Post-Vedic period. Again, in the modem period, it rose.

Education is milestone of women empowerment because it enables them to responds to the challenges, to confront their traditional role and change their life. Women Education is the only way to remove the gender discrimination in the society.

Definition and Conceptual Framework

The meaning of the 'empowerment' is to give power to make them able. The Oxford Dictionary defines empowerment as the *'action of empowering, the state of being empowered'*. We can say that 'Empowerment' is a process aimed at changing the nature and directions of systematic forces, which marginalize women and other disadvantaged sections in a given context.

The World Bank defines empowerment as *"the process of increasing the capacity of individuals or groups to make choices and transform those choices into desired actions and outcomes. Central to this process is action which both builds individual and collective assets and improves the efficiency and fairness of the organization and institutional context which govern the use of these assets."*

Empowerment means to make one powerful or to equip one with the power to face challenges of life, to overcome the difficulties, handicaps and inequalities. Empowerment is an active multi-dimensional process, which would enable women to realize their full identity and powers-in all spheres of life. It would consisting in providing greater access to knowledge and resource, greater autonomy in decision making, greater ability to plan the lives, greater control over the circumstances that influences their lives and freedom from the shackles imposed on them by custom, belief and practice. Empowerment does not means setting women against men. Indeed, it means making both men and women realize their changing roles and status and develop a consensus for harmonious living in the context of an egalitarian society. It means redistribution of work roles, redistributing their values to the changing world and attitudes and evolving new kinds of adjustments, understanding and trust with each other. Empowerment of women is a new ideology for carrying democratic values into the family and society.

Women Empowerment refers to increasing and improving the social, economic, political and legal strength of the women, to ensure equal-right to women, and to make them confident enough to claim their rights, such as:

1. Freely live their life with a sense of self-worth, respect and dignity.
2. Have complete control of their life, both within and outside of their home and workplace.
3. To make their own choices and decisions.
4. Have equal rights to participate in social, religious and public activities.
5. Have equal social status in the society.
6. Have equal rights for social and economic justice.
7. Determine financial and economic choices.
8. Get equal opportunity for education.
9. Get equal employment opportunity without any gender bias
10. Get safe and comfortable working environment.

Reasons for Women Empowerment

According to Kamela Basin (1992), the reasons for women empowerment are as follows:

1. Empowerment means recognizing women contribution and development knowledge.
2. It means helping women fight against their own fears, feelings of inadequacy and inferiority.
3. It means enhancing their self-respect and self-dignity.
4. It means women controlling their own bodies.
5. It means women becoming economically independent and self-reliant.
6. It means women controlling resources like land prosperity.
7. It means reducing omen's burden of work especially within the house.

8. It means creating and strengthening women's group and organizations.
9. It means promoting equalities of nurturing.

Characteristics of Women Empowerment

1. Women empowerment enables a greater degree of self confidence and sense of independence among women.
2. Women empowerment gives the capacity or power to resist discrimination imposed by the male dominated society.
3. Women empowerment enables women to organize them selves to increase their self-reliance.
4. Women empowerment provides greater economy to women.
5. Women empowerment means women's control over material assets, intellectual resources and ideology.
6. Women empowerment abolishes all gender based discrimination in all institutions and structure of society.
7. Empowerment of women is an ongoing dynamic process which enhances women's abilities to change the structures and ideologies that keep them subordinate.
8. Women empowerment is a process of creating awareness and capacity building
9. Women empowerment means participation of women in policy and decision making process at domestic and public levels.
10. Women empowerment challenges traditional power equations and relations.
11. Women empowerment means exposing the oppressive power of existing gender and social relations.
12. Empowerment of women makes them more powerful to face the challenges of life, to overcome the disabilities, handicaps and inequalities.
13. Empowerment of women enables women to realize their full identity and power in all spheres of life.
14. Women empowerment is a process of acquiring power for women in order to understand her rights and to perform her responsibilities towards oneself and others in a most effective way.
15. Empowerment also means providing greater access to knowledge and resources, greater autonomy in decision making, greater ability to plan their lives and freedom from the shackles imposed on them by custom belief and practice.
16. Women empowerment occurs within sociological, psychological, political, cultural, familiar and economic spheres and various levels such as individual, group and community.

Importance of Women Empowerment

Importance of women empowerment can be seen through following direction:

Equally Competent and Intelligent: Women are equally competent. Nowadays, women are even ahead of men in many socio-economic activities.

Capable: Women are as capable as men. Previously, women were not allowed higher education like men and hence their capabilities were wasted. But, nowadays, they are also allowed to go for higher studies and it encourages women to show their capabilities which will not only benefit her individually but to the whole world at large.

Overall Development of Society: The main advantage of Women Empowerment is that there will be an overall development of the society. The money that women earn does not only help them and or their family, but it also help develop the society.

Economic Advancement: Women Empowerment also leads to more economic benefits not to the individuals but to the society as well. Unlike earlier days when they stayed at home only and do only kitchen stuffs, nowadays, they roam outside and also earn money like the male members of the society. Women empowerment helps women to stand on their own legs, become independent and also to earn for their family which grows country's economy.

Reduce Poverty: Women Empowerment also reduces poverty. Sometimes, the money earned by the male member of the family is not sufficient to meet the demands of the family. The added earnings of women help the family to come out of poverty trap.

Under-employed and Un-employed: Women population constitutes around 50% of the world population. A large number of women around the world are unemployed. The world economy suffers a lot because of the unequal opportunity for women at workplaces.

National Development: Women are increasingly participating in the national development process. They are making the nation proud by their outstanding performances almost every sphere including medical science, social service, engineering, etc.

Major Issues Concerning Women Empowerment in India

Empowering Women: For women's empowerment and equality, it is therefore fundamental that women have the right to decide upon their choices without coercion or violence and have the freedom to participate more fully and equally in society.

Importance of Gender Equality: Gender equality ensures same opportunities, rights and obligations for women in every sphere of life. This in turn implies equality in opinion, equal opportunities, financial independence and equal access to facilities.

Identification of Needs and Concerns: To address any issue regarding women, firstly, the role that they play needs to be determined. This is governed by factors such as age, urban/ rural orientation, social status and educational attainment. While women in general may have many common interests, the choices that they have may widely vary from region to region but certain groups need more attention in order to address their specific concerns.

Education for the Girl Child: Although education is important for all, it is more so for the girl child as it helps them to know about their rights and privileges and makes them more aware of health care and better caretakers. An educated mother takes better care of all. Government has realized that investing in girls' education leads to overall reduction of poverty.

Giving Women More Autonomy: Women's empowerment deals with the entire gambit of day to day life which includes right to education, health and an equal status in work environment.

It should also include the political empowerment that would guarantee women equality in basic human and legal rights, control of resources and an equal opportunity in employment and earning.

Ways and Means of Achieving Women Empowerment

Through Social Empowerment: Awareness programmes need to be organized for creating awareness among women especially belonging to weaker sections about their rights and for checking the spread of sexually transmitted diseases like HIV/AIDS and infections/ communicable diseases like TB nearby. The social stigma like child marriage, female foeticide, child abuse and child prostitution must be eradicated immediately.

Through Education: Education is a powerful tool of social transformation i.e. empowering women with the knowledge, skills and self-confidence necessary to participate fully in the development process. However, women's literacy rates are significantly lower than men's in most developing countries. Gender sensitivity must be developed. A watch has to be kept on dropout rate of girls with corrective measures.

Through Science and Technology: Science and technology can be effectively used to ease women's work load inside and outside the house involving them as equal partners, recognizing their knowledge, experiences and the significant role they can play in sustainable development with organized Orientation and training, there is a great potential for empowering women with appropriate and sustainable technologies.

Through Economic Participation: Women's quantitative participation in the workforce is important not only in addressing the disproportionate levels of poverty among women, but also as a key step towards raising household income and encouraging economic development. The Government of India set aside some reasonable amount of money which encouraged women having business ideas to borrow money in order to start businesses and have their own source of income thus they can become independent

Through Political Empowerment: Effective political involvement includes the equitable representation of women in decision-making structures, both formal and informal and their engagement in formulation of policies affecting the socio-economic groups in which they live.

Through Women's Organization: Women's organizations have come to be recognized as the main source of power, position and strength for women in modem India. A women fight injustices perpetrated by men single handed or also. But, she can do the same collectively through organizations.

Government Initiatives for Women Empowerment in India

Government Policies, Schemes and Programmes

- Integrated Child Development Services (ICDS)
- Rajiv Gandhi Scheme for Empowerment of Adolescent Girls (RGSEAG)
- The Rajiv Gandhi National Creche Scheme for Children of Working Mothers
- Integrated Child Protection Scheme (ICPS)
- Support to Training and Employment Programme for Women (STEP)
- National Mission for Empowerment of Women
- Rashtriya Mahila Kosh
- Rajiv Gandhi Mahila Vikas Pariyojana (RGMVP)

Legislative Measures for Safeguarding Women's Interest

- The Special Marriage Act (1954)
- The Hindu Marriage Act (1955)
- The Hindu Succession Act (1956)
- The Hindu Adoption and Maintenance Act (1956)
- The Suppression of Immoral Traffic of Women and Girls Act (1956)
- The Dowry Prohibition Act (1961)
- The Medical Termination of Pregnancy Act (1971)
- The Criminal Law Amendment Act (1983)
- The Family Court Act (1984)
- Indecent Representation of Women (Prohibition) Act (1986)

Constitutional Provisions for Empowering Women in India

- Article 14: Equality before law for all persons
- 15(3): special provisions may be made by the state in favour of women and children

- Article 16: Equality of opportunity for all citizens relating to employment or appointment to any office under the state
- Article 39(a): State policy to be directed to securing for men and women equally the right to an adequate means of livelihood
- Article 39(d): Equal pay for equal work for both men and women
- Article 42: Provisions to be made by the state for securing just and humane conditions of work and relief
- Article 51A (e): Promotion of harmony by every citizen of India and renouncement of such practices which are derogatory to thy dignity of women etc.

Key Challenges for Women Empowerment in India

Several challenges that are plaguing the issues of women empowerment in India are:

1. Unpredictable attitude of society towards women.
2. Patriarchal society is one of the major challenges for women empowerment. Patriarchy is a social system of privilege in which men are the primary authority figures, occupying roles of political leadership, moral authority, control of property, and authority over women and children.
3. Discrimination against girls is another barrier for women empowerment.
4. The lower enrolment of girls in schools and playing the role of second mother by shouldering the responsibilities of household work such as looking after the siblings are the critical areas to be given attention to in India.
5. Incompetent laws and amendments as the fundamental problems lie in the attitude of the society which is highly biased against women.
6. Child marriage is one of the detriments to empowerment of women.
7. In social field, women are suppressed domestically and do not enjoy respectable position. They are not regarded as intelligent and powerful enough as men.
8. Early marriage is one of the barriers to empowerment of women.

9

Gender Equality and Equity

In Relation with Caste, Class, Race, Religion, Region, Ethnicity and Disability

We, proud Indians of 21st century, rejoice in celebrations when a boy is born, and if it is a girl, a muted or no celebrations is the norm. Love for a male child is so much so that from the times immemorial we have been killing our daughters at birth or before birth, and if, fortunately, she is not killed we find various ways to discriminate against her throughout her life. Though our religious beliefs make women a goddess but we fail to recognize her as a human being first; we worship goddesses but we exploit girls. We are a society of people with double-standards as far as our attitude towards women is concerned; our thoughts and preaching are different than our actions.

Gender Inequality

Gender inequality refers to the broad range of conditions by which women have been disadvantaged, including their economic opportunities, political standing, legal status, personal freedom, familial obligations, access to education, and cultural representation. Thus, gender inequality refers to the obvious or hidden disparity between individuals due to gender.

Definition and Concept of Gender Inequality

Gender Inequality, in simple words, may be defined as discrimination against women based on their sex. Women are traditionally considered by the society as weaker sex. She has been accorded a subordinate position to men. She is exploited, degraded, violated and discriminated both in our homes and in outside world. This peculiar type of discrimination against women is prevalent everywhere in the world and more so in Indian society.

Characteristics of Gender Inequality

1. Gender inequality dwells not only outside the household but also centrally within it;
2. Gender inequality stems not only from pre-existing differences in economic endowments (wealth, income, etc.) between women and men, but also from pre-existing gendered social norms and social perceptions, i.e., the inequalities are also ideologically embedded; and
3. Gender inequalities not only pre-exist in the noted forms, but they can also arise from newly defined rules and procedures that structure the functioning of the governance institution itself.

Different Facets of Gender Inequality

Gender inequality has many distinct and dissimilar faces. Amarty Sen (2001) has opined that *"gender inequality exists in most of part of the world, from Japan to Morocco, from Uzbekistan to United States. Yet inequality between men and women is not everywhere the same. It can take many different forms. Gender inequality is not one homogeneous phenomenon, but a collection of different and interlinked problems..."*. Further, he has identified seven types of gender inequalities viz:

- Mortality inequality,
- Natality inequality,
- Basic facility inequality,
- Special opportunity inequality,
- Professional inequality,
- Ownership inequality and
- Household inequality.

Thus, different facets of gender inequality colour our life from the day we are born until the day we die. These different forms of gender inequalities impose adversities not only on the lives of women and girls, but also on men and boys.

Determinants of Gender Inequality

The major determinants of gender inequality include the:

- social setup,
- culture,
- religion,
- geographical conditions,
- economic setup,
- moral standards and
- educational level of the society.

All these factors individually or in combination make up the face of gender discrimination. But, the conflict of gender inequality is divergent in nature as it originates from a single point with different angles.

Gender Inequality in India

Gender inequality in India refers to health, education, economic and political inequalities between men and women in India. Various international gender inequality indices rank India differently on each of these factors, as well as on a composite basis, and these indices are controversial. Gender inequalities, and its social causes, impact India's sex ratio, women's health over their lifetimes, their educational attainment, and economic conditions. Gender inequality in India is a multifaceted issue that concerns men and women alike. Some argue that some gender equality measures, place men at a disadvantage. However, when India's population is examined as a whole, women are at a disadvantage in several important ways.

Gender Statistics: The following table compares the population wide data for the two genders on various inequality statistical measures, according to the World Bank's Gender Statistics database for 2012.

Table 9.1: Measures of Gender Statistics

Gender Statistic Measure	*Females (India)*	*Males (India)*	*Females (World)*	*Males (World)*
Infant mortality rate, (per 1,000 live births)	44.3	43.5	32.6	37
Life expectancy at birth, (years)	68	64.5	72.9	68.7
Expected years of schooling	11.3	11.8	11.7	12.0
Primary school completion rate, (%)	96.6	96.3	*	
Lower secondary school completion rate, (%)	76.0	77.9	70.2	70.5
Secondary school education, pupils (%)	46	54	47.6	52.4
Ratio to males in primary and secondary education (%)	0.98	1.0	0.97	1.0
Secondary school education, gender of teachers (%)	41.1	58.9	51.9	48.1
Account at a formal financial institution, (% of each gender, age 15+)	26.5	43.7	46.6	54.5
Deposits in a typical month, (% with an account, age 15+)	11.2	13.4	13.0	12.8
Withdrawals in a typical month, (% with an account, age 15+)	18.6	12.7	15.5	12.8
Loan from a financial institution in the past year, (% age 15+)	6.7	8.6	8.1	10.0

Table 9.1 Continued

Table 9.1 Continued

Gender Statistic Measure	*Females (India)*	*Males (India)*	*Females (World)*	*Males (World)*
Outstanding loan from banks for health or emergencies, (% age 15+)	12.6	15.7	10.3	11.6
Outstanding loan from banks to purchase a home, (% age 15+)	2.26	2.35	6.6	7.4
Unemployment, (% of labour force, ILO method)	4	3.1	*	–
Unemployment, youth (% of labour force ages 15–24, ILO method)	10.6	9.4	15.1	13.0
Ratio to male youth unemployment rate (% ages 15–24, ILO method)	1.13	1.0	1.14	1.0
Employees in agriculture, (% of total labour)	59.8	43	*	–
Employees in industry, (% of total labour)	20.7	26	*	–
Self-employed, (% employed)	85.5	80.6	*	–
Cause of death, by non-communicable diseases, ages 15–34, (%)	32.3	33.0	29.5	27.5
Life expectancy at age 60, (years)	18.0	15.9	*	–

Source: 'Gender Statistics', The World Bank (2012).
Note: * Global average data not available.

Gender Equality and Gender Equity

In the gender literature, we often come across two concepts: 'gender equality' and 'gender equity'. They are sometimes used interchangeably, but they do not quite refer to the same thing. We shall briefly explain the difference between them.

Gender Equality

"Gender equality requires equal enjoyment by women and men of socially-valued goods, opportunities, resources and rewards." In other words, gender equality refers to equal access to social goods, services and resources and equal opportunities in all spheres of life for both men and women. When there is gender inequality, it is women that are more likely to be disadvantaged and marginalized; but we should not ignore the negative impact that gender inequality can have on men as well. For example, societal norms regarding the appropriate behaviour for men tend to put them under pressure as regards the need to provide materially for their family, and also deny them opportunities of being more nurturing towards their children and wife. Therefore, gender equality is the concern of all and changes must be brought about for both men and women. However, this

is not to say that men and women are equally affected by gender inequality. It remains true that women have the greater share of disadvantages.

Role of Schools in Reinforcing Gender Equality

The gender inequities pervading society are carried into the school environment. This is evidenced in school processes such as teaching, teacher–student interaction, school management, and the plan and design of the physical infrastructure. Teaching and learning materials, for example, may contain gender stereotypes. Teachers are not always aware of the gender specific needs of both girls and boys. School management systems may not sufficiently address gender constraints such as sexual harassment, and many schools do not have adequate or separate toilets for girls and boys. As a result, the schools do not provide a gender responsive environment for effective teaching and learning to take place.

A gender responsive school is one in which the academic, social and physical environment and its surrounding community take into account the specific needs of both girls and boys. This implies that the teachers, parents, community leaders and members, and the boys and girls are all aware of and practice gender equality. It also assumes that school management systems, policies and practices recognize and address the gender- or sex-based needs of both girls and boys. In addition, in a gender responsive school the academic delivery, including teaching methodologies, teaching and learning materials, classroom interaction, and management of academic processes, is gender responsive. The students, both girls and boys, are empowered to practice gender equality and to protect the democratic and human rights of both genders. The concept extends right to the physical environment in the school – including buildings, furniture and equipment that are also gender friendly.

Making a School Gender Responsive

In order to arrive at such a school, a holistic approach involving various interventions is required. The holistic intervention package can include the following elements:

1. Undertaking gender sensitization of parents, community leaders and members, teachers, girls and boys in order to raise their awareness and understanding of the need to support girls' education.
2. Training teachers in the skills for making teaching and learning processes responsive to the specific needs of girls and boys.
3. Empowering girls with skills for self-confidence, assertiveness, speaking out, decision making and negotiation in order for them to overcome gender-based constraints to their education.

4. Empowering boys with skills to de-link from gender oppressive attitudes and practices such as macho-ism, bullying and sexual affronts and to develop the self-confidence needed to accept gender equality positively.
5. Training the school community in the skills necessary to improve their reproductive health and protect themselves against sexually transmitted diseases, particularly HIV/AIDS.
6. Training the school community to manage sexual maturation issues of both girls and boys with particular emphasis on menstruation management.
7. Training teachers and students in guidance and counselling skills.
8. Establishing guidance and counselling desks in order to provide services for the social and psychological development of girls and boys.
9. Providing scholarships and support to needy girls and boys to ensure that they do not drop out of school.
10. Providing gender responsive infrastructure including:
    a. Boarding facilities in case of long distances from school.
    b. Separate and adequate toilets for girls and boys.
    c. Adequate and clean water and sanitation, especially to enhance menstruation management and the overall health of the school community.
11. Carrying out activities to promote the participation of girls in science, mathematics and technology (SMT) subjects.
12. Establishing a gender responsive school management system that ensures gender equality in the governance and operation of the school.
13. Undertaking gender training of the school management team, including the school board parent–teacher association, heads of departments and prefects, in order to raise their awareness on the need to support girls' education.
14. Involving the community and other stakeholders in monitoring and taking action to ensure improved enrolment, attendance and performance of girls.
15. Establishing a database to track student performance and welfare as well as the levels of gender responsiveness of all aspects of the school

Gender Equity

"Gender equity is the process of being fair to women and men." Women and men should not only be given equal access to resources and equal opportunities, but they should also be given the means of benefiting from this equality. This is where the concept of 'gender equity' comes into play. Gender equity implies fairness in the way women and men are treated. The different life experiences and needs of men and women are taken into consideration and compensation is made for women's historical and social disadvantages. The lower status of women in society often constitutes a handicap and provisions should be made

to redress this inequality before they can take advantage of the opportunities provided. Gender equity thus serves to level the playing field and empower women. Therefore, we can say that equity is essential to achieve true equality.

Social Stratification

In all societies people differ from each other on the basis of their age, sex and personal characteristics. Human society is not homogeneous but heterogeneous. Apart from the natural differences, human beings are also differentiated according to socially approved criteria. So, socially differentiated men are treated as socially unequal from the point of view of enjoyment of social rewards like status, power, income etc. That may be called social inequality. The term social inequality simply refers to the existence of socially created inequalities.

Social stratification is a particular form of social inequality. All societies arrange their members in terms of superiority, inferiority and equality. Stratification is a process of interaction or differentiation whereby some people come to rank higher than others.

In one word, when individuals and groups are ranked, according to some commonly accepted basis of valuation in a hierarchy of status levels based upon the inequality of social positions, social stratification occurs. Social stratification means division of society into different strata or layers. It involves a hierarchy of social groups. Members of a particular layer have a common identity. They have a similar life style.

The Indian Caste system provides an example of stratification system. The society in which divisions of social classes exist is known as a stratified society. Modern stratification fundamentally differs from stratification of primitive societies. Social stratification involves two phenomena:

1. Differentiation of individuals or groups on the basis of possession of certain characteristics whereby some individuals or groups come to rank higher than others,
2. The ranking of individuals according to some basis of evaluation.

Types of Social Stratification

The major types of stratification are:

Caste: Caste is a hereditary endogamous social group in which a person's rank and its accompanying rights and obligations are ascribed on the basis of his birth into a particular group. For example Brahmins, Kshyatryas, Vaishyas and Sudra Caste.

Class: Stratification on the basis of class is dominant in modern society. In this, a person's position depends to a very great extent upon achievement and his ability to use to advantage the inborn characteristics and wealth that he may possess.

Estate: Estate system of medieval Europe provides another system of stratification which gave much emphasis to birth as well as to wealth and possessions. Each estate had a state.

Slavery: Slavery had economic basis. In slavery, every slave had his master to whom he was subjected. The master's power over the slave was unlimited.

Caste and Gender Issues

Gender equality in Indian society is another area that needs active affirmation. Women at the grassroots already disadvantaged by their marginalized community status are further compromised by caste and gender hierarchies. Women and girls find themselves victims of not only violence of various kinds, but also haplessly dispossessed and voiceless. In a country where the feminine principle has been traditionally revered, it is ironic that millions of women and girls are brutally victimized - socially, physically, mentally, economically and sexually.

To assess the position of women in ancient society, a reference to stratification system which includes Varna and caste system is essential. Caste endogamy as mechanism of recruiting and retaining control over the labor and sexuality of women existed. Concept of purity and pollution segregating groups and also regulating mobility of women are also important. Caste not only determines social division of labor but also sexual division of labor. Certain tasks have to be performed by women that certain other tasks are meant for men.

Income, Class and Gender Issues

Class refers to a status group in a society and the economic prosperity defines a person's class. The word Class has been defined in numerous ways—for Sociologist class is one of the fundamental type social stratification. Individuals are grouped into classes according to their economic positions and similar political interest with in the stratification. Most societies have their own notion of social class.

Income and class has always played an important role in shaping academic success. Parents of a higher socio-economic status generally intervene on behalf of their children to acquire better grades or more qualified teachers and willingly donate large sums of money to a certain institution to better improve their child's chances of acceptance, along with other extravagant measures. This creates an unfair advantage and distinct the class barrier.

Gender-based inequity in education is not just a phenomenon in developing countries. Boys and girls are often taught with different approach which tends children to think that they are different and deserve different treatment. However, studies show that boys and girls learn differently and therefore should be taught differently. Boys learn better when they are kept moving while girls learn better sitting in one place with silence. Therefore, segregation of gender for this reasoning promotes gender equity in education as both boys and girls have optimized learning

Race and Gender Issues

From a scientific point of view, the human species is a single species. It is therefore misleading to use divisive terms such as races and racial groups. Nevertheless, the term racial group is enshrined in legislation, and phrases such as race equality and race relations are in widespread official use. Racial equity in education means the assignment of students to public schools and within schools without regard to their race. This includes providing students with a full opportunity for participation in all educational programmes regardless of their race

Discrimination emanating from categorical distinctions on the basis of sex and race have historically intersected in multiple and diverse ways, and have taken specific forms during particular historical conjunctures, such as in the contexts of slavery and colonialism. The dominant structures of power often relied on violence to sustain their patriarchal and racial boundaries.

When a woman's race is factored in to her experience, the double burden of gender and racial discrimination and related intolerance becomes evident. Areas of particular concern include the disadvantages faced by minority women in the labour market, trafficking in women, and race-based violence against women.

Religion and Gender Issues

Religion is a system of faith and worship, which provides adherents with meaning and purpose in their lives. It is one of the major institutions in society, with almost every human civilization producing a system of religious belief. Religions may or may not include a belief in a supreme being, but all are concerned with the transcendent, the spiritual, and with aspects of life beyond the physical world. Major religions, such as Buddhism, Christianity, Hinduism, Islam and Judaism are practiced throughout the world, but there are also numerous minor religious groups, and indigenous religions particular to specific regions. Within each organized religion, one generally finds a large number of different denominations, sects, and cults, each with their own interpretations, beliefs and practices.

Religion, tradition and culture are often used to justify women's subordinate position in society. In all the world's major religions, religious texts have been interpreted to reinforce the power of men in society. Recently, there has been a rise in conservative or fundamentalist religious movements, often associated with conservative nationalism or right-wing politics. These movements are generally opposed to the concept of gender equality. Their attitudes towards gender issues include: a belief that women's proper place is in the home; opposition to reproductive rights; blaming women for the decline in moral values; vilifying women who step outside traditional roles; and active homophobia.

In most religions, women are the majority of believers, but it is men who claim to hold the positions of authority and have the rights, including the authority to interpret religious texts. In many religions, women have historically not held leadership positions, and, in some where women have held leadership positions in the past, they are now denied the same leadership position today. Some religions still bar women from holding leadership positions.

For millions of women around the world, religion is a source of identity, belonging, and comfort in times of hardship, but paradoxically, it is often a force, which encourages them to accept violence and oppression as part of life, and discourages potentially positive social change.

Region and Gender Issues

A region is a large area where there are a good many resemblances among the inhabitants. Region can be defined as "an area within which the people and the different constituent communities are conspicuously more inter-dependent than they are with people of other areas". The community feeling within a region is called regionalism. Gender discrimination can be occurring on the basis of region. Women/girls face many problems in comparison to males. In India, there are some states where women's crime is very high in comparison to other states.

Ethnicity and Gender Issues

The term ethnicity has been defined in broader sense to signify self-consciousness of a group of people united or closely related by shared experience such as language, religious belief, common heritage etc. While race usually denotes the attributes of a group, ethnic identity signifies creative response of a group who consider themselves marginalized in society. The identity of a group is defined vis-à-vis another community and how this identity becomes psychologically and socially important for a member of or members of a community.

In all societies women are disadvantaged in relation to men. Matrilineal societies like the Khasis are often cited to rebuff the idea that women in all societies are discriminated. Recent writings have shown how even among a matrilineal society like Khasis control of property and decision-making within the family often resides with the male head the brother. Despite differences in a very important sense ethnic groups and women are marginal in decision making, less powerful, less visible and more often than not prejudiced against.

The importance of logical distinctions not withstanding differences is hierarchized. Both ethnic minorities and women face a great deal of antagonism, prejudices and discrimination. Prejudice operates mainly through the use of stereotypical thinking. Both women and ethnic groups have high visibility. They look different. A woman is supposed to shorter than man, weaker but also dress, walk, speak, and gesticulate differently. Both the ethnic minority and women are also attributed with other qualities that are not obvious. For Giddens ethnicity refers to cultural practices and outlook that distinguishes a given community of people. Members of ethnic groups see themselves as culturally distinct from other groupings in a society. Many different characteristics may serve to distinguish ethnic groups from one another but the most usual are language, history or ancestry, religion and styles of dress.

Disability and Gender Issues

Gender is one of the most important categories of social organization, yet people with disabilities are often treated as asexual, genderless human beings. However, women with disabilities and men with disabilities have different life experiences due to biological, psychological, economic, social, political and cultural attributes associated with being female and male. Patterns of disadvantage are often associated with the differences in the social position of women and men. These gendered differences are reflected in the life experiences of women with disabilities and men with disabilities. Women with disabilities face multiple discriminations and are often more disadvantaged than men with disabilities in similar circumstances.

Women with disabilities are often denied equal enjoyment of their human rights, in particular by virtue of the lesser status ascribed to them by tradition and custom, or as a result of overt or covert discrimination. Women with disabilities face particular disadvantages in the areas of education, work and employment, family and reproductive rights, health, violence and abuse.

Women with disabilities have been described as being doubly marginalized on account of their disability and their gender. They may be more vulnerable to poverty and social exclusion, and often have limited social, political and economic opportunities and lack of access to basic services. Women with disabilities may also be at greater risk of sexual and physical violence and abuse. Girls with disabilities often experience discrimination, for example in education and family life.

However, to address these issues it is necessary to understand the social roles of and between women and men both with and without disabilities. The exclusion experienced by women and girls with disabilities is not simply a women's issue or a women with disabilities issue, but a social issue that requires active participation of women, men, girls and boys. This can be described as a gender and development, rather than women in development, approach.

10

Changing Status of Women in India

The status of women in India has been subject to many great changes over the past few millennia. From equal status with men in ancient times through the low points of the medieval period, to the promotion of equal rights by many reformers, the history of women in India has been eventful. In modern India, women have held high offices in India including that of the President, Prime Minister, Speaker of the Lok Sabha and Leader of the Opposition.

Women Education in Indian History

Education is a ladder of development. It dispels darkness and brings s light. It is a base of all Human Resource Development, a stepping stone for the onward march of culture, the bedrock of all human progress. An ancient proverb lays down:

"If you are planning for one year, plant rice; if you are planning for five years, plant trees; If you are planning for the future, educate your children".

According to Jawaharlal Nehru *"Education of one boy is education of one person by education of a girl the education of the whole family"*. This statement amply and to a great extent explains the importance of women education. In India, the condition of women education has always remained deplorable. Women' education was badly neglected in the past. While her position in Vedic times or even the Upanishadic Era was good, there is no doubt that period after 1000 A.D. was a dark age for her. Whatever the historic reasons, her social position began to deteriorate during the period and had considerable repercussions on her education.

Indian Women Education during Vedic Period

During Vedic period, the women were considered as complementary of man. She has the equal status as man. They had full rights for their education but, maximum education was done at their homes. This was the earlier condition of education of women in Vedic Period. Afterwards the women education was neglected. There was no arrangement for their education in Gurukul.

Indian Women Education during Buddhist Period

In the beginning of Buddhist Period the women education was neglected. When Mahatma Buddha allowed the ladies monk in Vihara then the women education flourished. They lived separately. The Acharya lectured them in the presence of special monk or monks. During Buddhist Period the women education was available to the high caste women. The general and low caste women have zero education.

Indian Women Education during Muslim Period

During Muslim Period the women education did not flourish because of Parda System. The low age girls could go to Maktab and could have education but for higher education, the guardians had to do arrangement at their homes for their education that is for the instruction of girls, there were separate schools but usually they received their education in their own houses or in those of their teachers, living in close proximity.

Indian Women Education during British Period

The East India Company did not consider it necessary to educate the fair sex, perhaps because lady clerks or officers were not required for administrative purposes. At the same time, a variety of odd superstitions held back girls education. Thus William Adams wrote about female education in 1838, *"All the established native institutions of education exist for the benefit of the male sex only, and the whole of the female sex is systematically consigned to ignorance and left wholly without even the semblance of a provision for their instruction."*

During the Company's rule there was no separate state Schools for girls and hardly a few girls were attending boys' schools. Most of the Girls School was run by missionaries and a few by private bodies. In 1851, the Protestant Missions were conducting 86 boarding schools and 285 day schools for girls with an enrollment of 2274 and 8919 respectively. According to the Educational Dispatch of 1854, the total number of girls' school was 256 in Madras (Chennai), 65 in Bombay (Mumbai), 288 in Bengal and 17 in North Western Provinces.

From 1857 to 1902

The Indian Education Commission of 1882, while examining the question of girls education remarked, *"Female education is still in an extremely backward condition and needs to be fostered in every legitimate way."* It recommended that it should receive a larger share of public funds. As a result, state funds were spent more freely on girls' education. There was a sharp rise in private efforts also. Owing to these two factors girls' education progressed. This was especially noticeable amongst Europeanized communities viz Brahmo Samaj, the Parsees and the Christians.

From 1902 to 1917

But very son the feeling of passive apathy was changed into active sympathy owing to sentimental and material causes. The Education Departments also took some active steps and devised new plans for spreading education viz separate schools for girls were started. Arrangements of conveyance for taking girls to schools were made. Inspectors were appointed, favourable grants were given to private girls schools, and steps were taken to attract ladies to the teaching profession.

The above steps gave a great encouragement to girls' education. In 1984, Mrs. Annie Besant established the Central Hindu Girls School at Banaras (Varanasi) with the object of importing Western Education to girls quite separately from boys in a modernized school of Hinduism. In 1916 the first Medical College Lady Hardinge College, Delhi was established for the fairer sex in the country. The Women (SNDT) University was also established in the same year. In 1917 there were 12 arts colleges, four professionals' colleges and 166 secondary schools for girls. The majority of girls however did not continue their studies in schools for a long period.

From 1917 to 1947

During this period development of women education took place very rapidly. At the time of Independence, there were thirty thousand institutions related with women education and approximately fifty lakh women were getting education from these institutions.

Indian Women Education during Modern Period

After Independence revolutionary changes came into the field of women education. Many committees and commissions were established for the welfare of women and their education, namely:

- Durga Bai Deshmukh Committee – 1958
- Hansa Mehata Committee – 1964
- National Policy on Education – 1986

There is considerable expansion in educational facilities for women all over the country at all levels. Major emphasis is given on women participation in vocational, technical and professional education at different levels. The special emphasis was lead on the removal of disparities and equalization of opportunity to women for attending their specific needs in acquiring education. Various steps were taken by State Governments and Central Government to remove prejudice and complexes present in Indian women in acquiring education. Special vocational training Institutions' for women were established by the State departments of vocational education.

During Modern Period women education has become a revolution. Now the women are present in the every field of education. The knowledge explosion has made them universal. During this period the women education has been treated at par with the men. They have equal opportunities and facilities for them. More facilities have been given to them by the governments. In this period the women education is far ahead in comparison to their Vedic Period.

Social Reform and Muslim Women

Similar movements began, within the Islamic community in the late nineteenth century. However, emphasis on purdah system and slow spread of education among women delayed the development of a progressive movement to improve the opportunities for Muslim women. People like Begum of Bhopal, Syed Ahmad Khan and Sheikh Abdullah in Aligarh and Karmat Hussain in Lucknow spearheaded a movement to improve women's education. In 1916 Begum of Bhopal formed the All-India Muslim Women's Conference. The traditionalists disapproved such activities and were enraged by the resolution passed by the Muslim Women's Conference in 1917 that polygamy should be abolished. In the later years several Muslim women joined the nationalist struggle and noncooperation movement against the British.

All these movements had a very limited perspective of changing the position of women. Gender equality was not on their agenda. The movement was not conceived as a radical onslaught on the religious orthodoxy, which subjugated women. Social reformers viewed women's question as a social problem. Almost all the socio-religious reform in the country focused their full attention on the problems facing women. Though they differed in their views regarding the nature and scope of the work, they were always unanimous that women's status in India needed to be improved.

Women's Participation in the Freedom Movement

Women's Movement in Pre-Independence Period

Freedom movement covered a period of 90 years starting from 1857 when the first attempt was made and up to 1974 when India attained independence. Women participated in the movement during the entire e period through the degree of participation varied across different stages of the movement. Many women freedom fighters have played a significant role in the various stages of the freedom struggle. Let us discuss the social background and contributions of prominent women participants in the freedom struggle.

The first attempt for freedom was made in 1857, popularly known as first war of Indian independence. Rani Lakshmi Bai of Jansi emerged as great heroine during this time. Rani's determined fight and death in battle field is an inspiration for all time, she lived and died for her country. Other prominent women who participated in the 1857 revolt were, Rani Tarabai, Begum Hazeat Mahal, Lalitha Bhakshi, Sundar Kasi bhai Motibai, Rani of Ramgrah and Rani of Ttulsipur. They were all elegant fighters of freedom. The self-respect, spirit of sacrifice dedication courage and devotion to mother land made them the champions of freedom. They may be little in number, but they mobilized the spirit and quality of Indian womanhood.

In 1885, Indian national congress was established, it provided the platform for the men and women to fight against the British and to achieve the freedom for the country. The member ship of Indian National Congress was opened to women because the political leaders were aware of women's worth. In 1889, ten women attended the fourth session of congress at Bombay.

With the spread of women's education among middle class several women became active in political life of India. Majority of them were from Calcutta and Bombay. Swarna Kumari Debi, first Indian woman editor and sister of Rabindranath Tagore joined the Indian National Congress and took keen interest in the welfare of Indian women. She started a Ladies Association to foster the women activities. The other women present were Pandit Rema Bai, Shevanthi Bai Kaniker, all of them worked as educationalist and social reformers. Thus the participation of women during the early phase of freedom struggle is limited in terms of the number of participants. Majority of the participants are hailed from the princely class and the upper caste.

During 1900-1913, the participation of women has increased. Women of different classes involved in mass struggles, militancy and publications. The period 1940-1980 is of great significance in the history of women movements. These years' women began to realize their exclusion from mainstream political movements. It was due the leadership of Annie Besant an organized movement for the emancipation of women and for political right came to be established. She prepared the ground for the Gandhian freedom movement in which women have played a prominent role.

Gandhiji's call played the most significant role in involving large number of women in the nationalist movement. It is important to understand the impact of Gandhian ideology on women's movement. He said "the women of India should have as much share in winning swaraj as men probably in this peaceful struggle". He believed women are the companion of men gifted with equal mental capacities. He proclaimed that "if women of India aroused, no one could stop the countries march to freedom." This is the way Mahatma appealed to the women of India to enter the struggle for the freedom. The involvement of really large number of women in the national movement began when Gandhi launched the first Non Co-operation Movement and gave a special role to women. Peasant women played an important role in the rural satyagrahas of Borsad and Bardoli. Women participated in the Salt Satyagraha, in the Civil Disobedience Movement, in the Quit India Movement and in all the Gandhian satyagrahas. They held meetings, organized processions, picketed shops selling foreign cloth and liquor and went to jail.

Women's participation in the freedom movement did not lead to a separate autonomous women's movement since it was part of the anti-colonial movement. While women who picketed shops, marched in processions or went to jail or threw bombs did not question male leadership or patriarchal values, it did generate in them a sense of self-confidence and a realization of their own strength. Many returned to their homes but others continued their activities in the public arena. It transformed the lives of many young widows such as Durgabai Deshmukh or Kamaladevi Chattopadhyaya. Women won respect for their courage and the large numbers in which they participated in the freedom struggle and at the Karachi session of the Indian National Congress in 1930, the resolution on Fundamental Rights gave equal rights to women.

Women's Movement In Post-Independence Period

The attainment of independence in 1947 ushered in a new era of hope. Indian National congress, which came to power, under the leadership of Jawaharlal Nehru initiated steps to put an end to the get old unequal status of women through the constitution of free India. Jawaharlal Nehru believed that 'without economic freedom other aspects of women's equality would not be realized'. He is agreed with the limited view that women's education alone can bring about the desired changes and he wanted women trained in all human activities. He said that "if women's struggles remained isolated from the general political, economic and social struggles, the women's movement would not gain strength and will remain confined to the upper classes". There cannot be any doubt that a single factor which contributed to the transformation of women's roles and status in the Indian society was their massive participation in the national freedom movement. Equality between men and women was accepted as one of the objectives in the Fundamental Rights Resolution of the Indian National Congress in 1931.

Women Social Reformers of India

Some of the important and leading social reformers pertaining to women are discussed below:

Raja Rammohun Roy

Raja Rammohun Roy was born on 22nd May 1772, in Radhanagar, West Bengal, in a Brahmin family. Raja Rammohun Roy is also known as the *"Maker of Modern India"*. He is considered as the pioneer of modern Indian Renaissance. That is why Raja Ram Mohan Roy is also known as the

"Father of Indian Renaissance". He was an educational reformer, a socialist reformer, and a religious reformer too. He is called *"The Father of Modern India"* because of his challenged and transformed Hindu culture on his new way. Raja Rammohun Roy was one of the key personalities of *"Bengal Renaissance"*. He founded "Brahmo Samaj" in the year of 1828.

Contribution in the Field of Social Reforms with Special Emphasis on Women Education

Abolition of Sati: His biggest achievement was the abolishment of *"sati pratha"*, a practice in the India of his times, where a widow was made to immolate herself at the funeral pyre of her deceased husband. He struggled for years to get this evil legally eradicated. Raja Rammohun Roy raised his voice against the Sati system. In the funeral pyre of the deceased husband, his wife was mercilessly thrown if she did not enter into the flame voluntarily. She was termed as Sati. The Brahmins and other higher castes in the society encouraged it.

Founder of Brahmo Samaj: He founded the Brahmo Samaj along with other enlightened Bengalis. The samaj was a highly influential socio-religious reform movement which fought against evils like caste system, dowry, ill treatment of women, etc.

Voice against Idolatry: Ram Mohan raised his voice against idolatry. In his book Tuhfat-ul-Muwahhidin' he championed the cause of Monotheism. He criticized idol-worship by the Hindus. He also opposed the principle of Trinitariasm' (God, Son Jesus and the holy spirit) of the Christianity. He rejected polytheism, idol-worship and rituals of different religions. He advocated monotheism or unity among gods. He also advised people to be guided by the conscience. He inspired men to cultivate rationality.

Liberty of Women: Raja Rammohun Roy advocated the liberty of Women. He was determined to give women her proper place in the society. Besides abolishing Sati, he advocated in favor of widow remarriage. He also told that like the sons, daughters have also their right over parental property. He also influenced the British government to bring necessary modification in the existing law. He raised voice against child-marriage and polygamy. He was the advocate of women education.

Opposition to Caste System: The caste system was a very ugly practice prevailing in Indian society right from the later Vedic age. Indian society was fragmented by the name of different castes. The higher castes like Brahmins and Kshatriyas looked down upon the Sudras, Chandalas and other aboriginals. Ram Mohan opposed this ugly system of the Indian society. To him everybody was a son or daughter of the God. So, there is no difference among men.

Advocate of Western Education: Raja Rammohun Roy was a great scholar having sharp intellect in the Vedas, Upanishads, Quran, Bible and several other holy scriptures. He very well realized the importance of English language. He could visualize the need of a scientific, rational and progressive education for the Indians.

He supported the move of Lord Macaulay and championed the cause of the English system of education in India. His motto was to take Indians the path of progress. He established English school in 1816 and Vedanta College in 1825. He wanted to introduce modem system of education. Of course, he could not live to see the introduction of English system of education in India in 1835. However, his efforts and dreams were materialized into reality even after his death.

Synthesizer of Religion and Morality: Raja Rammohun Roy was a noble soul. He brought a perfect blending between religion and morality. According to him a man must possess virtues like merry, morality, catholicity, forgiveness and so on. These qualities will purify his soul. Further, man will be regulated by these qualities.

Education for Women: Raja Rammohun Roy promoted the growth and prosperity of the women education. He strongly believed that unless the womenfolk were educated, the society would not be liberated from the evils. Raja Rammohun Roy promoted the Western education and India during that time witnessed a great progress in the field of education.

Father of Indian Journalism: Raja Rammohun Roy was the *'Father of Indian Journalism'*. He believed in the freedom of press. He edited a newspaper in Bengali named *'Sampled Kaumudi'*. He was also the editor of Mirat- ul-Akbar. When restrictions were imposed on the publications of newspapers, he reacted sharply and criticized the British authorities vehemently.

Ishwar Chandra Vidyasagar (1820-1891)

Ishwar Chandra Vidyasagar (1820-1891) was as one of the pillars of Bengal renaissance who managed to continue the social reforms movement that was started by Raja Rammohan Roy in the early 1800s. Vidyasagar was a well-known writer, intellectual and above all a staunch supporter of humanity.

Contribution in the Field of Social Reforms with Special Emphasis on Women Education

Women's Education: He was an ardent advocate of women education. He rightly viewed education as the primary way for women to achieve emancipation from all the societal oppression they had to face at that time. He exercised his power and lobbied hard for opening of school for girls and even outlined suitable curriculum that not only did educate them, but also enabled them to be self-reliant through vocations like needlework. He went door to door, requesting heads of families to allow their daughters to be enrolled in schools. He opened 35 schools for women throughout Bengal and was successful in enrolling 1300 students. He even initiated Nari Siksha Bhandar, a fund to lend support for the cause.

Mass Education: Another significant contribution of Vidyasagar was the spread of mass education. On witnessing the pervading darkness and superstitions in which people of Bengal lived in the absence of education, Vidyasagar explored local popular support and participation in the spread of mass education. He appealed to the people who responded positively and it was decided that schools would be set up at chosen localities where the financial burden of erecting school buildings were to come from the locality. Vidyasagar got quite a number of schools constructed in this way in areas under his official jurisdiction.

Widow Remarriage: Vidyasagar was always vocal about the oppression that the society inflicted on women at that time. He was very close to his mother who was a woman of great character, who directed him once to do something to alleviate the pain and helplessness of Hindu widows, who were forced to live a life of abnegation. They were denied basic pleasures of life, marginalized in the society, often exploited unfairly and treated as a burden by their family. Vidyasagar's compassionate heart could not take their plight and he made it his mission to improve the quality of life for these helpless women. He faced raging opposition from orthodox society which termed the concept as something heretic. He challenged the Brahminical authorities and proved that widow remarriage is sanctioned by Vedic scriptures.

Swami Vivekananda (1863-1902)

One of the chief disciples of Ramakrishna Paramahamsa, Swami Vivekananda was born as Narendra Nath Datta on January 12, 1863 in Kolkata, West Bengal to Vishwanath Datta and Bhuvaneswari Devi. He took the name Swami Vivekananda after becoming a monk. He was a good student, besides being proficient in music and sports. He stood up against many of the superstitions prevalent during that time and had great affection and respect for ascetics.

Contribution in the Field of Social Reforms with Special Emphasis on Women Education

Man-Making Education: Swamiji does not accept information as education. He advocates a type of education, which is manmaking, life-building and character-formation. Education should also help in the development of originality. It should unfold all the hidden powers in man. A child should learn to accept pleasure and pain, misery and happiness as equal factors in the formation of character. Man-making education is inherent in character development as well as vocational development. What India needs today is character and strengthening of the will. This can be achieved through man-making education.

Women's Equality: Education plays a vital role in liberating women from the society. Swami Vivekananda had held Indian women in high esteem and has appreciated their typical Indian features like spirit of service, compassion, affection, contentment and reverence. Swami Vivekananda felt that no nation can grow without taking care of the interest of women. He said, *"All nations have attained greatness by paying proper respect to women. That country and that nation which does not respect women have never become great, nor will ever be in future."* He felt that Indian women must be given the liberty to live an independent life. They must have the right to take decisions and, when faced with problems, should learn to solve it themselves.

Women Education: According to Swamiji, *"The real strength or 'Shakti' of a country are its women."* He quotes Manu, *"Daughters should be supported and educated with as much care and attention as the sons."* He wanted women to be free from all fetters as self-respecting persons, with their own individuality, and was in favour of women being gives such training as would infuse them with strength so that they can tackle the problem that face them.

Sir Syed Ahmad Khan (1817-1898)

Sir Syed Ahmad Khan, one of the architects of modern India was born on October 17, 1817 in Delhi and started his career as a civil servant. The 1857 revolt was one of the turning points in Syed Ahmed's life. He clearly foresaw the imperative need for the Muslims to acquire proficiency in the English language and modern sciences, if the community were to maintain its social and political clout, particularly in Northern India.

He was one of those early pioneers who recognized the critical role of education in the empowerment of the poor and backward Muslim community. In more than one ways, Sir Syed was one of the greatest social reformers and a great national builder of modern India. He began to prepare the road map for the formation of a Muslim University by starting various schools. He instituted Scientific Society in 1863 to instill a scientific temperament into the Muslims and to make the Western knowledge available to Indians in their own language.

Contribution in the Field of Social Reforms with Special Emphasis on Women Education

- He worked hard to raise the status of the Muslim women.
- He was against the "purdah" system, polygamy, easy divorce and lack of education among the girls. Though he was opposed by the orthodox Muslims.

- He made commendable efforts in promote women's education.
- He tried to interpret the "Quran" in the light of reason and spoke out against fanaticism and ignorance.
- He also initiated social reforms for uplifting Muslim society.
- He believed that the decline of the Muslim was due to their reluctance to adopt western-style education Khan advocated modern education for both men and women.
- He also opposed polygamy, talking the view that since a man could not treat all his wives equally polygamy must be absolutely and definably restricted monogamy should be the rule.
- He also challenge the orthodox view that Islam advocated purdah for women or that it discouraged women's education.
- Sir Syed Ahmed Khan was the first Muslim leader who realized the importance of education for his people. In order to equip Muslim with the ornament of knowledge, he opened many educational institutions and societies which revolutionized the life of the Muslims.
- Sir Syed Ahmed khan established Muhammadan Educational Conference in 1886 in order to bring political awareness among the Muslims. The Conference held its annual conferences regularly till 1906 when in its Dhaka session All-India Muslim League was founded.
- Sir Syed's greatest achievement was his Aligarh Movement, which was nothing but an educational venture. He established schools at Moradabad in 1859 and Ghazipur in 1863. He also founded a scientific society in 1864. When Sir Syed was posted at Aligarh in 1867, he started the Muhammadan Anglo-Oriental School in the city. During his visit to England in 1869, he studied the British educational system and appreciated it.
- Sir Syed Ahmad Khan was a great votary of women's right to education was evident from his views on Muslim personal law, he greatly differed from other Muslim scholars on questions of divorce and women rights, and he also condemned domestic violence against women in the strongest words. The fact that he could not complete his commentary on Quran during his lifetime has obscured many of his modern and advanced views on gender equality and empowerment of women.
- Apart from establishing institutions with distinctly liberal spirit Sir Syed Ahmad Khan also did some scholarly legal work in the field of civil rights for women. He held a firm view that the educating the women will have a positive chain reaction on the Indian society and that if tour women are educated the whole society will get educated, however because of ill health Sir Syed Ahmad Khan could not

theorize much on the subject of women's education which led some critics to believe that he was not a great supporter thereof. We all know that actions speak louder than words it is amply clear from Sir Syed's actions that he was one of the early proponents of the need for women's education in India. The Civil Rights Act of 1866 (empowerment of women) could not have been passed without the legal scholarly help that Sir Syed Ahmad extended to the bill.

Mahatma Jotiba Govindrao Phule (1827-1890)

Mahatma Jyotirao Govindrao Phule was born on 11 April 1827 in Satara, Maharashtra in a family of vegetable vendors. He could not complete his education due to family's poor condition but later completed it with the help of a few persons who had recognized his potential. Jyotirao was married at the age of 12 with Savitribai Phule.

Contribution in the Field of Social Reforms with Special Emphasis on Women Education

His first and foremost work was in the field of women's education; and his first disciple was his wife herself who always shared his dreams and supported him all through life.

To fulfill his ideals and aspirations of creating a just and equitable society, in 1848, Jyotiba opened a school for girls; it was a first girls' school ever in the country. His wife Savitribai taught there as a teacher. But, for trying to educate girls, a highly unthinkable act at that time, Jyotiba was forced to leave his home. However, such threats and pressures by the society would not deter him from doing his work and he kept creating awareness among people about social evils.

In 1851, he started a bigger and better school for girls which became very popular; there was no discrimination on the lines of religion, caste or creed and everyone was welcomed to study there.

Jyotiba was also against child-marriages and was a great supporter of widow remarriage; he was very sympathetic to the cause of distressed women and opened a home for such poor and exploited women where they could be taken care off.

Jyotiba was also actively involved in the emancipation of so-called lower castes and especially the Untouchables; in fact he was perhaps the first person who gave untouchables the name Dalit as signifying someone who is broken, depressed or exploited and is outside the so-called Varna system.

For uplifting the so-called lower caste people and untouchables, on 24 September 1873, he formed the Satya-shodhak Samaj (the Society of Truth Seekers); the main objective of the Samaj was to create a just and equitable social order free of discrimination on the basis of caste, religion or gender. Satya-shodhak Samaj was also opposed to religious dogmas and superstitions such as idolatry need for priests and irrational rituals etc.

Thus, Jyotiba Phule devoted his whole life for the weaker and depressed section of society; in his thinking and works, he was well ahead of his times.

Swami Dayanand Saraswati

The Arya Samaj founded by Swami Dayanand Saraswati in 1875 undertook the task of reforming Hindu religion and women's condition in north India. Arya Samaj advocated social reform and worked improve the condition of women. It fought untouchability and the rigidities of the hereditary caste system and promoted social equality and specially to women.

Gandhi and Women's Rights

Gandhi basic ideas on women's rights were equality in some spheres and opportunity for self-development and self-realization. He believed that women are the companion of men, gifted with equal mental capacities and realized that her contemporary subordinate position was the result of domination by man.

In this connection, Gandhi said men have not realized this truth in its fullness in their behaviour towards women. They have considering them as their friends and co-workers. Gandhi was equally aware that the position and role of women differed from class to class and that, for example in the village generally they hold their own with their men folk and in some respects even rules them. But, he was convinced that the legal and customary status of women is bad enough throughout and demands radical alteration.

Gandhi believed that every man and women had a duty to perform in the interest of self-realization and social well-being while arguing that she should labour under no legal disability not suffered by men and denouncing the „sheer force of vicious circumstances by means of which even the most ignorant and worthless men have been enjoying a superiority over women which they do not deserve and ought not to have, he still thought that there was a particular sphere appropriate for women. This is most clearly illustrated in his ideas on female education. He was all in favour of educating women, but the emphasis must be different for men and for women.

He had similar ideas on female morality and divorce, and in 1926 spoke against double standards for men and women and why is there all this morbid anxiety about female purity? We hear nothing of women's anxiety about men's chastity. Why should men arrogate to themselves the right to regulate female purity? To Gandhi, self-restraint in sexual matters was a great virtue, but it had to come from within the individual. Marriage was a sacrament; the dowry system should be abolished because it debased marriage, reducing it to an arrangement for money. Divorce was preferable to the continuance of a marriage which had ceased to be a vehicle for self-realization.

Gandhi's ideal woman was the mythical Sita, the self-sacrificing monogamous wife of the Ramayana, who guarded her chastity and remained loyal to Rama in spite of many provocations. Sita was promoted as the model for Indian women. Gandhi was perhaps hardly conscious of the fact that his ideal of womanhood, which he considered to be a revival of the Hindu ideal, contained in fact many traits of the puritan. Victorian ideal of women, as it was preached by the English bourgeoisie. Gandhi was very conscious of the power that women could have in a struggle based on the concept of non-cooperation. He stressed the importance of their participation in political and social matters and exhorted them to join the nationalist struggles.

Gandhi placed particular stress on the issue on the issue of non-violent struggle, claiming that women had great ability to endue suffering and could therefore play a key part in the movement. He claimed that the principle of non-violence and political non-violent resistance was suited to women as they were by nature non-violent. I do believe he wrote in 1938, that women are more fitted than man to make ahimsa.

Nehru and Women's Rights

Nehru particularly emphasized the necessity for women to work outside the home, to be economically independent, and not to regard marriage as a profession. Freedom depends on economic conditions even more than political and if a woman is not economically free and self-earning. She will have to depend on her husband or someone else and dependents are never free. He realized that this economic bondage was the root cause of the troubles of the Indian women and clearly perceived that superficial reforms would not serve the cause of their emancipation. The joint family system of the Hindus, a relic of a feudal age utterly out of keeping with modern conditions, must go and also many other customs and traditions. But, the ultimate solution lies only in complete refashioning our society.

Nehru's more progressive attitude is also revealed in his about female education. He took part in the foundation laying ceremony for a women's college at Allahabad, but discovered that its prospectus laid down that women's place was in the home, that her duty was to be a devoted wife, brining up her children skillfully, and dutifully obedient to her elders. He was quite outspoken in his criticism of these ideals. Nehru also argued women to participate in the nationalist struggle. In 1931 he stated in a national war, there is no question of either sex of community. Whoever is born in this country ought to be a soldier. Nehru spoke with great enthusiasm about the women who took part in the nationalist movement, of the thousands who braved police charges and prisons. However, he was quite conscious that women had to engage in a double struggle, against imperialism and against oppression by men and that these struggles were intimately linked.

Impact of the Reforms Movement

The British wanted to appease the orthodox upper section of society. As a result only two important laws were passed. Some legal measures were introduced to raise the status of women. For example, Sati was declared illegal (1829). Infanticide was declared illegal. Widow re-marriage was permitted by a law passed in 1856. Marriageable age of girls was raised to ten by a law passed in 1860. A law passed in 1872, sanctioned inter-caste and inter-communal marriages. The other law passed in 1891, aimed at discouraging child marriage. For preventing child marriage, the Sharda Act was passed in 1929. According to it a girl below 14 and a boy below 18 could not be married. In the 20th century and especially after 1919 the Indian national movement became the main propagator of social reform. Increasingly, the reformers took recourse to propaganda in the Indian language to reach the masses. They also used novels, dramas, short stories, poetry, the Press and in the thirties (1930's), the cinema too spread their views.

Numerous individuals, reform societies, and religious organizations worked hard to spread education among women, to prevent marriage of young children, to bring women out of the purdah, to enforce monogamy, and to enable middle class women to take up professions or public employment. Due to all these efforts Indian women played an active and important role in the struggle for independence of the country. As a result many superstitions disappeared and many others were on their way out. Now, it was no longer a sin to travel to foreign countries.

II

Issues and Concerns of Transgender

Who are Transgender People?

Transgender people are individuals of any age or sex whose appearance, personal characteristics, or behaviors differ from stereotypes about how men and women are 'supposed' to be. Transgender people have existed in every culture, race, and class since the story of human life has been recorded. The contemporary term 'transgender' arose in the mid-1990s from the grassroots community of gender-different people. In contemporary usage, transgender has become an 'umbrella' term that is used to describe a wide range of identities and experiences, including but not limited to transsexual people; male and female cross-dressers (sometimes referred to as 'transvestites,' 'drag queens' or 'drag kings'); inter-sexed individuals; and men and women, regardless of sexual orientation, whose appearance or characteristics are perceived to be gender atypical. In its broadest sense, transgender encompasses anyone whose identity or behavior falls outside of stereotypical gender norms. That includes people who do not self-identify as transgender, but who are perceived as such by others and thus are subject to the same social oppressions and physical violence as those who actually identify with any of these categories. Other current synonyms for transgender include 'gender variant,' 'gender different,' and 'gender non-conforming.'

In India there are a host of socio – cultural groups of transgender people like hijras/ kinnars, and other transgender identities like – shiv-shaktis, jogtas, jogappas, Aradhis, Sakhi, etc. However, these socio-cultural groups are not the only transgender people, but there may be those who do not belong to any of the groups but are transgender persons individually.

In India, there are a wide range of transgender related identities which includes the Hijras, Aravanis, Kothis, Jogtas/ Jogappas, Shiv Sakthis. In the past, they were treated with great respect.

- *'Hijra'* is a Persian word translated as eunuch which is used in common parlance for transgender community in India.

- *'Aravani'* is a term used for male-to-female transgender who undergo genital modification through SRS (Sex Reassignment Surgery) or perform Nirwaan which is a traditional mode of castration.
- *Kothi* is used for those who adopt a feminine role in same sex relationships, but do not live in communes as Aravanis.
- *Jogtas/ Jogappas* found in Maharashtra and Karnataka are male to female transgender who devote themselves to the service of a particular god.
- *Shiv Shakthis* found in Andhra Pradesh are males who are considered married to gods particularly Lord Shiva. They usually work as spiritual healers or astrologers.

Problems Faced by Transgender in India

There are so many problem which are faced by the transgender in India are as:

1. The main problems that are being faced by the transgender community are of discrimination, unemployment, lack of educational facilities, homelessness, lack of medical facilities: like HIV care and hygiene, depression, hormone pill abuse, tobacco and alcohol abuse, and problems related to marriage and adoption.
2. They are shunned by family and society alike.
3. They have restricted access to education, health services and public spaces.
4. Recently, they were excluded from effectively participating in social and cultural life.
5. Politics and decision-making processes have been out of their reach.
6. They do not have their fundamental right.
7. Reports of harassment, violence, denial of services, and unfair treatment against transgender persons have come to light.

Rights Granted under Indian Law to Transgender

The Constitution of India In essence, the Constitution of India is 'sex blind', that is to say, the basic premise of equality before the law and equal protection of the law is based on a Constitutional mandate that the sex of a person is irrelevant save where the Constitution itself requires special provisions to be made for women [Article 15(3)].

Right of Transgender Persons Bill, 2014: The Bill was introduced in Rajya Sabha on 12th December, 2014 which is passed on 24th April, 2015 unanimously, with cross-party support. This was a private member's bill introduced by the MP from Tamil Nadu, Tiruchi Siva. 24th April is celebrated as Transgender day following the passage of the Bill in the Rajya Sabha.

The rights guaranteed under the Bill are mostly substantive rights such as the right to equality and non-discrimination, life and personal liberty, free speech, to live in a community, integrity, along with protection from torture or cruelty and abuse, violence and exploitation. There is a separate clause for transgender children.

India Court Recognizes Transgender People as Third Gender

On 15 April 2014 justices K.S. Radhakrishnan and A.K. Sikri granted legal recognition to transgenders or eunuchs as "third gender" and directed the centre and states to treat them as socially and educationally backward classes for the purposes of quotas in admission to educational institutions and public appointments.

Challenges for Education of Transgender

The main challenges for education for Transgender are given below:

Inclusion in School/ college and University: Inclusion of transgender with school and college is a big challenge. It is so challenging to provide equal opportunity of education to transgender because there is a problem of inclusion with male and female gender students.

Use of Disrespectful Names and Pronouns: When a transgender youth identifies as a particular gender (irrespective of biological sex), it is respectful to the youth's human dignity to use the name chosen and the pronouns appropriate to that particular gender. To persevere intentionally in the use of a prior name and other pronouns is to be deliberately disrespectful. Transgender youth can understand and sympathize with some confusion, so long as there is continuous, good faith progress in using the proper name and pronouns.

Lack of Access to Appropriate Restroom Facilities: Transgender people often lack safe access to public restrooms. They may be assaulted if they use the restroom that conforms to their gender identity or forced to use a restroom that does not conform to their gender identity. Transgender people often have no safe access to locker room facilities that conform to their gender identity. Wherever dress codes are enforced, they may create problems for transgender youth.

Confidentiality: Transgender youth may have unsupportive families and may even face violence and/or ejection from their home if their gender identity or gender expression is disclosed to the family.

Lack of Ideal Personality: Transgender youth often feel alone in the world. Few programmes for youth employ transgender people; few libraries offer information about biological sex and gender, gender identity, or being transgender.

Strategies or Solutions for Transgender

Made Effort for Inclusion: There is a need for prepare an environment where transgender feels secure. Teacher and community people can play an important role in inclusion. There is a need to provide vocational education and training to teachers and other school members. At the secondary and higher secondary levels vocational training should be provided to the transgender that they preparefor their jobs.

Names and/or Pronouns: Use the name and/or pronouns appropriate to the young person's chosen gender identity. Remember that it is everyone's essential dignity to be called by our chosen name and it iseveryone's right to be recognized as the person we see ourselves to be.

Access to Restroom Facilities: Educate staff and youth about gender identity. Make sure that everyone understands that transgender youth. If possible, designate gender-neutral restrooms and locker rooms (toilet facilities that anyone may use, irrespective of gender identity or gender expression). Educate staff and youth about gender identity.

Confidentiality: Make sure that the programme maintains confidentiality with regard to the gender identity, gender expression, sexual orientation, and sexual behavior ofallthe youth in the programme.

Ideal Personality: Search out transgender support groups and GLBTQ youth-serving organizations in your area. Make sure that these groups and organizations are included on your resource lists.

Provide Financial Assistance: Government should provide fee-waiver, fee-reimbursements, scholarships, free textbooks, free hostel accommodation and other facilities at subsidized rates for students belonging to the transgender in order to make higher education and professional education accessible by the community. Special coaching should be provided to the candidates for competitive examinations.

Establishment of Anti-discrimination Cell: All the educational institutions/universities should establish an anti-discrimination cell to monitor any form of discrimination against the transgendercommunity. On the line of strict anti-ragging cell, there should be zero tolerance towards any incidence of the discrimination or complain.

Research: There is need for a focused institutionalized mechanism of research and academic activities to generate more data/information to identify and understand the problems related to various aspects of their life and help frame policies through research and academic programme that would bring an effective and long-term change in their lives.

India's First Transgender School

India's first transgender school opened in Kochi on 30th December, 2016. Residential school for transgender people has been opened in the Indian city of Kochi, to help adults who dropped out of school finish their education. The school, named 'Sahaj International', was inaugurated by transgender activist, writer and actor Kalki Subramaniam at Thrikkakara in Kerala's Ernakulam district. This alternative learning centre works in collaboration with National Institute of Open Schooling (NIOS). The school, the first of its kind in the country, is expected to go a long way in ensuring equal opportunities for transgenders who have dropped out from school. The new learning centre will help them continue their education and appear for Class X and XII examinations.

The transgender school is headed by six transgenders and a woman under the Transgender Foundation. "The school will initially start with 10 students including a migrant and a differently abled transgender. There will be a pool of 60 trainers which includes teachers, social workers, doctors and engineers to support the educationally disadvantaged to strengthen their community's social status

12

Violence against Women

Women constitute half of our population and play specific and crucial role either visible or invisible, in society and history. A woman creates life, nurtures it, guards and strengthens it. In these tasks as a role player they have a vital role in the development of the nation. It is a matter of great pride for all of us to live in a country which is the world's largest democracy, a sovereign socialist republic with a comprehensive charter of right written into its constitution, a signatory to most treaties for struggle against colonialism, imperialism and racism.

It is ironical that in a country where womanhood has been put on pedestal for worship, incidence of wife battering, molestation of women in various forms like rape, eve-teasing, abduction and bride burning among women keep as increasing year to year.

Meaning of Violence

According to United Nations Declaration of Elimination of Violence against Women in the book "Women in the Third World" (1998); Violence is defined as any act of gender based violence that results in, or is likely to result in physical, sexual or psychological harm or suffering to women, including threats of such acts, coercion or arbitrary deprivations of liberty whether occurring in public or private life. It shall be understood to encompass but not be limited to physical, sexual and psychological violence occurring in the family and in the community including battering, sexual abuse of female children, dowry violence, marital rape and other traditional practices harmful to woman. Violence can be further classified in two categories:

Violence within Home

Girl Child Abuse

It is one area in which very little amount of evidence is available. Girl child abuse within the home takes place in various forms. The various forms are sexual aggression, beatings and child labour. All available studies on girl child abuse have shown that the abuse is of physical and emotional nature.

Table 12.1: Types of Violence

VIOLENCE	
Within Home	Outside Home
Girl Child Abuse	Witch Hunting
Wife Beating / Battering	Rape
Mental Abuse	Molestation
Female Foeticide	Eve-teasing

The causes of the girl child abuse are the environment at home, social environment as well as life situations. All these three factors are significant in nature. One of the most common forms of girl child abuse at home is sexual molestation and rape. Families rarely talk about issues such as rape very openly. If a daughter has been raped, there is a tendency to suppress the matter. If the rapist is a family member such as father, brother or an uncle, the chances of reporting the rape case is almost nil.

Girl child abuse can be differentiated into four major categories:

- Physical abuse
- Emotional abuse
- Neglect
- Sexual abuse

Wife Beating and Battering

Wife beating and battering is one of the most common forms of violence within home. Indian women are socialized to be submissive and inferior. Hence a significant number of them accept wife beating and battering as a normal process. This form of violence does not take place only in the case of poor and illiterate women but also in the case of educated, middle and upper class women. Feelings of guilt and shame prevent women from sharing their problem. This is more commonly observed in the case of educated, middle and upper class women. Hence they silently bear the trauma.

Wife Beating

Definition: 'Wife beating is physical abuse of a woman by her present or former husband or male companion. It consists of repeated blows inflicted with intent to do harm. Threats and verbal abuse that were preceded by beating are part of a pattern of control of a wife by her husband that is basic to wife beating."

There have been very few attempts to deal with and understand the problem of violence against women in the family. In order to understand the nature and extent of wife beating in Indian society, it would naturally imply that marital violence is mostly directed by the husband against the wife causes of wife beating may be stated as—Arguments over money; Jealousy and suspicion regarding wife's character; Instigation by in-laws; House work; Alcohol; Wife's desire to work outside the home or wife's high self-esteem; Dispute over children; Extra marital affairs on the part of husband.

Form of Violence: The form of violence may include

- Beating with hand and fist.
- Beating with articles like iron-rod
- Kicking the abdomen while the woman is pregnant.
- Using knives or blades to cause cuts and bruises.
- Causing burns with any hot objects or cigarette buds.
- Throwing women against objects and banging her head against the wall.
- Excessive sexual demands or sexual perversions.

Wife Battering

Definition: "Wife battering refers to violent acts—psychological, sexual and/or physical assault—by an assailant against his wife and/or partner made with the intent of controlling the partner by inducing fear and pain."

A common name given to wife battering is silent crime. It is the most under-reported crime in India. No woman wants to relate the agony of her personal life to court room and throw herself open to having her bonafides questioned and her character maligned. She would rather prefer to cling on to a broken marriage. Here, two points emerge at once: that the violence is located at home and the offender is the husband. The site of violence being the home and the attacker being the husband has distorted, confused and is responsible for the gross trivialization of the crime. Violence by man against their partners is an old problem, it is assumed by some to have begun with the first monogamous pairing. What is new is that the fact that the public admission of violence against women occurs in a civilized society and the insistence by the government and responsible citizens that such violence is no longer acceptable; therefore we are compelled to discuss such a problem and search for solution to alleviate it.

Causes of Wife Beating and Battering

1. When a woman is incapable of adjusting to the emotional, intellectual and most importantly the physical needs of her husband, it can result in violence.
2. Bad habits in a husband such as alcoholism, drug addiction are the common cases.
3. Certain personality types in husbands may also result in violence. For e.g. if a husband is extremely jealous, this may create insecurity in marriage and can result in violent behaviour.

4. If a husband has excessive ego and if the wife happens to be more successful then him, the husband can develop inferiority complex. He may want to show his power and superiority over his wife through wife beating and battering.
5. When the wife is extremely submissive, under confident and totally dependent on her husband, she may become a victim of violent behaviour.
6. If a husband has been a victim of child abuse, this can cause emotional disturbance. He may become violent towards his wife.
7. Wife beating and battering can have serious consequences for the victims. It indicates aggressive behavior not only to the physical body but also towards her self-respect and her self-confidence.
8. If a woman is financially independent, wife beating and battering can lead to separation and divorce. However if she is totally dependent on her husband, the situation can be very problematic.
9. Wife beating and battering is a criminal offence and the husband can be punished to three years of imprisonment and a fine.
10. It has been observed that the attitude of the Indian women is to accept male domination and hence cases of wife beating and battering are not always reported.
11. This type of violence within home is considered as minor by the women themselves as well as by the society. Hence not much seriousness is attached to it.
12. In a study conducted on wife beating and battering, it was noted that women rarely reported this form of violence. It was also found out that only when the beatings became very severe that the women considered themselves as abused. It means a single slap or a single blow once in a while were regarded as routine husband – like behavior.
13. It has been observed that the social atmosphere and socialization of women give a kind of justification to the problem of wife beating and battering. The general attitude is that men have absolute control over their wives and can treat them in any way that they think is the most suitable.
14. To conclude, it can be said that wife beating and battering is common among all classes. This is because it shows the power relationship between husbands and wives.

Mental Abuse

Definition:"Psychological abuse (also referred to as psychological violence, emotional abuse, or mental abuse) is a form of abuse, characterized by a person subjecting, or exposing, another person to behavior that may result in psychological trauma, including anxiety, chronic depression, or post-traumatic stress disorder. It is often associated with situations of power imbalance in abusive relationships including bullying, gas lighting and abuse in the workplace."

"Mental abuse is a form of violence that affects the mind, often leaving the abused feeling worthless and lacking empowerment"

Mental or emotional abuse is as damaging as physical abuse, though it is often harder to recognize and therefore even to recover from. Mental abuse causes long term self-esteem issues and profound emotional repercussions for the partners of abusers. Abusive relationships are characterized by extreme jealousy, emotional withholding, lack of intimacy, raging, sexual coercion, infidelity, verbal abuse, threats, lies, broken promises, physical violence, power plays and control games.

When people think of domestic abuse, they often picture battered women who have been physically assaulted. But not all abusive relationships involve violence. Unfortunately, emotional abuse is often minimized or overlooked-even by the person being abused.

A woman may be mentally abused by either her husband or in-laws or both. It may occur in the following way:

Dominance: It is the abuser who wants to take charge of the relationship. The women will be expected to obey the command without any questions.

Humiliation: Insults, name calling, shaming and public put downs are all weapons of abuse designed to erode the self-esteem & make the women feel powerless.

Isolation: In order to increase the wife's dependence, the abusers will try to cut off the women from the outside world. She may not be allowed to see family, friends or even neighbors one may also be prevented from going out of the house for work. Permission may be required to do anything which may include simple eating or drinking.

Threats: Abuser commonly use threats to keep the women from leaving them or to scare them using false charges, she may be threatened to hurt, Kiel any family members or abuse their children.

Intimidation: The abuser may use a variety of intimidation tactics designed to scare the women into submission. Such tactics include making threatening looks or gestures, smashing things in front of them, destroying property, hurting or putting weapons on display. This clear message is that if the woman does not obey there will be violent consequences.

Denial and Blame: Abusers are very good at making excuses for the inexcusable. They will blame the behaviour on the women.

Female Foeticide and Infanticide

Female Foeticide: Female foeticide is the practice of aborting a foetus when a person finds out that the foetus is female after undergoing a sex determination test known as prenatal diagnostic tests.

Female Infanticide: Female infanticide is the deliberate killing of girl babies. It is also described as gender-selective killing or "gendercide". (Similar words like 'gynocide' and 'femicide' are used to describe the killing of females of any age.)

This form of violence within home is the one which brings shame to humanity. It is the cold-blooded murder of a baby girl (infanticide) as well as female fetus (foeticide). In the male-dominated Indian society, the birth of a boy is always welcome but the birth of a girl is looked down upon as a burden.

Difference between Female Foeticide and Infanticide

These two are two different roads to one common goal – killing a girl child. Let us take a look at the differences between the two in a tabular format given below:

Table 12.2: Difference between Female Foeticide and Infanticide

Female Foeticide	*Female Infanticide*
The girl is not yet born. She is still in foetus stage. It is at this stage the foetus is killed.	The girl is born, that is, delivery happens and then the infant is killed.
Killing takes place by removing the foetus from the womb. Basically abortion. Sometimes, a more indirect method is used where a pills is inserted into the genitals of a pregnant woman and within a few hours, the foetus dies and disintegrates and comes out while passing urine.	Killing takes place after birth. A number of methods can be used for the same.

Religious and Social Causes of Female Infanticide and Foeticide

Several religious and social causes of female infanticide and foeticide are as follows:

1. The son is important to carry forward the family name and the family lineage. Girls are married into different families and hence cannot carry forward the family name.
2. The son is important to light the funeral pyre of the parents as well as to perform the Shraddha ceremony which will give salvation to the souls.
3. A son is important to look after the parents in their old age.
4. A very important reason which is related to girls being considered as a burden, is the practice of dowry. Due to this, birth of a girl is associated with financial burden whereas boys are treated as post-dated cheques.

5. A combination of all these religious and social factors led to the practice of female infanticide. The killing of baby girls was sometimes done immediately after birth and sometimes over a period of time. This practice is prevalent in rural India to a significant extent even today.
6. Education and modernization have not created significant changes in the attitudes of the society. Even today boys are given more preference over girls.
7. The practice of female infanticide has taken a new form in the modern society and it is called as female foeticide. It means terminating the pregnancy if the pregnant woman is carrying a female foetus. The sex of the foetus can be known through a medical test known as Amniocentesis. It is also called as sex-determination test. The main intention of using this test is to detect abnormality in the foetus. However, the test has been misused to detect the sex of the foetus. If the foetus is a female foetus, then it is aborted sometimes with the consent of the mother and most of the times without her consent.
8. Due to practices of female infanticide and female foeticide, the sex ratio in our country has been affected tremendously.
9. The consequences of female infanticide and foeticide are extremely serious. The table mentioned above clearly the imbalance in sex ratio which is in favour of men.
10. If there is a constant and continuous decline in the number of females as compared to the males, it can lead to several social problems. For e.g. there can be some places which can experience a severe shortage of females in the marriage market. Brothers may have to share a wife and this situation can lead to major moral and value degradation. The problem of sexual violence against women will also increase.
11. Many a times it is noted that female infanticide and female foeticide are carried out without the consent of the mother. This can result in feelings of server guilt, depression and helplessness for the mother.
12. Studies conducted have shown that the threat of desertion, divorce and ill-treatment force the women to agree for female infanticide and female foeticide. If the woman is completely dependent on her husband, these threats have a more strong impact on the women.
13. The question we need to ask is can we allow Indian women to become an endangered species? There are people who believe that it is better to kill a baby girl or abort a female foetus rather than allow her to grow and spend on her dowry later on.
14. There are open advertisements such as *"Better Rs. 5,000 now that Rs. 5 Lakhs later"*. This advertisement clearly promotes the message that it better to spend less amount of money on female foeticide than spending a large amount on the daughter's dowry.

15. An awareness is extremely important to change the mindset of the male – dominated society. Social evils such as dowry as well as age-old religious practices favouring only a son, should be completely eliminated. It is more important to invest in a daughter's education and health to make her self – reliant rather than killing her brutally.

Violence Outside Home

Witch Hunting

Definition: A witch-hunt is an attempt to find and punish a particular group of people who are being blamed for something, often simply because of their opinions and not because they have actually done anything wrong.

One of the most important examples of violence in communities against women is witch-hunting. Incidents of women being labeled as witches or as keepers of evil spirits and the violence against them were large scale in nature. These incidents of labeling as witches and of witch-hunting are mainly associated with the tribal communities. Witch-hunting is common in a tribal group called as 'Santhals'. The Santhal tribe is found in central – eastern part of India in the state of Jharkhand. Witches among Santhals can only be women and they are considered as the main danger to the Santhal community. The Santhal society has some definite rules about women. Women were totally prevented from participating in the worship of family spirits. They were not allowed to perform any religious rituals. Women were also excluded from the village group rituals. It means women were not allowed to participate in any family and public rituals.

Rape

Definition: Rape is a type of sexual assault usually involving sexual intercourse or other forms of sexual penetration carried out against a person without that person's consent. The act may be carried out by physical force, coercion, abuse of authority, or against a person who is incapable of giving valid consent, such as one who is unconscious, incapacitated, has an intellectual disability or is below the legal age of consent.

One of the most serious crimes committed against women and whose effects are extremely painful is rape. Rape can be defined in various ways. The legal definition of rape is as follows:

According to section 375 of the IPC (Indian Penal Code), a man is said to commit rape on a woman under any of the following circumstances:

1. Against her will
2. Without her consent (permission)

3. With her consent, when her consent has been obtained by putting in her fear of death or harm
4. With her consent, when the consent is given because she believes the man to be her married husband
5. With her consent, if she gives consent because of intoxication or unsoundness of mind.
6. With her consent, if she is under 16 years of age.

Rape is not just a physical violence against a woman but it is also psychological and emotional violence. It is the ultimate humiliation for a woman in which her self-respect and her dignity are attacked.

Causes of Rape

There are several important causes of rape which are as follows:

1. When a man needs to show his superiority over a woman, he does it by physically dominating her. He feels that this is the only way of indicating his domination.
2. Sometimes young girls or small girls act as easy targets and they become victims of rape.
3. Emotional disturbance in a man can also lead to rape. Sometimes the man himself may have been a victim of violence or molestation. This can develop a sense of sadism in him. He may enjoy giving physical and psychological pain to others and to women who are easy victims.
4. Violence and vulgarity shown through media can impact the younger generation to a great extent. Those with aggressive tendencies may commit rape to give vent to such tendencies.
5. A weak legal system can act as an important cause for rape. The rapist may roam about scot-free and it is the rape victim who becomes the target of social humiliation and rejection.

Suggestions

1. One of the most important suggestions need to be introduced is amending the law in favor of women.
2. Rape victims should not be maltreated at the hands of the police whose assistance has been sought during the crisis. They should not be submitted to the countless questions about her own sexual mores and behaviour by the police investigator.
3. In the hospital, the victims should be thoroughly examined by as expert doctor and immediate cure of physical injuries, prevention of veneral diseases and prevention of pregnancy should be taken.

4. The victims of rape should not be treated like the offender.
5. Report of rape victims should be recorded by women police officers & women investigators are to be appointed to investigate such cases.
6. Rape stigma should not be attached with the victim and his family rather it should be shifted from the victim to the offender.
7. Victims of the rape deserve emotional support and sympathy by family members for post – rape adjustment.
8. Sex education should be imparted to adolescents and youths in order to prevent the crime against women.

If the society wants to escape from sex anarchy of rape of women, changes must be brought in the mind, heart and behaviour of men and women in the various compartments of our culture and in our social institutions.

Molestation

Definition: Molestation is a crime that involves "sexual acts with children up to the age of 18, including touching of private parts, exposure of genitalia, taking of pornographic pictures, rape, inducement of sexual acts with the molester or with other children, and variations of these acts by pedophiles. Molestation may include incest or unwanted sexual acts by a relative, but is short of rape.

Molestation is considered as a crime against women and it fall under the category of sexual harassment. Molestation can be understood as a crime which makes use of forced assault to outrage the modesty of the women. It means it is physical in nature. Section 354 of the IPC deals with molestation. Since molestation involves physical touch, it becomes serious. Molestation is the sexual exploitation of a child or a woman by an adult for sexual gratification or for profit. Molestation may include:

- Fondling of private parts like breast and genitals
- Mutual masturbation
- Coitus
- Pornography and Prostitution.

Thus, molestation is the act of subjecting someone to unwanted or improper sexual advances or activity especially for women and children.

Signs of Molestation

When an adult women is molested, there are certain signs which may suggest that molestation took place.

Physical Signs: Bruises or lacerations on parts of the body; Unexplained injuries; Torn, strained or bloody clothing or undergarments: Irritation or pain in the genital area; Symptoms of a sexually transmitted disease or a venereal disease; Difficulty in urinating; Symptoms of pregnancy.

Behavioural Signs: Depression or loneliness; Self-abuse or suicidal behavior; Drug of alcohol abuse; Nightmares; Unexplained or unpredicted behaviour patterns; Sudden loss or increase in sexual behavior

In case of children, it is difficult to identify because they may be scared to talk about such an incident. It is important to be very supportive of them as they might feel that it is their fault and would shudder from the experience. Molestation is a heinous crime; it shows the mentality of the men living in the society. Stricter laws should be made against women's violation to keep women safe and maintain a healthier environment. It the Union Women and Child Development Ministry has its way, molesters will face a hard time as the government is planning to make the laws stricter for the culprits.

Eve-Teasing

Definition: The making of unwanted sexual remarks or advances by a man to a woman in a public place.

Eve-teasing is not a myth but a reality. It exists and exists everywhere. It has been a serious menace in our society. The commission of this crime is an indicator of how far the women folk are in secured in our society. The miscreants hurl indecent remarks. In daily life if not all men are potential eve-teasers, all women are potential victims. Women suffer from the fear of being teased, irrespective of her age, health, appearance, mental state etc. This has affected the peace of mind of women and they are not able to move freely and participate in the public life of the community.

The eve-teasers disposable deeds cover the following:

1. Indulging in cat- calls, waving, wolf, whistling, winking and uttering indecent remarks about female anatomy or singing absence songs in such a way so as to be heard by women. Songs are deliberately chosen from popular film so that these could appear innocuous if it came to an argument.
2. Nudging past hurriedly, pressing against women. Trying to pinch the bottoms or the breasts and disappearing in the crowd. If caught they pretend that rubbing was all accidental. They get a free hand during the breakdown of power. In the process sometime even the aged women are not spared from this kind of menace.
3. Eve-teasers got up in crowded buses & trains, prefers to stand or sit next to ladies & depending on the situation, the teaser sometimes gets himself sandwiched with her in the crowded and leans on her.

4. In recent years, in some universities these forms of eve-teasing have replaced with brazen acts as dupatta snatching, back patting & in some cases even forced kissing.
5. Eve-teasing has also taken the form of telephoning a girl and uttering absence and suggestive words.
6. Mailing anonymous love letters in the filthiest languages.
7. Exhibiting male genital in front of women and thereby deriving strange perverted sexual pleasure of it.

Causes of Eve Teasing

Several causes of eve-teasing can be identified as follows:

1. A male-dominated patriarchal society is a significant cause of eve-teasing. Men consider themselves as superior and hence take the freedom to humiliate or insult any woman according to their wish.
2. Influence of media is another important cause. Different forms of eve-teasing are shown through our films and television serials. This can influence the boys and the men. They consider eve-teasing as harmless when they see their favorite actors indulging in the same behavior on the screen.
3. Eve-teasing is considered as the easiest way to attract attention of the girls. Since it is only verbal in nature, boys also consider it as the safest way to attract attention or to humiliate the girls.
4. One of the most important causes of eve-teasing is the fact that girls or women are considered as temptresses. It means men feel that it is the women who like to attract or invite their attention by the kinds of clothes and the kinds of attitudes they carry. Thus men conveniently put the blame on women and justify eve-teasing and even molestation to a great extent.
5. Because of its non-physical nature, eve-teasing is considered as insignificant, mild and funny. Hence it is treated as a normal behavior of men with women. It means violence is normalized and not considered as an offence.
6. In the modern society, many aspects of the value system have degenerated. The kind of modern life style which is followed by both boys and girls can encourage eve-teasing and molestation. Example can be cited of date-rape.

Suggestions

1. There is a need to create awareness in society so that the attitude of general public may be more sympathetic towards the victim.

2. The girls have to be bold and their own and must get themselves trained in art forms like judo or karate for self-defense.
3. Whatever the incident, it must be reported to the police as an eve-teaser who remains un-reported gets encouraged in his exploits and this encourages other also.
4. The public has to also play an important role in curbing the evil. Public opinion also has to build up against the eve-teasers.
5. It is also worthwhile for the parents to discuss sex with the children and remove from their mind the unhealthy curiosity about it.

There is a continuous increase in the cases of violence against women. The burden of tradition, a prevailing ideology of male superiority and a society that condone violence creates a chamber of horrors where even angles would year to tread Spreading of Education and creating social awareness can be two important measures taken against violence. The media should play an important role in enhancing the status of women by outlining the contribution of female child and women would make to the family and to society at large. Only when a many pronged attack is launched against the evil the menace can be minimized considerably, if not eradicated absolutely.

13

Gender Equality and Constitutional Framework of India

The rights available to woman (ladies) in India can be classified into two categories, namely as constitutional rights and legal rights. The constitutional rights are those which are provided in the various provisions of the constitution. The legal rights, on the other hand, are those which are provided in the various laws (acts) of the Parliament and the State Legislatures.

Constitutional Rights/Provisions to Ensure Dignity of Women

Lots of provisions have been introduced through constitution to ensure dignity and self-respect to the women at large. As mentioned earlier Dr. B. R. Ambedkar, author of Indian Constitution, make sure that Constitution of India safeguard the social and legal rights of women. The rights and safeguards enshrined in the Constitution for women in India are listed below:

Article 14: Article 14 of constitution of India ensures equality before the law or the equal protection of the laws within the territory of India. This is a very important provision which provides equal legal protection to women against any women based crime. This provision also paves way for the introduction of various laws and acts to ensure protection and enforcement of legal rights of women in India.

Article 15: Article 15 of constitution of India ensures that no one should create any sort of discrimination only on the grounds of religion, race, caste, sex or place of birth or any of them within the territory of India. At the time of Independence there was lots of discrimination in India against women which gradually abolished after introduction of article 15.

Article 15(1): The state shall not discriminate against any citizen of India on the ground of sex.

Article 15(3): The state is empowered to make any special provision for women. In other words, this provision enables the state to make affirmative discrimination in favour of women.

Article 16: Article 16 of constitution of India ensures equal employment opportunity to every citizen of India. As per article 16, there should not be any discrimination in respect of employment opportunity under the State only on grounds of religion, race, caste, sex, descent, and place of birth, residence or any of them. Now we can see women are doing really good work in politics and in corporate sector. Presently they are holding responsible positions in Government and Government run institutions. Let me share few good names from political and corporate field. These names are Chanda kochhar, Indira nooyi, Sonia Gandhi, Sushma Swaraj and this never ending list goes on.

Article 16(2): No citizen shall be discriminated against or be ineligible for any employment or office under the state on the ground of sex.

Article 23(1): Traffic in human beings and forced labour are prohibited.

Article 39: Article 39 of constitution of India ensures the benefit of the directive principles of state policy to the women. Directive principles of state policy mean *guiding principles* for the framing of laws by the government at state level.

Article 39(a): The state to secure for men and women equally the right to an adequate means of livelihood. Article 39(a) of directive principles of state policy ensures and directs a state to apply policies which focus on a men and women have an equal right of adequate means of livelihood

Article 39(c): Article 39(c) ensures equal pay for equal work for both men and women.

Article 39(d): The state to secure equal pay for equal work for both Indian men and women.

Article 39(e): The state is required to ensure that the health and strength of women workers are not abused and that they are not forced by economic necessity to enter avocations unsuited to their strength.

Article 42: Article 42 of constitution of India caste a duty on every employer to ensure just and humane conditions of work and for maternity relief. In reality the position and treatment of women in corporate offices is really bad and in fact they are exploited by their seniors and bosses. In this scenario the provisions of article 42 are very important and now it is duty of employer to provide good working conditions to all the employees. The state shall make provision for securing just and humane conditions of work and maternity relief.

Article 51-A(e): It shall be the duty of every citizen of India to renounce practices derogatory to the dignity of women.

Article 243-D (3): One-third of the total number of seats to be filled by direct election in every Panchayat shall be reserved for women.

Article 243-D (4): One-third of the total number of offices of chairpersons in the Panchayats at each level shall be reserved for women.

Article 243-T (3): One-third of the total number of seats to be filled by direct election in every Municipality shall be reserved for women.

Article 243-T (4): The offices of chairpersons in the Municipalities shall be reserved for women in such manner as the State Legislature may provide.

Article 243: Article 243 of constitution of India ensures reservation of seats in gram panchayat for women. This opportunity of being a part of local level arbitration process has improved the social conditions of women in village areas.

Legal Rights to Women

Protection of Women from Domestic Violence Act (2005): It is a comprehensive legislation to protect women in India from all forms of domestic violence. It also covers women who have been/are in a relationship with the abuser and are subjected to violence of any kind—physical, sexual, mental, verbal or emotional.

Immoral Traffic (Prevention) Act (1956): It is the premier legislation for prevention of trafficking for commercial sexual exploitation. In other words, it prevents trafficking in women and girls for the purpose of prostitution as an organised means of living.

Indecent Representation of Women (Prohibition) Act (1986): Indecent Representation of Women (Prohibition) Act (1986) prohibits indecent representation of women through advertisements or in publications, writings, paintings, figures or in any other manner.

Commission of Sati (Prevention) Act (1987): It provides for the more effective prevention of the commission of sati and its glorification on women.

*Dowry Prohibition Act (1961):*Dowry Prohibition Act (1961) prohibits the giving or taking of dowry at or before or any time after the marriage from women.

Maternity Benefit Act (1961): Maternity Benefit Act (1961) regulates the employment of women in certain establishments for certain period before and after child-birth and provides for maternity benefit and certain other benefits.

Medical Termination of Pregnancy Act (1971): It provides for the termination of certain pregnancies by registered medical practitioners on humanitarian and medical grounds.

Pre-Conception and Pre-Natal Diagnostic Techniques (Prohibition of Sex Selection) Act (1994): It prohibits sex selection before or after conception and prevents the misuse of pre-natal diagnostic techniques for sex determination leading to female foeticide.

Equal Remuneration Act (1976): It provides for payment of equal remuneration to both men and women workers for same work or work of a similar nature. It also prevents discrimination on the ground of sex, against women in recruitment and service conditions.

Dissolution of Muslim Marriages Act (1939): Dissolution of Muslim Marriages Act (1939) grants a Muslim wife the right to seek the dissolution of her marriage.

*Muslim Women (Protection of Rights on Divorce) Act (1986):*It protects the rights of Muslim women who have been divorced by or have obtained divorce from their husbands.

Family Courts Act (1984): Family Courts Act (1984) provides for the establishment of Family Courts for speedy settlement of family disputes.

Indian Penal Code (1860): It contains provisions to protect Indian women from dowry death, rape, kidnapping, cruelty and other offences.

Code of Criminal Procedure (1973): It has certain safeguards for women like obligation of a person to maintain his wife, arrest of woman by female police and so on.

Indian Christian Marriage Act (1872): Indian Christian Marriage Act (1872) contain provisions relating to marriage and divorce among the Christian community.

Legal Services Authorities Act (1987): Legal Services Authorities Act (1987) provides for free legal services to Indian women.

Hindu Marriage Act (1955): It introduced monogamy and allowed divorce on certain specified grounds. It provided equal rights to Indian man and woman in respect of marriage and divorce.

Hindu Succession Act (1956): It recognizes the right of women to inherit parental property equally with men.

Minimum Wages Act (1948): Minimum Wages Act (1948) does not allow discrimination between male and female workers or different minimum wages for them.

Mines Act (1952) and Factories Act (1948): Mines Act (1952) and Factories Act (1948) prohibits the employment of women between 7 P.M. to 6 A.M. in mines and factories and provides for their safety and welfare.

National Commission for Women Act (1990): National Commission for Women Act (1990) provided for the establishment of a National Commission for Women to study and monitor all matters relating to the constitutional and legal rights and safeguards of women.

Sexual Harassment of Women at Workplace (Prevention, Prohibition and Redressal) Act (2013): It provides protection to women from sexual harassment at all workplaces both in public and private sector, whether organised or unorganized.

The following other legislation's also contain certain rights and safeguards for women:

- Employees' State Insurance Act (1948)
- Plantation Labour Act (1951)
- Bonded Labour System (Abolition) Act (1976)
- Legal Practitioners (Women) Act (1923)
- Indian Succession Act (1925)
- Indian Divorce Act (1869)
- Parsi Marriage and Divorce Act (1936)
- Special Marriage Act (1954)
- Foreign Marriage Act (1969)
- Indian Evidence Act (1872)
- Hindu Adoptions and Maintenance Act (1956)

Parliamentary Provisions to Ensure Dignity of Women

After Independence, there was need to introduce some statutory laws to ensure safety and protection of women. Keeping in view this requirement, just like constitutional provisions, various parliamentary steps have also been taken by the law of India in order to ensure dignified life to the Indian Women. Parliamentary steps means and includes the enactment of various laws and statutory acts to protect the interest of women and to stop the crime against women. These acts have proved really useful towards progress and safety of women in society.

In order to ensure adherence to constitutional provisions for women welfare, there was a need to enact specific laws by the state and central Government. Although a women can be victim of any crime in society and in fact all crimes cannot be classified as a crime against women except few crimes which affects a women largely. However major steps have been taken by the legislation which has proved as weapons for women and helped them to stand in male dominating country. Now we will discuss major crimes against women along with the legal provision which penalize the criminal.

Major Crimes against Women

Few crimes which are recognized as crime against women are:

Adultery: Adultery is a very serious crime against women in India and affects married women by and large. In simple words, adultery means having voluntary sexual relationship with a married person other than the spouse. The offence of adultery is dealt with by section 497 of the Indian penal Code, 1860, which says adultery means sexual intercourse of a man with a married woman without the consent of her husband when such sexual intercourse does not amount to rape. However, we may find different meaning of adultery in different laws in different countries. Initially only men were punished under the law of adultery in India but now men and women both are equally responsible for committing the crime of adultery. As per section 497, the offender shall be punished with imprisonment for a term which may extend to five years, or with fine, or with both. In such case the wife shall not be punishable as a partner in crime.

Child Marriage: Child marriage is a very awful offence against child as it does not only harm the future of child but also damage social values. Further, the doctors have also revealed that child marriage is a very big reason for bad health condition for girl child. Child marriage restricts the social development along with reduction in the educational and employment opportunities in the global market. It was like a burden on society to practice this unwritten custom. The major step was taken by the Law Commission of India by fixing the minimum age for marriage which is 18 years for girls and 21 years for boys. Another major step was mandatory primary education and moreover for girls provision for free education provided by the Government of India.

Female Feticides: Female feticide means identifying and killing of female foetus before they take birth. This is the most brutal way of killing women. The custom of female feticide is practiced by the society form ancient times and it is really shameful to note that even today, when we considers ourselves educated and civilized, this custom is practiced in a big manner. Government has taken so many steps to spread awareness among people about the consequences of this crime.

Trafficking and Prostitution: Trafficking means import and export of humans for sex business. It is indeed very sad to learn that in India, where women are recognized as Devi and prayed by all Indian's as Devi Shakti, they are also treated as a source of earning by unethical means. Prostitution is one of the biggest problems in this world which is damaging the women in many ways. In general, the term prostitution means offer of sexual services for earning money. Prostitution is a problem which exists across the world. There are quite a few laws in India in order to prevent the crime of prostitution like Suppression of Immoral Traffic in Women and Girl Act 1956 and Immoral Traffic (Prevention) Act 1956. There are few commissions are made by state Government to save women and specially girls to protect them from this practice.

Domestic Violence: Domestic violence means cruelty by husband or family towards women. For the purpose of domestic violence family includes spouse, his mother, father, brother, sister, his relatives and sometimes even friends. Domestic violence is recognized as a criminal offence under section 498A of Indian Penal Code, 1860. Cruelty can be done by physically, mentally, economically or emotionally.

An act called Domestic violence Act, 2005 was introduced to handle the cases of Domestic violence in India. This act is a very noteworthy attempt in India to recognize domestic violence as a punishable offence. Before the introduction of this act two kinds of remedies were available to a women affected by Domestic violence. These two remedies were divorce through civil courts and application of section 498A through criminal courts.

Eve Teasing: It is a general perception that eve teasing is not a big crime like rape or murder and may be because of that we don't take it seriously. But from a women's point of view eve teasing is also a big crime as this activity does make her feel uncomfortable most of the times. In case of eve teasing girl should not remain silent and raise her voice. She should inform her family members and simultaneously file a complaint in the nearest police station. In this case family should also support the women instead of locking her at home.

Acid Throwing: Recently the issue of acid throwing on girls has also become a big issue. There are few types of acids and all are very dangerous for human flash and burn. This acid attack sometimes is so dangerous that even bones and eyes are also got damaged due to acid. Few victims are forced to leave their education or occupation due to the results of acid throwing. Now a days this has become very easy for people to get these acids and the cases of acid throwing has become very regular in daily life.

Dedicated and specific law to deal with such cases, a draft of the Prevention of Offences (by Acids) Act, 2008, is to be tabled in Parliament. After the approval in Parliament it will become applicable as law.

Fraudulent Marriage: Before going into the details of Fraudulent Marriage let us understand the general meaning of fraud in relation to crime against women. Fraud means hiding something or giving false impression about something which a person knows that knowing the fact may harm his prospective marriage. The scope of fraudulent marriage has increased in the recent past as in India parents. This is not necessary that fraudulent marriages only take place in case of NRIs even Indian grooms also do the same for money or for boy child or for any other reason.

Exploitation at Work Place: Though, we all accept the truth that in today's world women has come out of her image of house wife and proved herself as a better administrator then a man. In all sectors women are working hard and getting awards and rewards for that. She has crossed all the boundaries and shut the mouth of all those peoples who has ever questioned her working caliber. But, she has to pay a very heavy price of her success as she has to face exploitation at work place do we ever think what boundaries she has crossed and how.

Rape, Murder: Rape is another very serious crime against women and this crime is increasing day by day. Reporting of rape and abduction cases has become very common in print and electronic media which is indeed a very sad affair for all of us. Increasing rape cases are enough to prove that our moral values are still very low and we still to learn how to respect the dignity of women at large.

In simple terms the word 'Rape' means sexual intercourse or sexual penetration, by another person without the consent of the other person or victim. Provisions related to rape are given in section 375 and 376 of the Indian Penal Code, 1860. Section 375 explains the pre-condition which are necessary to prove the offence of rape whereas section 376 provides punishment for the offence of rape. As per section 376, whoever commits the offence of rape shall be punished with imprisonment of either for a term which shall not be less than seven years (7) but which may be **for life** or for a term which may extend to ten years and shall also be liable to fine.

Dowry: The system of dowry is another social evil which dragging women back from 100 of years as this evil has a very long history especially in India. Various dowry based domestic violence cases has been reported by media. There are ample legal provisions in India to provide relief to women in case of dowry based domestic violence cases. Civil law of India has prohibited the payment of dowry in the year 1961. Further Indian Penal Code, 1860 has introduced Sections 304B and 498A, which allows women to file complaint and seek restoration of her rights from serious harassment by the husband's family.

Dowry is one of the strong and biggest reasons of increasing domestic violence. Every year thousands of dowry deaths along with mental trauma cases reported and registered in India. In case of inadequate dowry, incidents like burning, suicides, physical and mental torture of women is very common by husband and his family. Keeping in view the increasing cases of dowry deaths another legislative provision called "Protection of Women from Domestic Violence Act 2005", was introduced in order to reduce domestic violence cases and to protect women's rights.

14

Resolving Issues Related to Women and Girl Child

Women face lots of social issues and problems all through the life which are big struggles for them right from their beginning of life. Female infanticide is the most common practice of killing girl child in mother's womb in the Indian society. Women are considered as burden for their parents and husbands as they think that women are here only to consume money whole life without earning a little bit. Another common problem for women is sex discrimination which they face from their birth and continues till their death. Illiteracy, lack of proper education, responsible for household works, rape, sexual harassment at work place, etc are some big issues for the women. However, a lot of positive changes has occurred in the women status as the number of educated people is increasing in the country. Some of the issues related to women or girl child in India are given below.

Female Foeticide and Infanticide

Female Foeticide

Female foeticide is a practice of selective elimination of the female foetus after prenatal sex determination or sex pre-selection, thus, avoiding the birth of a girl child. Sex of the baby could be detected through pre-conception and post-conception methods. The pre-conception methods include Ericsson method (X and Y chromosome separation), and pre-implantation genetic diagnosis. However, it is the post-conception methods that are in much wide use, namely: amniocentesis, chronic villussampling and ultra-sonography. Female foeticide in India is the abortion of a female foetus outside of legal channels. It occurs in India for assumed cultural reasons that span centuries.

Female Infanticide

Discrimination does not end with the sex-selective abortion of female foetus. In most cases, it continues beyond birth. Female infanticide is a deliberate and intentional act of killing a female child within one year of its birth either directly by using poisonous organic and inorganic chemicals or indirectly by deliberate neglect to feed the infant by either the parents or other family members. It is unfortunate that the parents also view her as a liability. Female infanticide is the deliberate killing of new born female children.

Causes of Female Foeticide

The important causes of female foeticide and infanticide are as follows:

Son Mania: Indian society is patrilineal, patriarchal and patrilocal. Among the Hindus, the reproduction and heredity beliefs are governed by the laws of Manu. Besides religious consideration, economic, social and emotional desires favour males, as parents expect sons but non daughters to provide financial support, especially in their old age.

Girl as a "Burden": The evil of dowry system has led to a belief that daughters have to be protected and sufficient financial resources have to be accumulated to support the marriage of the girl. Boys on the other hand are considered as assets, who fetch a fabulous dowry for the parents. This has created a stereo-type notion of girl as a "burden" on the household.

Education and the Gender Skew: The more educated a women is, the more likely she is to actively choose a boy, assuming that she decides to have one child. The only educated women likely to keep daughters are the very independent minded. Educated men, especially in the business class, also want to have sons to carry on their business.

Marginalisation of Women in Agriculture: Although women contribute far more to the agricultural production, they are by far largest group of landless labourers with little real security. Modernisation of agriculture alleviates the burden of tasks that are traditionally men's responsibility leaving women's burden unrelieved.

Misuse of Technology: The tests like Amniocentesis and ultra-sonography, which were originally designed for detection of congenital abnormalities of the foetus, are being misused for detecting the sex of the foetus with the intention of aborting it if it happens to be that of a female. Thus, female foeticide and infanticide is receiving fillip through misuse of technology, done surreptitiously with the active connivance of the service providers.

Weak Implementation of Laws: The Pre-natal Diagnostic Techniques (Regulation and Prevention of Misuse) Act, 1994, prohibits determination of sex of the foetus. It also provides for mandatory registration of genetic counselling centres, clinics, hospitals, nursing-homes, etc. However, the implementation of the law is weak and it has not been used to the fullest. The focus has been only on the registration of the number of ultrasound machines and not on the actual act of abortions of female foetuses.

Sex Ratio

Sex is an easily identifiable characteristic and its dichotomous nature presents few problems of classification. The sex structure of any population can be measured through the percentage of males in the population or masculinity proportion or the sex ratio. The sex ratio of the population thus may either be expressed as the number of males per thousand females or as the number of females per thousand males. The former definition is followed all over the world but the Indian census followed the later definition. The sex ratio above thousand indicates a high sex ratio while that below thousand indicates a low sex ratio.

Factors Affecting Overall Sex Ratio

The overall sex ratio is the result of the factors such as, the sex ratio of the new born babies are sex ratio at birth, the sex ratio of the deceased persons and the sex ratio of the net migrants.

Sex ratio at Birth: There is no 1:1 ratio of male and female births. The number of male babies is always slightly higher. Sex ratio of birth is above thousand. There are 105 male babies per thousand female babies. Sex ratio of birth is determined biologically. Nature is slightly more favourable to male at birth. The sex ratio at birth depends upon the sex ratios of two biological antecedent events that is sex ratio at the time conception and sex ratio of fetal losses of deaths. The sex of fetus is determined at the time of fertilization but there is no direct means of observing this ratio at conception.

Sex Ratio of Deceased Persons: Differential mortality of the males and females is an important factor affecting the overall sex ratio and the sex ratio at various wages. In other words more than thousand males per thousand females. The male fetus is biologically, more delicate than the female fetus. It means that even after the birth the male baby continues to be biologically disadvantaged. The fact is reflected in the higher male mortality rates not only in the first day, in the first week and in the first month and in the first year but throughout life. In fact, in most countries the crude death rates for males are higher than those of females.

Sex Ratio at Net Migrants: The third factor affecting the overall sex ratio of any population is sex ratio of the net migrants which essentially socio economic in nature. Migration is ordinarily sex selective but it cannot have significant impact on the sex structure of the population. In India, the sex ratio in urban areas is favourable to males because of male domination in internal migration.

Sexual Harassment of Women at Work Place

"Sexual Harassment" includes anyone or more of the following unwelcome acts or behaviour (whether directly or by implication), namely:

- Physical contact or advances;
- A demand or request for sexual favours;
- Making sexually coloured remarks;
- Showing pornography;
- Any other unwelcome physical, verbal or non-verbal conduct of a sexual nature.

A work place is defined as "any place visited by the employee arising out of or during the course of employment, including transportation provided by the employer for undertaking such a journey."

Work place sexual harassment is sexual, unwelcome and the experience is subjective. It is the impact and not the intent that matters and it almost always occurs in a matrix of power. It is possible that a woman may experience a single instance of sexual harassment or a series of incidents over a period of time. It is important also to remember that each case is unique and should be examined in its own context and according to the surrounding circumstances as a whole.

Behaviour that Constitute Sexual Harassment at Workplace

Below are examples of behaviour that may or may not constitute workplace sexual harassment in isolation. At the same time, it is important to remember that more often than not, such behaviour occurs in cluster. Distinguishing between these different possibilities is not an easy task and requires essential training and skill building. Some examples of behaviour that constitute sexual harassment at the workplace:

1. Making sexually suggestive remarks or innuendos.
2. Serious or repeated offensive remarks, such as teasing related to a person's body or appearance.
3. Offensive comments or jokes.
4. Inappropriate questions, suggestions or remarks about a person's sex life.
5. Displaying sexist or other offensive pictures, posters, MMS, SMS, WhatsApp, or e-mails.
6. Intimidation, threats, blackmail around sexual favours.
7. Threats, intimidation or retaliation against an employee who speaks up about unwelcome behaviour with sexual overtones.
8. Unwelcome social invitations, with sexual overtones commonly understood as flirting.
9. Unwelcome sexual advances which may or may not be accompanied by promises or threats, explicit or implicit
10. Physical contact such as touching or pinching.

11. Caressing, kissing or fondling someone against her will (could be considered assault).
12. Invasion of personal space (getting too close for no reason, brushing against or cornering someone).
13. Persistently asking someone out, despite being turned down.
14. Stalking an individual.
15. Abuse of authority or power to threaten a person's job or undermine her performance against sexual favours.
16. Falsely accusing and undermining a person behind closed doors for sexual favours.
17. Controlling a person's reputation by rumour-mongering about her private life.

Honour Killing

An honor killing or shame killing is the homicide of a member of a family by other members, due to the perpetrators' belief that the victim has brought shame or dishonor upon the family, or has violated the principles of a community or a religion, usually for reasons such as refusing to enter an arranged marriage, being in a relationship that is disapproved by their family, having sex outside marriage, becoming the victim of rape, dressing in ways which are deemed inappropriate, engaging in non-hetero sexual relations or renouncing a faith.

Honor killings are acts of vengeance, usually death, committed by male family members against female family members, who are held to have brought dishonor upon the family. A woman can be targeted by (individuals within) her family for a variety of reasons, including: refusing to enter into an arranged marriage, being the victim of a sexual assault, seeking a divorce - even from an abusive husband - or (allegedly) committing adultery. The mere perception that a woman has behaved in a way that "dishonors" her family is sufficient to trigger an attack on her life.

Methods of killing include stoning, stabbing, beating, burning, beheading, hanging, throat slashing, lethal acid attacks, shooting and strangulation. The murders are sometimes performed in public to warn the other women within the community of possible consequences of engaging in what is seen as illicit behavior.

Causes of Honor Killings

The following are some of the Specific triggers of Honor killings

Refusal of an Arranged Marriage: Refusal of an arranged marriage is often a cause of an honor killing. The family which has prearranged the marriage risks disgrace if the marriage does not proceed.

Seeking a Divorce: A woman attempting to obtain a divorce or separation without the consent of the husband/extended family can also be a trigger for honor killings. In cultures where marriages are arranged and goods are often exchanged between families, a woman's desire to seek a divorce is often viewed as an insult to the men who negotiated the deal. By making their marital problems known outside the family, the women are seen as exposing the family to public dishonor. Allegations and rumors about a family member. In certain cultures, an allegation against a woman can be enough to tarnish her family's reputation, and to trigger an honor killing: the family's fear of being ostracized by the community is enormous.

Victims of Rape: In many cultures, victims of rape face severe violence, including honor killings, from their families and relatives. In many parts of the world, women who have been raped are considered to have brought 'dishonour' or 'disgrace' to their families. This is especially the case if the victim becomes pregnant.

Homosexuality: There is evidence that homosexuality can also be perceived as grounds for honor killing by relatives. It is not only same-sex sexual acts that trigger violence - behaviors that are regarded as inappropriate gender expression (e.g. a male acting or dressing in a "feminine way") can also raise suspicion and lead *to* honor violence.

Views on Women: Honor killings are often a result of strongly patriarchal views on women, and the position of women in society. In these traditional male-dominated societies women are dependent first on their father and then on their husband, whom they are expected to obey. Women are viewed as property and not as individuals with their own agency. As such, they must submit to male authority figures in the family – failure to do so can result in extreme violence as punishment.

Dowry

Dowry refers to the property, movable and or immovable, that is received by the bridegroom or his parents from the bride's parents.

The Dowry system refers to the durable goods, cash, and real or movable property that the bride's family gives to the bridegroom, his parents, or his relatives as a condition of the marriage. It is essentially in the nature of a payment in cash or some kind of gifts given to the bridegroom's family along with the bride and includes cash, jewellery, electrical appliances, furniture, bedding, crockery, utensils and other household items that help the newly weds set up their home.

The Dowry Prohibition Act, 1961 defines dowry as 'any property or valuable security given or agreed to be given either directly or indirectly

1. By one party a marriage to the marriage; or
2. By the parents of either party to marriage or by any other person to either party of the marriage or to any other person; at or before or after the marriage as consideration for the marriage of the said parties.

In ancient times the parents sent their daughter to her husband's home by paying a dowry in the form of certain material gifts and the daughter entrusted it to her husband. The dowry came as a boon to the girls in those days. In those days, the girls were not literate. They were not earning. They were financially helpless and so they depended solely on their husbands. The dowry safe guarded and helped them to support themselves in times of calamities like widowhood or some sudden misfortune and thus it acted as a security against contingencies of life.

Determinants of Dowry System

Determinants of dowry system has happened to our India in the following ways:

Educational Qualification and Profession of the Boy: The size of dowry paid depends on the educational qualifications and profession of the boy. The amount of cash paid in dowry scales up as the educational qualification rises. The boy with a professional degree ordinarily fetches a higher sum of dowry than an ordinary graduate. The financial status of the boy's family also acts as an important consideration in the stipulation of the amount of dowry.

Economic Status of Boy's Family: When the family of the boy is propertied and economically well-off, it puts up a demand for a high rate of dowry 'to maintain its prestige and status'. When the educational qualification, profession and property combine together, the sky becomes the limit for the dowry demanded.

Social Status of the Boy's Family: The social status of the family of the boy also plays a role in determining the rate of dowry.

Demerits of the Girl: The size of dowry scales up and down not only the merits of the boy, but also according to the disqualifications and demerits of the girl. For instance if the bride is dark-skinned or if she is short or squint-eyed or has any thing negative, she pays more.

Ways to Eradicate the Dowry Systems

We try to eradicate the dowry systems by applying the following ways.

Education: By imparting education, the practice of dowry could be minimized but cannot be solved by educating them.

Refuse to Marry: It is also suggested that the girls must refuse to marry the boys who demand dowry. But the girls feel that if they do so they may be left as maids and their prospects of marriage may come to an end once and for all.

Registration of Marriages: Compulsory registration of marriages is also suggested to put down this evil. At the time of registration, the parents of both the bride and bridegroom must be asked to take an oath, 'not offered' and 'not accepted' dowry in cash or kind and to sign a prescribed form to that effect. This will help gradual elimination of this evil.

Political Parties and Service Organizations: Political parties and service organizations like the clubs must also take up the programmes of propagation of the evil of dowry and ordain its members not to give or to take dowry.

Child Marriage

Child marriage is a formal marriage or informal union entered into by an individual before reaching the age of 18. The legally prescribed marriageable age in some jurisdictions is below 18 years, especially in the case of girls; and even when the age is set at 18 years, many jurisdictions permit earlier marriage with parental consent or in special circumstances, such as teenage pregnancy. In certain countries, even when the legal marriage age is 18, cultural traditions take priority over legislative law. Child marriage affects both, boys and girls, though the overwhelming majority of those affected are girls, most of whom are in poor socioeconomic situations. Child marriage in India, according to the Indian law, is a marriage where either the woman is below age 18 or the man is below age 21. Most child marriages involve under-age women, many of whom are in poor socio-economic conditions.

Factors Responsible for Child Marriages

Many factors have been responsible for child marriages. The causes of child marriage are explained below

Illiteracy: India is an agricultural country. Here peasants generally like to marry their sons in an early age so that an additional member may be available to assist in domestic and agricultural work.

Low Status of Woman: It was recognized that a woman should always remain under control. Before marriage, father is her guardian, after marriage, husband is considered her guardian and after death of husband, her sons or any other male member of the family is her guardian.

Opposition to Inter-caste Marriage: Opposition to the inter-caste marriages is another factor that has encouraged child marriages. To avoid nothing is left to attract inter-caste marriage, parents marry their daughter and sons in an early age of ignorance.

Joint Family System: In patriarchal family there is no place for women's voice. In order to avoid the burden of a daughter or to bring an additional member for work by marrying his sons they marry their daughters in an early age.

Religious Factors: It is a general belief among all uneducated and orthodox religious people that a daughter should be married before her menstruation.

Property Rights

Women's property rights are property and inheritance rights enjoyed by women as a category within society at any point in time. The patterns and rights of property ownership vary between societies and are influenced by cultural, racial, political, and legal factors. The lack of control over both productive and non-productive resources that is apparent in both rural and urban settings places women at a reduced level of advantage in areas of security of home, maintaining a basis for survival, and accessing economic opportunities. Development-related problems faced across the globe have been increasingly linked to women's lack of property and inheritance rights, especially in regards to land and property ownership, encompassing areas such as low levels of education, hunger, and poor health.

In India, Women's access and rights of ownership over family property (both moveable and immovable), in the absence of a will, is governed by succession laws based on religion. Under Hindu law prior to 1937, a woman did not have the right to own any property at all, except what she received from her parents at the time of her wedding. The Hindu Succession Act, 1956 was a breakthrough in terms of giving Hindu women a full and equal share of their husbands' property as the children; yet, the male bias persisted. An amendment to this Act in 2005 took the progressive step of making daughters coparceners at par with sons, such that they receive an equal birthright to a share in the natal family's ancestral property, i.e. parents' property. Laws are giving importance to the woman's rights. But, still women not get the equal property rights because of some of the social believes and not changes people attitude towards the women.

Divorce

Divorce (or dissolution of marriage) is the termination of a marriage or marital union, the canceling and/or reorganizing of the legal duties and responsibilities of marriage, thus, dissolving the bonds of matrimony between a married couple under the rule of law of the particular country and/or state. Divorce laws vary considerably around the world, but in most countries divorce requires the sanction of a court or other authority in a legal process, which may involve issues of alimony (spousal support), child custody, child visitation /access, parenting time, child support, distribution of property, and division of debt. A divorce happens after a husband and wife decide not to live together anymore and that they no longer want to be married to each other. They agree to sign legal papers that make them each single again and allow them to marry other people if they want to. Relationships have become complex in the modern days.

Reasons for Divorce

The following are some of the reasons for divorce in modern days.

Infidelity: Mutual trust is the base of most of the relationships. Relationships do break up when either of the partners deceive to other. Infidelity is the important reason for divorce. When partners become unfaithful to one another the relationship will end up and divorce become the solution to enjoy legal freedom.

Communication Break down: Lack of communication creates lot of gaps among couples. Such gaps lead to lot of misunderstandings between them. Communication problem is not because they can't express their feelings to one another. The 'ego' stops them to be open up to one other. If they don't speak for a longer time that stops two ways communication then there is a danger of ending their relationship.

Physical, Emotional or Psychological Abuse: Any abuse brings lot of pain in all the relationships. Marriage is the bond which is completely made up of mutual dependencies and expectations. Physical abuse, including bullying, manhandling, or violence is quite unbearable and has clear grounds for divorce. Emotional or psychological abuse hurts the emotions of a partner and the chances are very less to stay back with an abusive person.

Marital Financial Issues: Financial strains are often the biggest reasons for the collapse of a marriage. Possible causes for the disagreement over unequal monetary status or financial responsibilities can cause so much of stress in their relationship that leads to their divorce.

Sexual Incompatibility: Sexual act contributes a lot to the successful marital life. Physical bond is necessary to build a strong emotional bond with the respective partner. Feel of satisfaction brings each other closer and avoids lot of complexities. Sexual dissatisfaction often leads to frustration leading to separation and divorce. Sexual and reproductive incompatibility could be the top of the reasons for divorce. But if the sexual drives of both partners are totally out of synchronization then it is better take any psychological or medical help.

Religious and Cultural Strains: Marriage between different religion, culture and ethnicity is a common trend in these days. Living with a different cultural background is not an easy thing at all. There has to be lot of adjustments and sacrifices from both the sides. The couples of a different religion, culture or ethnicity sometimes do not take up the expectations of their partner's religion and often cause resentment among them. The differences are mainly due to the several taboos posed by a culture. Mutual compromise can only solve this issue and save partners too.

Child Rearing: Child rearing is one of the sensitive issues causing rifts in the marriages and contributing as one of the major reasons for splitting or divorce. If one of the partners is totally reluctant towards child-rearing issues, then the reason can be enough to provoke the petition of divorce by the parent. It is not fair to blame only the mother since her role has been extending and responsibility should be felt equally from both the parents.

Addiction: Over use of alcohol, drug or gambling are usually all forms of addiction, which can ruin relationships. The problem becomes worst when combined with physical or verbal abuse, and can leave devastating emotional scars on the whole family, including children also. Addiction will definitely make you to lose your interests in the family affairs. It is better to be conscious about our habits before getting addict.

Differences in Expectations and Priorities: It is difficult to get reflexive partner in the life. Each person thinks differently since each one have unique backgrounds. As everyone has got different personality traits, the different priorities, perceptions and expectations towards life are also found to be alike. Sometimes the couples are so drastically different that they cannot cope up living together and wish their marriage to an end. One can avoid it by understanding each other's differences over a course of time and there will be ways to solve such differences. Divorce is not the only solution for all couples problems. It can relieve the individuals from the suffocative state but not from the suffering.

Widowhood

A widow is a woman whose spouse has died, while a widower is a man in that situation. The state of having lost one's spouse to death is termed widowhood. These terms are not applied to a person after he or she becomes divorced from their former spouse, though they may sometimes be used after the former spouse has died. This term "widowhood" can be used for either sex. Widowhood is one of the normal stages in the life cycle of women. It is a natural occurrence. But the Hindus believe that the widowhood of woman is the result of sins, she committed in her previous life. Even the widows themselves entertain such a notion and bear with their status. Widowhood is considered as an inauspicious thing and therefore a widow faces a miserable and inhuman existence. Being economically dependent on the members of her husband's family, she has to live at their mercy for her subsistence. She is ill-treated, abused and sometimes blamed and cursed for any unhappy occurrence in the family. For the very death of her husband, she is held responsible and abused. She is considered as a woman of ill. Consequently she has to keep herself away or at a distance on the occasions of family festivities including the occasions of marriage of her own children.

Identification of Sexual Abuse/Violence and Its Verbalization

Sexual abuse is any type of sexual activity that you do not agree to, including:

- inappropriate touching
- vaginal, anal, or oral penetration
- sexual intercourse that you say no to
- rape

- attempted rape
- child molestation

Sexual assault can be verbal, visual, or anything that forces a person to join in unwanted sexual contact or attention. Examples of this are voyeurism (when someone watches private sexual acts), exhibitionism (when someone exposes him/herself in public), incest (sexual contact between family members), and sexual harassment. It can happen in different situations, by a stranger in an isolated place, on a date, or in the home by someone you know. Women who are sexually abused may suffer serious health problems, such as sexually transmitted infections, stomach problems, and ongoing pain. They also are at risk for emotional problems, like depression, anxiety, and post-traumatic stress disorder.

The following are the some of the identification signs for sexual abuse women:

- Self-injury (cutting, burning)
- Inadequate personal hygiene
- Drug and alcohol abuse
- Sexual promiscuity
- Running away from home
- Depression, anxiety
- Suicide attempts
- Fear of intimacy or closeness
- Compulsive eating or dieting

15

Gender and Law

Women's rights are the rights and entitlements claimed for women and girls of many societies worldwide, and formed the basis to the women's rights movement in the nineteenth century and feminist movement during the 20th century. In some countries, these rights are institutionalized or supported by law, local custom, and behavior, whereas in others they may be ignored or suppressed. They differ from broader notions of human rights through claims of an inherent historical and traditional bias against the exercise of rights by women and girls, in favour of men and boys. Issues commonly associated with notions of women's rights include, though are not limited to, the right: to bodily integrity and autonomy; to be free from sexual violence; to vote; to hold public office; to enter into legal contracts; to have equal rights in family law; to work; to fair wages or equal pay; to have reproductive rights; to own property; to education. The present chapter deals about the laws related to women issues.

Laws related to Rape

Rape means an unlawful intercourse done by a man with a woman without her valid consent. (Section 375 of the Indian Penal Code, 1860). Indian Panel Code, 1860, as per Section 375 of IPC a man is said to commit the offence of rape with a women under the following six circumstances:

1. Sexual intercourse against the victim's will.
2. without her/victim's consent.
3. with her consent, when her consent has been obtained by putting her or any person in whom she is interested in fear of death or of hurt.
4. with her consent, when the man knows that he is not her husband, and that her consent is given because she believes that he is another man to whom she is or believes herself to be lawfully married.
5. with her consent, when, at the time of giving such consent, by reason of unsoundness of mind or intoxication or the administration by him

personally or through another of any stupefying or unwholesome substance, she is unable to understand the nature and consequences of that to which she gives consent.

6. with or without her consent, when she is under sixteen years of age.

Laws related to Dowry

Section 2 of the Dowry Prohibition Act, 1961 as amended by the Dowry (Prohibition) Amendment Act, 1984 and 1986 defines dowry as follows:

"Dowry", means any property or valuable security given or agreed to be given either directly or indirectly,

- by one party to a marriage to the other party to the marriage; or
- by the parents of either party to a marriage; or
- by any other person, to either party to the marriage or to any other person;

at, or before, or any time after the marriage, in connection with the marriage of the said parties.

Dowry Prohibition Act, 1961

The punishment for giving and taking dowry or abetting the give and take of dowry was earlier punishable by imprisonment up to 6 months, or a fine up to Rs. 5,000. Demanding dowry directly or indirectly from the parents or guardian of a bride was also liable for similar punishment. This punishment was later enhanced by the amendment act and now these offences are punishable with a minimum of six months and maximum ten years of imprisonment. The fine limit has been enhanced to Rs 10,000 or to an amount equivalent to the dowry given, taken or demanded whichever is more. The court has been given the discretion to reduce the minimum punishment though in doing so the court is required to record in writing adequate and special reasons for doing so.

Laws related to Remarriage

Remarriage is allowing the women to remarry after the death of the spouse or divorced the spouse on proper legal grounds. The Hindu Widows' Remarriage Act, 1856, also Act XV, 1856, enacted on 26 July 1856, legalized the remarriage of Hindu widows in all jurisdictions of India under East India Company rule. To protect what it considered family honour and family property, upper-caste Hindu society had long disallowed the remarriage of widows, even child and adolescent ones, all of whom were expected to live alife of austerity and abnegation. The Hindu Widows' Remarriage Act of 1856, enacted in response to the campaign of Pandit Ishwar Chandra Vidyasagar, provided legal safeguards against loss of certain forms of inheritance for a remarrying Hindu widow, though, under the Act, the widow forsook any inheritance due her from her deceased husband. Especially targeted in the act were Hindu child widows whose husbands had died before consummation of marriage.

The Hindu widow re-marriage Act of 1856 validated on widow's remarriage. Given below are the features of this Act:

1. Widow re-marriage and the children born of such a marriage have been declared valid.
2. After re-marriage, the widow loses right over the property of her deceased husband.
3. There are two views in regard to the rights of widow over the property of her deceased husband, if she changes her religion before her re-marriage. The views of the various high courts are conflicting in this regard.
4. In case a widow is a minor, she will have to obtain permission from her parents or guardians for remarriage.
5. In addition to these provisions, the Hindu Succession Act 1956 and the Hindu Marriage Act 1955, also contain provisions relating to widow remarriage.

Laws related to Divorce

Divorce (or dissolution of marriage) is the termination of a marriage or marital union, the canceling and/or reorganizing of the legal duties and responsibilities of marriage, thus dissolving the bonds of matrimony between a married couple under the rule of law of the particular country and/or state. A wife can obtain divorce on the following grounds:

1. The husband has been guilty of rape, sodomy or bestiality
2. In a suit under section 18 of the Hindu Adoptions and Maintenance Act, 1956 or in proceeding under section 125 of the Cr. P.C. 1973, a decree or order has been passed against the husband awarding separate residence and maintenance to her after the passing of such a decree or order there is no resumption on cohabitation for one year on upwards.

Under this Act, there is a provision for divorce by mutual consent of both parties as in under the Hindu Marriage Act 1955. (Section 28, Special Marriage Act, 1954). With the passing of the Hindu Marriage Act in 1955 dissolution of marriage was provided for on an all India scale. A wife can seek divorce on the ground of the following:

Adultery: Where the husband "has after the solemnization of the marriage had voluntary sexual intercourse with any person other than his spouse", the wife can petition for divorce.

Cruelty: Where the husband "has after the solemnization of the marriage, treated the petitioner with cruelty", the wife is entitled to get a degree of divorce.

- Continually used abusive and insulting words which bring shame and mental agony to her
- Indulged in excessive sexual intercourse or in unnatural sexual behavior against her wishes
- Unreasonably refused and persisted in the refusal for long time
- Indulged in drunkenness or intoxicating drugs
- Forced her to have intercourse with a stranger
- Brought into the house another woman for his carnal satisfaction and indulged in sexual orgy with her
- Deliberately ill-treated the children in her presence with a view to give her mental pain.

Desertion: Where the husband "has deserted the petitioner for a continuous period of not less than two years immediately presentation of the petition" the wife can obtain divorce.

Conversion: Where the husband "has ceased to be a Hindu by conversion to another religion" the wife can seek divorce.

Unsound Mind: Where the husband "has been incurably of unsound mind or has been suffering continuously or intermittently form mental disorder of such a kind and to such an extent that the petitioner cannot reasonably be expected to live with the respondent", the wife can obtain divorce.

Leprosy: Where the husband "has been suffering from a virulent and incurable form of leprosy", the wife can obtain divorce.

Venereal Disease: Where the husband "has been suffering from venereal disease in a communicable form", the wife can obtain divorce.

Renunciation of the World: Where the husband "has renounced the world by entering any religious order", the wife can obtain divorce.

Presumed Death: Where the husband "has not been heard of as being alive for a period of seven years or more by those persons who would naturally have heard of it, had that part been alive", the wife can obtain divorce.

Judicial Separation: Where there "has been no resumption of cohabitation as between the parties to the marriage for a period of one year or upwards after passing of a decree for judicial separation in a proceeding to which they were parties", wife can seek divorce.

Bigamy: A wife can seek divorce from her husband if he had married again before the commencement of this Act.

Rape and Unnatural Offence: If the husband has since the solemnization of the marriage been guilty or rape, sodomy or bestiality, the wife may seek divorce.

Marriage while being a Minor: Where "her marriage was solemnized before she attained the age of fifteen years and she has repudiated the marriage after attaining that age but before attaining the age of 18 years, the wife may seek divorce.

Laws related to Property Inheritance

The general law relating to the inheritance and succession can easily be referred to The Indian Succession Act, 1925. Under this Act every Indian is entitled to equal shares on inheriting the property on the death of a person. In India, Women's access and rights of ownership over family property (both moveable and immovable), in the absence of a will, is governed by succession laws based on religion. Under Hindu law prior to 1937, a woman did not have the right to own any property at all, except what she received from her parents at the time of her wedding. The Hindu succession Act, 1956 was a breakthrough in terms of giving Hindu women a full and equal share of their husbands' property as the children; yet, the male bias persisted. An amendment to this Act in 2005 took the progressive step of making daughters coparceners at par with sons, such that they receive an equal birthright to a share in the natal family's ancestral property, i.e. parents' property. Laws are giving importance to the woman's rights. But still women not get the equal property rights be cause of some of the social believes and not changes people attitude towards the women.

Laws Related to Trafficking

Human trafficking is a crime of crimes. It is a basket of crimes. In this basket one can dig out the elements of abduction, kidnapping, illegal detainment, illegal confinement, criminal intimidation, hurt, grievous hurt, sexual assault, outraging modesty, rape, unnatural offences, selling and buying of human beings, servitude, criminal conspiracy, abetment etc. Therefore, multiple abuse and abusers located at different points of time and place together constitute the organized crime of trafficking. A host of human rights violations like denial of privacy, denial of justice, denial of access to justice, deprivation of basis rights and dignity etc constitute other part of the exploitation. Therefore, there is no doubt that trafficking is an organized crime.

In the existing scenario, trafficking is usually confused with prostitution and therefore, there is no proper understanding of the seriousness of trafficking. It would be appropriate here to list out the wrongs, violations, harms and crimes that are committed by various persons on a trafficked victim. These violations can be realized only during a careful interview of a trafficked person. Once the victim is allowed, facilitated and promoted to speak, the unheard story will reveal a long list of violating acts perpetrated on her. Displaced from her community, which tantamount to kidnapping/ abduction (Sections 361, 362, 365, 366 IPC may apply)

- Procured illegally (S.366 A IPC)
- Sold by somebody (S.372 IPC)
- Bought by somebody (S.373 IPC)
- Imported from a foreign country (if she hails from a foreign country, or even from J & K State, and is under 21 years of age – S.366 B IPC)
- Wrongfully restrained (S.339 IPC)
- Wrongfully confined (S 340 IPC)
- Physically tortured/injured (S.327, 329 IPC)
- Subjected to criminal force (S. 350 IPC)
- Mentally tortured/harassed/assaulted (S. 351 IPC)
- Criminally intimidated (S.506 IPC)
- Outraged of her modesty (S 354 IPC)
- Raped/gang raped/repeatedly raped (S 375 IPC)
- Subjected to perverse sexual exploitation ('unnatural offences') (S.377 IPC).
- Subjected to unlawful compulsory labor (S.374 IPC)

Indian Constitution

The rights available to woman (ladies) in India can be classified into two categories, namely as constitutional rights and legal rights. The constitutional rights are those which are provided in the various provisions of the constitution. The legal rights, on the other hand, are those which are provided in the various laws (acts) of the Parliament and the State Legislatures. The following section deals about the Indian constitutions and legal rights of women.

Women's Reservation Bill

The Women's Reservation Bill was passed by the Rajya Sabha on 9 March 2010 by a majority vote of 186 members in favour and 1 against. As of March 2013, the Lok Sabha has not voted on the bill. Critics say gender cannot be held as a basis for reservation alone other factors should also be considered e.g. economic, social conditions of woman candidate especially when applying reservation for educated women.

Parliamentary Standing Committee Report on the Constitutional (108th Amendment) Bill "Achieving the goal of equal participation of women and men in decision making will provide a balance that more accurately reflects the composition of society and is needed in order to strengthen democracy and promote its proper functioning. Without the active participation of women and the incorporation of women's perspectives at all levels of decision-making, the goals of equality, development and peace cannot be achieved."

The Indian Constitution and Provisions for Women

(Please refer Chapter 13)

Human Rights and Women's Right

India's Constitution makers and our founding fathers were very determined to provide equal rights to both women and men. The Constitution of India is one of the finest equality documents in the world. It provides provisions to secure equality in general and gender equality in particular. Various articles in the Constitution safeguard women's rights by putting them at par with men socially, politically and economically. The Preamble, the Fundamental Rights, DPSPs and other constitutional provisions provide several general and special safeguards to secure women's human rights.

Preamble: The Preamble to the Constitution of India assures justice, social, economic and political; equality of status and opportunity and dignity to the individual. Thus it treats both men and women equal.

Fundamental Rights: The policy of women empowerment is well entrenched in the Fundamental Rights enshrined in our Constitution. For instance:

- Article 14 ensures to women the right to equality.
- Article 15(1) specifically prohibits discrimination on the basis of sex.
- Article 15(3) empowers the State to take affirmative actions in favour of women.
- Article 16 provides for equality of opportunity for all citizens in matters relating to employment or appointment to any office.
- These rights being fundamental rights are justifiable in court and the Government is obliged to follow the same.

Legal Aspects related to Women

Women in India have faced significant violations of their human rights for centuries. From rape and domestic violence to forced labor and denial of educational opportunities, the struggle for rights and empowerment is a daunting one for Indian women. In the world's second-largest country, hundreds of millions of women are still affected by some of these issues. The followings are the essential Legal Rights every Indian women should know--

- *Right to Equal Pay*: According to provisions under the Equal Remuneration Act, one cannot be discriminated on the basis of sex when it comes to salary or wages.
- *Right against Harassment at Work*: The enactment of the Sexual Harassment of Women at Workplace Act gives you the right to file a complaint against sexual harassment.

- *Right to Anonymity*: Victims of sexual assault have a right to anonymity. To ensure that her privacy is protected, a woman who has been sexually assaulted may record her statement alone before the district magistrate when the case is under trial, or in the presence of a female police officer.
- *Right against Domestic Violence*: The act primarily looks to protect a wife, a female live-in partner or a woman living in a household like a mother or a sister from domestic violence at the hands of a husband, male live-in partner or relatives.
- *Right to Maternity-related Benefits*: Maternity benefits are not merely a privilege of the working woman, they are a right. The Maternity Benefit Act ensures that the new mother does not suffer any loss of earnings following a period of twelve weeks after her delivery, allowing her to rejoin the workforce.
- *Right against Female Foeticide*: It is a duty imposed on every citizen of India to allow a woman to experience the most basic of all rights - the right to life. The Conception and Pre-Natal Diagnostic Techniques (Prohibition of Sex Selection) Act (PCPNDT) ensures her right against female foeticide.
- *Right to Free Legal Aid:* All female rape victims have the right to free legal aid, under the Legal Services Authorities Act. It is mandatory for the Station House Officer (SHO) to inform the Legal Services Authority, who arranges for the lawyer.
- *Right to Dignity and Decency*: In the event that an accused is a woman, any medical examination procedure on her must be performed by or in the presence of another woman.
- *Right to Property:* The Hindu Succession Act allows women and men equal share in inheritance, thereby setting new rules and regulations.
- *Right not to be arrested at Night:* A woman cannot be arrested after sunset and before sunrise, except in an exceptional case on the orders of a first class magistrate.

Declining Sex Ratio

Sex ratio is an important parameter that reflects the status of women in society. Some of the worst gender ratios, indicating gross violation of women's rights are found in South and East Asian countries such as India and China. In India sex-ratio is declining it is a fact, but more important and serious thing is that it is declining in spite of social, educational, economic development,. In 2015, the sex ratio in India was 943 females for 1000 males. Sex ratio varies from region to region. In the latest census, Kerala has 1084 females per 1000 males, making it the best state to have a good sex ratio. With a ratio of 877 females per 1000 males, the state of Haryana suffers from the lowest sex ratio. There has been a great improvement in the sex ratio of India. In 2012, India had a ratio of 940 females per 1000 males.

List of Laws/Constitutional guarantees that are relevant declining sex ratio:

- Pre-Natal Diagnostic Techniques (Regulation and Prevention of Misuse) Act,1994
- Pre-Conception And Pre-Natal Diagnostic Techniques (Prohibition of sex selection) Act 2002
- Medical Termination of pregnancy Act, 1971
- Article 21 of the Constitution - right to live
- Article 14 of the Constitution - right to equality

PNDT (Pre Natal Diagnostic Techniques) Act

Pre-Conception and Pre-Natal Diagnostic Techniques (PCPNDT) Act, 1994 is an Act of the Parliament of India enacted to stop female foeticides and arrest the declining sex ratio in India. The act banned prenatal sex determination. Offences under this act include conducting or helping in the conduct of prenatal diagnostic technique in the unregistered units, sex selection on a man or woman, conducting PND test for any purpose other than the one mentioned in the act, sale, distribution, supply, renting etc. of any ultrasound machine or any other equipment capable of detecting sex of the foetus. Main provisions in the act are:

1. The Act provides for the prohibition of sex selection, before or after conception.
2. It regulates the use of pre-natal diagnostic techniques, like ultrasound and amniocentesis by allowing them their use only to detect:
    - genetic abnormalities
    - metabolic disorders
    - chromosomal abnormalities
    - certain congenital malformations
    - haemoglobinopathies
    - Sex linked disorders.
3. No laboratory or Centre or clinic will conduct any test including ultrasonography for the purpose of determining the sex of the foetus.
4. No person, including the one who is conducting the procedure as per the law, will communicate the sex of the foetus to the pregnant woman or her relatives by words, signs or any other method.
5. Any person who puts an advertisement for pre-natal and pre-conception sex determination facilities in the form of a notice, circular, label, wrapper or any document, or advertises through

interior or other media in electronic or print form or engages in any visible representation made by means of hoarding, wall painting, signal, light, sound, smoke or gas, can be imprisoned for up to three years and fined Rs. 10,000.

Pre-Natal Diagnostic Techniques (Regulation and Prevention of Misuse) Act, 1994(PNDT), was amended in 2003 to The Pre-Conception and Pre-Natal Diagnostic Techniques (Prohibition Of Sex Selection) Act (PCPNDT Act) to improve the regulation of the technology used in sex selection. Implications of the amendment are:

- Amendment of the act mainly covered bringing the technique of pre conception sex selection within the ambit of the act
- Bringing ultrasound within its ambit
- Empowering the central supervisory board, constitution of state level supervisory board/Provision for more stringent punishments
- Empowering appropriate authorities with the power of civil court for search, seizure and sealing the machines and equipments of the violators
- Regulating the sale of the ultrasound machines only to registered bodies.

Female Foeticide

Female foeticide in India is the abortion of a female foetus outside of legal channels. It occurs in India for assumed cultural reasons that span centuries. Female foeticide has been linked to the arrival, in the early 1990s, of affordable ultrasound technology and its widespread adoption in India. Obstetric ultrasonography, either transvaginally or transabdominally, checks for various markers of fetal sex. It can be performed at or after week 12 of pregnancy. At this point, 34 of fetal sexes can be correctly determined, according to a 2001 study. Accuracy for males is approximately 50 per cent and for females almost 100 per cent. When performed after week 13 of pregnancy, ultra sonography gives an accurate result in almost 100 per cent of cases.

The Medical Termination of Pregnancy (MTP) Act, 1971, legalizes abortion –however, under certain conditions. It states that pregnancy can be terminated by at least one registered medical practitioner (if the length of the pregnancy does not exceed 12 weeks) and by at least two registered medical practitioners (if the length of the pregnancy is between 12 and 20 weeks) who are of the opinion, formed in good faith, that

- the continuation of the pregnancy shall expose the woman to risk to her life or of grave physical or mental health

- (this includes women subjected to rape, and pregnancy induced by the failure of any contraceptive device or technique used by a married couple)
- there is substantial risk that if the child is born s/he shall suffer from severe physical or mental abnormalities

Violence against Women

Violence against Women (VAW), also known as gender-based violence, is, collectively, violent acts that are primarily or exclusively committed against women. Sometimes considered a hate crime, this type of violence targets a specific group with the victim's gender as a primary motive. This type of violence is gender-based, meaning that the acts of violence are committed against women expressly because they are women.

Domestic Violence Act

The Protection of Women from Domestic Violence Act 2005 differs from the provision of the Penal Code, Section 498A of the Indian Penal Code, in that it provides a broader definition of domestic violence. Domestic violence is defined by Section 3 of the Act as "any act, omission or commission or conduct of the respondent shall constitute domestic violence in case it:

- harms or injures or endangers the health, safety, life, limb or well-being, whether mental or physical, of the aggrieved person or tends to do so and includes causing physical abuse, sexual abuse, verbal and emotional abuse and economic abuse; or
- harasses, harms, injures or endangers the aggrieved person with a view to coerce her or any other person related to her to meet any unlawful demand for any dowry or other property or valuable security; or
- has the effect of threatening the aggrieved person or any person related to her by any conduct mentioned in clause (a) or clause (b); or
- Otherwise injures or causes harm, whether physical or mental, to the aggrieved person."

The Protection of Women from Domestic Violence Act 2005 is an Act of the Parliament of India enacted to protect women from domestic violence. It was brought into force by the Indian government from 26 October 2006. The Act provides for the first time in Indian law a definition of "domestic violence", with this definition being broad and including not only physical violence, but also other forms of violence such as emotional/verbal, sexual, and economic abuse. It is a civil law meant primarily for protection orders and not meant to penalize criminally.

Sexual Harassment at Work Place Act

The Sexual Harassment of Women at Workplace (Prevention, Prohibition and Redressal) Act, 2013 is a legislative act in India that seeks to protect women from sexual harassment at their place of work. The Act came into force from 9 December 2013. This statute superseded the Vishakha Guidelines for prevention of sexual harassment introduced by the Supreme Court of India. The introductory text of the Act is:

- An Act to provide protection against sexual harassment of women at workplace and for the prevention and redressal of complaints of sexual harassment and for matters connected therewith or incidental thereto.
- Where as sexual harassment results in violation of the fundamental rights of a woman to equality under articles 14 and 15 of the Constitution of India and her right to life and to live with dignity under article 21 of the Constitution and right to practice any profession or to carry on any occupation, trade or business which includes a right to a safe environment free from sexual harassment;
- And where as the protection against sexual harassment and the right to work with dignity are universally recognised human rights by international conventions and instruments such as Convention on the Elimination of all Forms of Discrimination against Women, which has been ratified on the 25th June, 1993 by the Government of India;
- And where as it is expedient to make provisions for giving effect to the said Convention for protection of women against sexual harassment at workplace.
- The Act defines sexual harassment at the work place and creates a mechanism for redressal of complaints. It also provides safeguards against false or malicious charges.
- The Act also covers concepts of 'quid pro quo harassment' and 'hostile work environment' as forms of sexual harassment if it occurs in connection with an act or behaviour of sexual harassment.

Indecent Representation of Women (Prohibition Act)

The Act prohibits indecent representation of women through advertisements or in publications, writings, paintings, figures or in any other manner and for matters connected therewith or incidental thereto. No person shall produce or cause to be produced, sell, let to hire, distribute, circulate or send by post any book, pamphlet, paper, slide, film, writing, drawing, painting, photograph, representation or figure which contains indecent representation of women in any form.

Cybercrime

Cybercrimes are any crimes that involve a computer and a network. In some cases, the computer may have been used in order to commit the crime, and in other cases, the computer may have been the target of the crime. Internet crime is crime committed on the Internet, using the Internet and by means of the Internet. Computer crime is a general term that embraces such crimes as phishing, credit card frauds, bank robbery, illegal downloading, industrial espionage, child pornography, kidnapping children via chat rooms, scams, cyber terrorism, creation and/or distribution of viruses, Spam and so on. All such crimes are computer related and facilitated crimes.

With advancement of technology, the type and methods of cyber-crime against females are also changing. One such offense increasing in cyber-crime in India is known as 'Cyberstalking', which can be defined to mean threatening, unwarranted behavior or advances directed by one net user to another user through the medium of Internet and other forms of online communication. It is a recent phenomenon and women generally are the main targets of this crime.

Sexual and Reproductive Health and Rights (SRHR)

Sexual and reproductive health and rights or SRHR is the concept of human rights applied to sexuality and reproduction. It is a combination of four fields that in some contexts are more or less distinct from each other, but less so or not at all in other contexts. These four fields are sexual health, sexual rights, reproductive health and reproductive rights. In the concept of SRHR, these four fields are treated as separate but inherently intertwined.

Distinctions between these four fields are not always made. Sexual health and reproductive health are sometimes treated as synonymous to each other, as are sexual rights and reproductive rights. In some cases, sexual rights are included in the term sexual health, or vice versa. Not only do different non-governmental organizations (NGOs) and governments use different terminologies, but different terminologies are often used within the same organization.

Some of the notable global NGOs that fight for sexual and reproductive health and rights include:

- IPPF (International Planned Parenthood Federation)
- ILGA (International Lesbian and Gay Alliance)
- WAS (World Association for Sexual Health - formerly known as World Association for Sexology) and
- International HIV/AIDS Alliance.

Sexual Health

The World Health Organization defines sexual health as *"Sexual health is a state of physical, mental and social well-being in relation to sexuality. It requires a positive and respectful approach to sexuality and sexual relationships, as well as the possibility of having pleasurable and safe sexual experiences, free of coercion, discrimination and violence."*

Sexual Rights

Unlike the other three aspects of SRHR, the struggle for sexual rights includes, and focuses on, sexual pleasure and emotional sexual expression. One platform for this struggle is the WAS Declaration of Sexual Rights.

The Platform for Action from the 1995 Beijing Conference on Women established that human rights include the right of women freely and without coercion, violence or discrimination, to have control over and make decisions concerning their own sexuality, including their own sexual and reproductive health. This paragraph has been interpreted by some countries as the applicable definition of women's sexual rights. The UN Commission on Human Rights has established that if women had more power, their ability to protect themselves against violence would be strengthened.

There is a growing consensus that sexual health cannot be achieved and maintained without respect for, and protection of, certain human rights. The working definition of sexual rights given below is a contribution to the continuing dialogue on human rights related to sexual health.

"The fulfillment of sexual health is tied to the extent to which human rights are respected, protected and fulfilled. Sexual rights embrace certain human rights that are already recognized in international and regional human rights documents and other consensus documents and in national laws.

Rights critical to the realization of sexual health include:

1. the rights to equality and non-discrimination
2. the right to be free from torture or to cruel, inhumane or degrading treatment or punishment
3. the right to privacy
4. the rights to the highest attainable standard of health (including sexual health) and social security
5. the right to marry and to found a family and enter into marriage with the free and full consent of the intending spouses, and to equality in and at the dissolution of marriage
6. the right to decide the number and spacing of one's children
7. the rights to information, as well as education
8. the rights to freedom of opinion and expression, and
9. the right to an effective remedy for violations of fundamental rights.

The responsible exercise of human rights requires that all persons respect the rights of others. The application of existing human rights to sexuality and sexual health constitute sexual rights. Sexual rights protect all people's rights to fulfill and express their sexuality and enjoy sexual health, with due regard for the rights of others and within a framework of protection against discrimination." (WHO, 2006a, updated 2010)

At the 14th World Congress of Sexology (Hong Kong, 1999), the WAS adopted the Universal Declaration of Sexual Rights, which includes 11 sexual rights:

1. The right to sexual freedom.
2. The right to sexual autonomy, sexual integrity, and safety of the sexual body.
3. The right to sexual privacy.
4. The right to sexual equity.
5. The right to sexual pleasure.
6. The right to emotional sexual expression.
7. The right to sexually associate freely.
8. The right to make free and responsible reproductive choices.
9. The right to sexual information based upon scientific inquiry.
10. The right to comprehensive sexuality education.
11. The right to sexual health care.

Reproductive Health

Within the framework of the World Health Organization's (WHO) definition of health as a state of complete physical, mental and social well-being, and not merely the absence of disease or infirmity, reproductive health, or sexual health/hygiene, addresses the reproductive processes, functions and system at all stages of life. Reproductive health, therefore, implies that people are able to have a responsible, satisfying and safer sex life and that they have the capability to reproduce and the freedom to decide if, when and how often to do so. One interpretation of this implies that men and women ought to be informed of and to have access to safe, effective, affordable and acceptable methods of birth control; also access to appropriate health care services of sexual, reproductive medicine and implementation of health education programmes to stress the importance of women to go safely through pregnancy and childbirth could provide couples with the best chance of having a healthy infant. On the other hand, individuals do face inequalities in reproductive health services. Inequalities vary based on socioeconomic status, education level, age, ethnicity, religion, and resources available in their environment. It is possible for example, that low income individuals lack the resources for appropriate health services and the knowledge to know what is appropriate for maintaining reproductive health.

Reproductive Rights

Reproductive rights are legal rights and freedoms relating to reproduction and reproductive health. The World Health Organization defines reproductive rights as follows:

"Reproductive rights rest on the recognition of the basic right of all couples and individuals to decide freely and responsibly the number, spacing and timing of their children and to have the information and means to do so, and the right to attain the highest standard of sexual and reproductive health. They also include the right of all to make decisions concerning reproduction free of discrimination, coercion and violence."

Women's reproductive rights may include some or all of the following:

1. the right to legal and safe abortion;
2. the right to birth control;
3. freedom from coerced sterilization and contraception;
4. the right to access good-quality reproductive healthcare; and
5. the right to education and access in order to make free and informed reproductive choices.

Reproductive rights may also include the right to receive education about sexually transmitted infections and other aspects of sexuality, and protection from practices such as female genital mutilation. Reproductive rights began to develop as a subset of human rights at the United Nation's 1968 International Conference on Human Rights. The resulting non-binding Proclamation of Teheran was the first international document to recognize one of these rights when it stated that: *"Parents have a basic human right to determine freely and responsibly the number and the spacing of their children."*

Issues related to reproductive rights are some of the most vigorously contested rights' issues world-wide, regardless of the population's socio-economic level, religion or culture. Reproductive rights are a subset of sexual and reproductive health and rights.

Sexual and Reproductive Health and Rights (SRHR)

The term "sexual and reproductive health and rights" (SRHR) was explored nearly 20 years ago at the Cairo International Conference on Population and Development (ICPD) and the 1995 Fourth World Conference on Women (FWCW) held in Beijing. Building on the World Health Organization's definition of health, the Cairo Programme defines reproductive health as:

> "a state of complete physical, mental and social well-being and... not merely the absence of disease or infirmity, in all matters relating to the reproductive system and to its functions and processes. Reproductive health therefore

> implies that people are able to have a satisfying and safe sex life and that they have the capability to reproduce and the freedom to decide if, when and how often to do so. Implicit in this last condition are the right of men and women to be informed and to have access to safe, effective, affordable and acceptable methods of family planning of their choice, as well as other methods of their choice for regulation of fertility which are not against the law, and the right of access to appropriate health-care services that will enable women to go safely through pregnancy and childbirth and provide couples with the best chance of having a healthy infant (para 72)."

Furthermore, the Cairo Programme of Action clearly spells out the concept of reproductive rights, which states in part that such rights "rest on the recognition of the basic right of all couples and individuals to decide freely and responsibly the number, spacing and timing of their children and to have the information and means to do so, and the right to attain the highest standard of reproductive and sexual health. It also includes the right of all to make decisions concerning reproduction free of discrimination, coercion, and violence as expressed in human rights documents.

While governments would not name sexual rights or sexual orientation explicitly at the Beijing Women's Conference, the result and the process proved more useful than anticipated. A change in norms had been underway in international law since then, as evidenced by the growing body of documentation and commentary on these issues at the UN and in regional human rights forums. The Platform for Action, which was adopted by 189 delegations in Beijing, reaffirmed the Cairo Programme's definition of reproductive health and advances women's wider interests, especially in the area of sexual rights. Paragraph 96 states:

> "The human rights of women include their right to have control over and decide freely and responsibly on matters related to their sexuality, including sexual and reproductive health, free of coercion, discrimination and violence. Equal relationships between women and men in matters of sexual relations and reproduction, including full respect for the integrity of the person, require mutual respect, consent and shared responsibility for sexual behaviour and its consequences."

What is Sexual and Reproductive Health (SRH)?

Sexual and reproductive health (SRH) is an essential component of the universal right to the highest attainable standard of physical and mental health, enshrined in the Universal Declaration of Human Rights and in other international human rights conventions, declarations, and consensus agreements. Sexual and reproductive health needs must be met for both men and women. Human rights standards require states to respect, protect, and fulfill the right to sexual and reproductive health, and states must also ensure that individuals have the opportunity to actively participate in the development of health care policy and in individual care decisions—including determining whether and when to have children and in protecting the rights of others to sexual and reproductive health, including through ensuring violence-free relationships and homes and in seeking information, education, and care for one's children.

Sexual and Reproductive Rights (SRR)

Sexual and reproductive health rights including access to sexual and reproductive healthcare and information, as well as autonomy in sexual and reproductive decision making are human rights; they are universal, indivisible, and undeniable. Such rights are grounded in other essential human rights, including the right to health, the right to be free from discrimination, the right to privacy, the right not to be subjected to torture or ill-treatment, the right to determine the number and spacing of one's children, and the right to be free from sexual violence.

Sexual and reproductive rights (SRR) are most clearly defined in the 1994 International Conference on Population and Development (ICPD) Programme of Action, which took place in

Cairo, Egypt. Among the elements of comprehensive SRR outlined in the Programme of Action are:

1. Voluntary, informed, and affordable family planning services;
2. Pre-natal care, safe motherhood services, assisted childbirth from a trained attendant (e.g., a physician or midwife), and comprehensive infant health care;
3. Prevention and treatment of sexually transmitted infections (STIs), including HIV and AIDS and cervical cancer;
4. Prevention and treatment of violence against women and girls, including torture;
5. Safe and accessible post-abortion care and, where legal, access to safe abortion services; and
6. Sexual health information, education, and counseling to enhance personal relationships and quality of life.

SRR assumes that all people have the right to a healthy, safe, consensual and enjoyable sexlife; to control heir bodies and have sufficient accurate information to use in making decisions and seeking healthy behaviors; and to have affordable, accessible services that keep them healthy, not only when pregnant but before and after and even if they choose never to get pregnant.

Gender Discrimination and Sexual and Reproductive Rights

At its core, universal access to SRH cannot be achieved without the realization of gender equality and women's rights. Women are disproportionately affected by poverty, violence, a lack of access to decision-making and political processes, and low social status, all of which arise from gender-based discrimination and lead to disproportionate human rights abuses, including of the right to health. Reproductive health is often linked to pregnancy, and women face unique challenges to achieving the highest attainable standard of health because of this link: they are often valued only as mothers, making them more vulnerable to human rights abuses, as they are valued less then men. Moreover, their reproductive capacity can be used as a tool for abuses ranging from domestic violence to genocide.

SRHR and Violence against Women

Violence against women violates women's bodily integrity. A woman's right to control her body, including her sexuality and reproduction, is a basic human right. Failure to recognize this right allows for practices that cause harm to women and sometimes privilege power and tradition over individual wellbeing. When reproductive rights are denied or limited, so are women's human rights. The fundamental rights to bodily integrity; the enjoyment of the highest standard of physical and mental health; access to healthcare services; the right to determine the number, timing, and spacing of children; the right to exercise one's sexuality free from discrimination, coercion, and violence; and other human rights recognized in international law are all part of reproductive rights. When these rights are denied to women, the rights of all people everywhere are threatened. Working to protect reproductive rights recognizes the equality and dignity of women and the universality of human rights.

16

Commissions and Committees on Girls Education

To accelerate the progress of women education different measures were taken in independent India. In the constitution of India it is categorically mentioned under section 16 (a) that

> "there shall be equality of opportunity to all citizens in matters relating to employment or appointment to any office under the state.... while special arrangements may be made for women and children there shall not be any discrimination against any citizen on the ground only of religion, race, caste, sex or place of birth".

This provision in the constitution inspired women greatly for their education and there has been a phenomenal development in the education of women. At the beginning of the nineteenth century, there was hardly any provision for the formal education of girls. Even at the opening of the present century, not much progress had been made. But remarkable progress both in raising their social status and in developing their education was made after independence.

After independence several commissions and committees were appointed to suggest measures for the improvement of education in general. Focusing on women education and empowerment, some of the major recommendations of the following commissions and committees are given below:

University Education Commission or Radhakrishnan Commission (1948-49)

University Education Commission appointed in 1948-49, recommended for the improvement of women's education at higher education level. Dr. Radhakrishnan very emphatically stated,

"Women are human beings and have as much right to full development as men have. The position of women in any society is a true index of its cultural and spiritual level".

Radhakrishnan Commission has given a very generous and sympathetic consideration to this problem, a fact which is amply evidenced by the recommendations made in connection with it.

The recommendations of University Education Commission with respect to women education and empowerment are given below:

1. The ordinary amenities and decencies of life should be provided for women in colleges originally planned for men, but to which women are being admitted in increasing numbers.
2. There should be no curtailment in educational opportunities for women, but rather a great increase.
3. There should be intelligent educational guidance, by qualified men and women, to help women to get a clearer view of their real educational interests, to the end that they shall not try to imitate men, but shall desire as good education as women as men get as men. Women's and men's education should have many elements in common, but should not in general be identical in all respects, as is usually the case today.
4. Women students in general should be helped to see their normal places in a normal society, both as citizens and as women and to prepare for it, and college programmes should be so designed that it will be possible for them to do so.
5. Standards of courtesy and social responsibility should be emphasized on the part of men in mixed colleges.
6. New colleges are established to serve both men and women students; they should be truly co-educational institutions, with as much thought and consideration given to the life needs of women as to those of men. Except as such colleges come into existence there are no valid criteria for com paring segregated education with co-education.
7. Women teachers should be paid the same salaries as men teachers for equal work

National Committee on Women's Education or Durgabai Deshmukh Committee (1958-1959)

The recommendations of National Committee on Women's Education or Durgabai Deshmukh Committee (1958-1959) with respect to women education and empowerment are given below:

1. The education of women should be regarded as a major and special problem in education for a good year to come, and that a bold and determinate effort should be made to face its difficulties.
2. Steps should be taken to constitute as early as possible a National Council for the Education of girls and women

3. A separate unit for Women's Education, under a Educational Adviser, should be set up at the Centre.
4. In each State, a woman should be appointed as Joint Director and placed in charge of education of girls.
5. Lady teachers should be appointed in all schools where there are no women.
6. There should be identical curricula for boys and girls at the primary stage. At the secondary stage, there is need for differentiation of the courses.
7. Vocational training courses with 'Primary' as basic qualification may be conducted in school during the day, alongside general education. Courses with 'Middle' and Secondary as basic qualifications may be organized in vocational sections of middle and secondary schools, in multipurpose schools, in separate vocational schools, in apprenticeship classes, in training centres, in workshops and/or in continuation schools.
8. Educational facilities for adult women in the form of condensed courses (i) that prepare women for the middle school examination, and (ii) those that prepare them for the high school or higher secondary examination should be provided more extensively in all States.
9. Part-time employment of women teachers should be encouraged as largely as possible in order to enable women to manage their responsibilities at home as well as to do some teaching work

National Council of Women's Education (1962)

The "National Council of Women's Education" (1962) was appointed under the chairmanship of Hans Mehta to look to the differentiation of curriculum between boys and girls.

Bhaktavatsalam Committee (1963)

Bhaktavatsalam Committee (1963) was appointed to study the problem of women's education in six states where the education of girls was less developed. The main recommendations of the committee were following:

1. Both government and public should act jointly and proceed in a planned manner with regard to the education of girls;
2. Co-education should be made popular at the primary stage;
3. The services of educated married women should be sought as part time basis for teaching work;
4. Provision of adequate central help for women's education;
5. Establishment of social education centres in rural areas for women;
6. Evolving a functional curriculum for educating adult women;
7. Reservation of seats for women in training institutions; provision of attractive pay, living accommodation, conveyance charge etc.

Indian Education Commission or Kothari Commission (1964-1966)

In early seventies came the turning point towards development of women's education in India when the Education Commission, 1964-66, also known as the Kothari Commission, endorsed the views of Durgabai Deshmukh Committee and Hansa Mehta Committee towards women's education and clearly stated in their report that...

> *"For full development of our human resources, for improvement of homes and for moulding the character of children during the most impressionable years of infancy, the education of women is of even greater importance than that of men. But, in the modern world, the role of women goes much beyond the home and the bringing up of children. She is now adopting of her own and sharing equally with men the responsibility for the development of society in all its aspects. This is the direction in which we shall have to move....".*

The Commission, therefore, emphasized on equalization of educational opportunities. The Commission's recommendations came into force in the form of education policy, known as the National Policy of Education, 1968.

The Commission suggested that:

1. Women's education should be regarded as a major programme in education for some years to come and a bold and determined effort should be made to face the difficulties involved and to close the existing gap between the education of men and women in as short a time as possible;
2. On priority basis funds required for them should be provided;
3. There should be a special machinery at the state and central level to look after the women's education and both official and non-officials should be included in chalking out the plan and implementation of programmes for women's education.
4. Greater attention will be paid to the problems of training and employment of women teachers.
5. Teaching, nursing and social service are well organized areas where women can have an useful role to play

National Council for Women's Education in its meeting held in 1968

The National Council for Women's Education in its meeting held in 1968 recommended:

1. Provision of special programmes for preparing girls for different vocations and occupations.
2. Provision of full time and part time work for educated unemployed women;

3. Vocationalisation of education at the secondary stage for diverting students into different walks of life;
4. Establishment of training centres to provide training for women in those fields where women personnel are needed.

National Policy on Education (1968)

The Resolution on the National Policy on Education (1968) stressed the importance of women education and opined "The education of girls should receive emphasis not only on grounds of social justice but also because it accelerates social transformation". However, different bodies appointed at different times analyzed and discussed the problems and issues in the way of women's education and the ways and means to be adopted for its development and progress. Considerable attention had also been paid for evolving a suitable curriculum for the education of girls at different stages of education.

Status of Women in India (1974)

Another landmark report titled the Status of Women in India (1974) for the first time recognized equality of sexes as a major value to be inculcated through the educational process. It underlined the role of education as an agent of empowering women. It noted wide gaps between the enrolments of girls and boys at all levels as the proportion of girls in the relevant age groups covered by the school system remained far below the constitutional target of universal education up to the age of 14 years. It also observed that these gaps were mainly due to ambivalent attitude regarding the purpose of educating girls and inadequate educational facilities for girls. The committee, therefore, recommended sustained campaigns by all types of persons, preferably women-officials and non-officials, social and political workers, to bring every girl child into school in class I preferably at the age of 6 years; free education for all girls up to the end of the secondary stage; and equality of sexes as a major value to be inculcated through the educational process, among others.

Setting up of National Core Group

Another significant move of the Government of India towards women development has been the setting up of national core group which highlighted that women are not the weaker segment of society or passive beneficiaries of the development process, but they are the source of unique strength for achieving national goals. Education was seen as the most important instrument to improve the status of women in India and, therefore, the forthcoming Plan and policies visualized a strong need to give top priority to the education of women.

National Policy on Education (NPE) - 1986

The recommendations of National Policy on Education (1986) with respect to women education and empowerment are given below:

1. By the 1995 every educational institution should be active in formulating programmes for promoting and enhancing women education.
2. Women should be encouraged to take up vocational, professional and technical oriented courses.
3. Every state should have a Women's Education Cell and ample number of employees should be employed in this section. Regarding education the male and the female ratio should be equal. Besides this, this policy of Education made recommendations with regard to the following dimensions:
    - Access to education and equality of learning.
    - Content of education and gender bias vocational education
    - Training of teachers and other educational personnel
    - Research and development of women's studies. Representation of women in the educational hierarchy.
    - Employment of Women
    - Adult Education for Women
    - Resources
    - Management

Programme of Action (POA) - 1992

The recommendations of Programme of Action (1992) with respect to women education and empowerment are given below:

1. Enhance self-esteem and self-confidence of women.
2. Building of positive image of women by recognizing their contribution to the society, policy and the economy.
3. Developing ability to think critically.
4. Fostering decision-making and action through collective processes.
5. Enable women to make informed choice in areas like education, employment and health.
6. Ensuring equal participation in developmental processes.
7. Providing information, knowledge and skill for economic independence.
8. Enhancing access to legal literacy and information relating their rights and entitlements in society with a view to enhance their participation on an equal footing in all areas.

National Commission for Women (1992)

The recommendations of National Commission for Women (1992) with respect to women education and empowerment are given below:

1. Women should enjoy equal educational rights as men.
2. An educational programme should be formulated sothat every women is literate.
3. There should be no gender discrimination in education all over the country.
4. Girls should be admitted to schools and programmes should be formulated related to that.
5. Professions like vocational education and technical education should be encouraged amongst girls and women.
6. Major steps should be taken for girls school dropout specially in Secondary and Higher Secondary level

National Perspective for Women's Education (1998-2000)

The recommendations of National Perspective for Women's Education (1998-2000)) with respect to women education and empowerment are given below:

1. Special steps should be organized to remove the barriers of education for Schedule Tribes and other backward castes.
2. Media's help should be sought in spreading and creating awareness about women education in the society.
3. Girls school should be founded at major places.
4. Girls belonging to schedule tribes and backward castes should be given proper education.
5. Women education should be implemented in the National Educational Programme.
6. Girls and boys ratio of admission in school should be same.
7. Regional discrimination should be eradicated and girls of remote areas should be encouraged to study.
8. To remove gender discrimination books should be introduced in the national level.

National Curriculum Framework for School Education (2000)

The views of national curriculum framework for school education (2000) on "Education of Girls" are as follows:

> "Equality among sexes is a fundamental right under the Constitution of India. The State, however, also has the right to exercise positive protective discrimination in favour of the disadvantaged population groups including

women. Emphasis in education has moved from 'Equality of Educational Opportunity' (NPE, 1968) to 'Education for Women's Equality and Empowerment' (1986). As a result, the curricular and training strategies for the education of girls now demand more attention. Besides, making education accessible to more and more girls, especially rural girls, removing all gender discrimination and gender bias in school curriculum, textbooks and the process of transaction is absolutely necessary. Moreover, it will be the most appropriate thing to recognize and nurture the best features of each gender in the best Indian tradition. After all, India gave her women the right to vote without any prolonged battle for it unlike in the west. There is a need to develop and implement gender inclusive and gender sensitive curricular strategies to nurture a generation of girls and boys who are equally competent and are sensitive to one another, and grow up in a caring and sharing mode as equals, and not as adversaries."

National Policy for the Empowerment of Women in 2001

Another important move towards women's equality and empowerment is the adoption of the National Policy for the Empowerment of Women in 2001 which focused on equal access to quality education at all levels and the need for career - vocational guidance to girls/women. Apart from this, the policy envisaged introduction of a gender perspective in the budgeting process as an operational strategy.

CABE Committee on Girls Education and Common School System (2005)

In 2005, the government of India set up the CABE Committee on Girls Education and Common School System to examine existing schemes, incentives and special measures aimed at reducing gender disparity and increasing the participation and retention of girls, in all sectors of education.

The recommendations of CABE Committee on Girls Education and Common School System (2005) with respect to women education and empowerment are given below:

1. It recommended free and compulsory education for girls up to the age of 18 years and emphasized that there should be 'no hidden costs' in girls' education.
2. The committee gave thrust to initiate measures to promote girls' education of such nature, force and magnitude that enable girls to overcome the obstacles posed by factors such as poverty, domestic/ sibling responsibilities, girl child labour, low preference to girls' education, preference to marriage over education etc.
3. It also recommended women teachers and women attendants in every institution with provision of suitable working conditions for them so that they can perform their duties effectively, especially in rural areas.

Five Year Plans- 1950

The government of India adopted Five Year Plans as a development strategy as early as in 1950. Women's education has been placed at the forefront of development programmes in these Plans.

First Five Year Plan: The very First Five Year Plan included a chapter on Education in which girls'/ women's education was given a prominent place.

Second Five-Year Plan (1956-61): It recognized girls' education as a most urgent concern. It pointed out that public opinion in every part of the country is not equally alive to the importance of girls' education. The Plan Programmes, therefore, needed to focus on special efforts at educating parents, combined with efforts to make education more closely related to the needs of girls. It also recognized the need to study the situation in each area separately, explore methods for overcoming the difficulties in the acceptance of co-education and alternative to separate schools for girls in some areas.

Third Five – Year Plan (1961-65): The Plan focused special attention on the education of girls and reducing the disparities in levels of development in education between boys and girls.

Fourth Five-Year Plan (1969-74): It gave utmost priority to the expansion of elementary education and the provision of facilities for backward areas and communities and for girls.

Sixth Five – Year Plan (1980-85): It was committed to achieve a larger measure of equalization of educational opportunities, both in regard to access and achievement.

Seventh Five – Year Plan (1985-90): The Seventh Plan declared that girls' education will be free upto the higher secondary stage. The strategies for educational programmes and training and their organizational designs particularly focussed on women. The focus of effort was on promotion of girls' education through appointment of women teachers, attachment of pre-school centres to primary schools, provision of free uniforms and other incentives.

Eighth Five – Year Plan (1992-97): It highlighted for the first time, a gender perspective and the need to ensure a definite flow of funds from the general developmental sectors to women. It stressed on expansion of secondary schools particularly to cater to the needs of deprived sections like girls and SCs / STs and in rural areas. Special programmes were implemented with greater gender sensitivity.

Ninth Five Year Plan (1997-2002): It recognized education of girls as a non-negotiable area. The National Agenda for Governance also stated that plans will be instituted for providing free education for girls up to college level i.e., under-graduate level including professional courses. Additional hostel facilities for girls, particularly in tribal and remote areas, to improve attendance were also proposed. Women's component plan was adopted as one of the major strategies and directed both the Centre and State governments to ensure that not less than 30 percent of funds/benefits are earmarked in all the women's related sectors.

Tenth Five-Year Plan (2002-2007): The Tenth Plan again viewed girls' education as a major area seeking attention. The plan proposed to create an enabling environment by providing easy and equal access to educational opportunities, free education and gender – sensitive educational system. The plan laid emphasis on Universalisation of Elementary Education (UEE) guided by five parameters i.e. universal access; universal enrolment; universal retention; universal achievement; and equity.

The major schemes of elementary education launched were Sarva Shiksha Abhiyan (SSA), Mid- Day Meal Scheme (MDMS) and Kasturba Gandhi Balika Vidayalays (KGBVs). The scheme of providing boarding and hostel facilities for girls, initiated in 1993, was revised with the intent of increasing girls' enrolment at the secondary/ higher secondary level. Under the re-cast programme of Balika Samridhi Yojna (BSY), the Tenth Plan focused on educating and empowering the girl child living below the poverty line with adequate financial support till she completes higher secondary education or gets equipped with the necessary skills to earn her livelihood. The report of the working group set up for the 11th five year plan on development of education for girls recommended special schemes like construction of hostels in and around educational institutions, more hostels especially for girls nearer to secondary schools, reservation of not less than 33% seats in all technical and other higher educational institutions, extension of KGBV Scheme up to class XII, essential provisions of infrastructure facilities including common rooms for girls in all schools and provisions of more scholarships for girls for taking up professional courses among others.

Eleventh Five Year Plan (2007-12): The Eleventh Five Year Plan placed highest priority on education as a central instrument for achieving rapid and inclusive growth. Referring to the CABE Committee report on Girls' Education and Common School System, the XI FYP states that looking into the shortage of secondary schools for girls (both co-educational and girls' schools), opening of schools exclusively for girls appears to be necessary to overcome the gender disparity. The Plan further emphasizes that the States have to undertake, on priority, school mapping for girls education, especially for Muslim girls. It is heartening to note that the XI Plan included that measured will be undertaken to overcome obstacles posed by the factors such as poverty, domestic/sibling responsibilities, girl child labour, low preference to girls education, preference to marriage over education of girls etc. This was also recommended in the CABE Committee report mentioned earlier. A new Initiative proposed in this Plan is launching of 'A Girl Child Incentive Scheme' on a pilot basis in the selected educationally backward blocks (EBBs).

Sarva Shiksha Abhiyan (SSA) - 2001-02

The major recent initiative of the Government of India in achieving the goal of Education For All has been the launching of the Sarva Shiksha Abhiyan (SSA) in 2001-02 as a national programme. The SSA is an effort to universalize elementary education by community ownership of the school system. Gender sensitivity is the basic guiding principle, be it planning and management, school improvement, pedagogical renewal, strategies for community mobilization and participation or specific interventions for girls' education. It also ensures that every child with special needs, irrespective of the kind, category and degree of disability, is provided education in an appropriate environment. It envisages adoption of a zero rejection policy so that no child is left out of the education system. Flexibility is an important aspect of the government's approach under SSA. Various strategies have been adopted like Education Guarantee Scheme, Bridge Courses, Summer Camps and other initiatives to make it possible to reach out to unreached categories. SSA ensures elementary schooling (education for all children up to class VIII) completely free across the country.

The Targeted Provisions for Girls under SSA are:

1. Distribution of free textbooks for all girls up to class VIII.
2. Support for construction of separate toilets for girls in schools.
3. Organization of Back to School Camps for out of school girls.
4. Organization of Bridge Courses for older girls.
5. Recruitment of 50% women teachers.
6. Opening of Early Child Care and Education Centres in / near schools in convergence with ICDS Programme.
7. Support for organization of Teacher's sensitization programmes to promote equitable learning opportunities.
8. Development of gender sensitive teaching – learning materials including textbooks.
9. Intensive efforts to mobilise community to generate a community demand for girls' education.
10. Provision of Innovation Fund per district for need based interventions for ensuring girls' attendance and retention.

National Programme of Education for Girls at Elementary Levels (NPEGEL) - July 2003

Within the ambit of Sarva Shiksa Abhiyan (SSA), a special thrust on women's education came from the government through the National Programme of Education for Girls at Elementary Levels (NPEGEL) in July 2003. The NPEGEL under the existing scheme of SSA provides additional components at the elementary level for education of underprivileged/ disadvantaged girls. The scheme is being implemented in Educationally Backward Blocks (EBBs) where the level of rural female literacy is less than the national averages and the gender gap is above the national averages, as well as in blocks of districts that have at least 5 per cent SC/ST population and where SC/ST female literacy is below 10 per cent based on 1991 census.

Kasturba Gandhi Balika Vidyalaya (KGBV) - 2004

Another scheme introduced on behalf of the government in 2004 is the Kasturba Gandhi Balika Vidyalaya (KGBV). The main aim of the scheme is to preferentially encourage backward classes and scheduled caste girls to be in schools. It became a part of SSA in 2007. Currently, the scheme is operational in 24 states and 1 Union Territory. KGBV provides support for opening of residential girls' schools in educationally backward blocks for drop out girls or those who have missed schooling due to various reasons. In the 11th plan, KGBV is seen as a special initiative for dropout and never enrolled girls.

Right to Education (RTE) Act, 2009

Above all, the Right of Children to Free and Compulsory Education Act, 2009, commonly known as the Right To Education (RTE) Act, is being seen with much hope to bring about the long awaited changes in education of children aged 6-14 years, addressing disparities of access and quality. The Act was notified on 27.8.2010 and is in force from 1.4.2010. While stating the duties of appropriate Government authorities at various levels, the Act has also included duties of parents and guardians to get their children /wards admitted for elementary education in neighborhood schools. The biased parental attitude towards girl child in general and to education of girls child in particular will hopefully register a change by enforcement of the Act.

Policy Initiatives (Including Current Laws) for the Recognition of the Concept of Transgender and Third Gender

Tamil Nadu and Kerala was first among the states to introduce the *'Transgender Person's Welfare Policy'* but that was not for equal rights but only for welfare. In 24.04.2015, a private bill called *'Right to Transgender Persons'* Bill was proposed to Rajya Sabha but since this Bill was incomplete in certain respects so it was not properly recognized. At present in 22.07.2016 a Bill named *'The Transgender Persons (Protection of Rights) Bill, 2016'* was approved by the Cabinet Ministry. The Supreme Court has held that the right to self-identification of gender is part of the right to dignity and autonomy under Article 21 of the Constitution. However, objective criteria may be required to determine one's gender in order to be eligible for entitlements. The Bill states that a person recognized as 'transgender' would have the right to 'self perceived' gender identity. However, it does not provide for the enforcement of such a right. A District Screening Committee would issue a certificate of identity to recognize transgender persons. The definition of *'transgender persons'* in the Bill is at variance with the definitions recognized by international bodies and experts in India. The Bill includes terms like *'trans-men'*, *'trans-women'*, persons with *'intersex variations'* and *'gender-queers'* in its definition of transgender persons. However, these terms have not been defined.

17

Addressing Sexual Harassment and Violence

In Family, Neighbourhood and other Formal and Informal Institutions

Women, who since ancient ages were respected and worshipped as incarnation of 'Sakti', are today victimized by crimes from *'Womb to Tomb'*. Several enactments have been passed in India and at international level to bring about changes in the status of women and to eradicate crimes against women, but we have not yet achieved the desired result.

In modem era, no place is safe for the women, the new place of work brought with it new problems. Their life in the womb is threatened by techniques such as amniocentesis. At the home they are harassed by the husband, in-laws etc. at the workplace, they are physically and sexually harassed by the employers and supervisors. Even women, who are not the victims of violence, have had their way of life profoundly affected by the fear of such violence. The issue of violence against women has been the most pervasive theme of women's liberation movement in India. Female is a victim even in the industrialized, globalised and technological era.

Sexual Harassment against Women

Meaning of Sexual Harassment

The term 'Sexual harassment' coined in 1910's by feminist activists and their conception of sexual harassment was socio-cultural. In 1975 US Congress Senate Committee on Labour and Human Resources stated at the institute's formation that, it coined the phrase *'sexual harassment'*.

Sexual Harassment is defined as any unwelcome behaviour towards women that bears directly any sexual advances or sexual expression or seeking favour. Sexual harassment is also defined as unwelcome sexual advances, request for sexual favour and other verbal and physical conduct of sexual nature that leads to creat a hostile or offensive work environment.

Sexual harassment is a form of prohibited harassment. It is defined as unwelcome sexual advances, requests for sexual favours and other verbal or physical conduct of a sexual nature when: Submission to such conduct is made either implicitly or explicitly a term or condition of employment. Submission to or rejection of such conduct is used as a basis for employment decisions. Such conduct has the purpose or effect of unreasonably interfering with an individual's work performance or creating an intimidating, hostile or offensive working environment. This definition also encompasses unwelcome display or communication of sexually offensive materials.

The first definition of sexual harassment was formulated by Farely and working women united. In order to discover the pervasiveness of sexual harassment, they distributed the first questionnaire ever devoted solely to the topic of sexual harassment in May 1975. The definition of sexual harassment used in the survey was *"Any repeated and unwanted sexual comments, looks, suggestions or physical contact that you find objectionable or offensive and causes you is comfort on your job."* This definition is nearly equivalent to current legal definitions of sexual harassment.

Catharine Mackinnon's sexual harassment of working women, published in 1979, was a major influence in the construction of the social and legal meaning of sexual harassment. Catharine Mackinnon was one of the first scholars to theorize the unfavourable conditions that so many women had experienced; Mackinnon defines sexual harassment as follows:

> *"Sexual harassment most broadly defined, refers to the unwanted imposition of sexual requirements in the context of a relationship of unequal power. Central to the concept is use of power derived from one social sphere to lever benefits or imposes deprivations in another."*

But, it was very unfortunate that before 1997, in Indian criminal law, sexual harassment of women has not been enunciated as a juridical category of crime. It was only in 1997 that, in the realm of juridical interpretation, sexual harassment of working women was named and defined.

The following may be considered the sexual behavior:

1. *Verbal Sexual Behaviour:* The verbal sexual behaviour include:
   - Comments of a sexual nature about figure, size, shape, body weight, unwelcome remark, rough and vulgar humour/jokes.
   - Insulting publicly saying something demeaning and humiliating.
   - Graphic sexual description, chatter of sexual nature.

- Telephone calls with sexual tones.
- Teasing and using names such as darling, honey, sweet heart etc.

2. *Non-verbal Sexual behaviour:* The non-verbal sexual behaviour includes:
   - Licking lips or teeth, holding or eating food provocatively.
   - Sexual looks such as leering and calling with sexual tones.
   - Obscene written materials, such as letters, e-mail, notes, invitations.

Types of Sexual Harassment

Types of sexual harassment are explained in table 17.1 given below:

Table 17.1: Types of Sexual Harassment

Visual Sexual Harassment	It includes showing pornography, nude poster, photo- graph and cartoon, sexually explicit picture.
Physical Sexual Harassment	It includes actual physical attempt for kissing, embracing, patting, squeezing breast and cheeks and other physical attempt.
Psychological Sexual Harassment	It includes calling every day for work and retain her for excessive hours, and staring on her face, breast, neck, eye and other part of the body; repeated unwanted invitation for dinner, drinks and movies, proposal for physical intimacy beginning with subtle hints which may lead to overt request for dates or sexual intercourse, sexual favour, requiring to wear sexiest and revealing or suggestive saree, suit, dress and to adopt suggestive hairstyle, lipstick etc.

Extensity of Sexual Harassment

Sexual Harassment at Home: Sexual harassment can cause within the family and the child mainly is the victim here. In married couples also, marital rape is one form of sexual harassment which occurs often. To avoid sexual harassment parents should take proper care of the child.

Sexual Harassment at Neighbourhood: Neighbourhood is another area where sexual harassment in prevalent. When one moves from home to school, college and other places he/she specially the female is prone of *'eve-teasing'*. Comments related to sex and vulgar languages are also very much prevalent. So, the neighbourhood should be properly maintained by senior as well responsible citizens to avoid sexual harassment.

Sexual Harassment at Educational Institutions: Though it is derogatory yet sexual harassment is very much prevalent in certain cases in educational institutions. There are many reports where a male teacher has abused a girl student or sexually harassed her. In this context the discipline of the school must be very much proper otherwise such acts could not be avoided.

Sexual Harassment at other Fields: Other fields such as clubs, dance classes, private tuitions, tutorial homes, shops and even in workplaces sexual harassment occurs and is very much prevalent.

Effects of Sexual Harassment

There are many negative effects of sexual harassment. They are as follows:

- Unstable mental health
- Wastage of Resource
- Pollution of Social environment
- Erosion of values

UNESCO has played a vital role regarding sexual harassment and the highest court of India i.e. the Supreme Court also has been strict to punish the cases of sexual harassment. In this context the *'Protection of Children's Right Act'* needs to be mentioned.

Steps to Address Sexual Harassment

The following steps are needed to prevent and address Sexual Harassment:

1. *Create a policy prohibiting sexual harassment of any kind:* Write policy broadly, in gender-neutral terms, so it applies to everyone, regardless of the sex of the alleged harasser and the victim.

Elements of a good anti-harassment policy:

- Broadly defines conduct that constitutes sexual harassment, plus specific examples
- States that offenders will be subject to appropriate discipline, up to discharge
- Encourages employees who feel victimized by sexual harassment to report it
- Requires employees and supervisors to report any offensive conduct they experience or witness.
- Provides assurance that there will be no retaliation against employees who report harassment
- Promises that all sexual harassment reports will be promptly and thoroughly investigated and that remedial action will be taken if harassment has occurred.

2. *Establish a complaint procedure:* Provide the names and phone numbers of contact people (preferably of both genders) to whom workers can report misconduct. Specify who will investigate and decide the outcome of a complaint. Set a time frame to process and resolve complaints quickly and fairly.
3. *Institute investigative procedures:* Take every sexual harassment complaint seriously and investigate it promptly. You'll need to interview the accused, the accuser and potential witnesses. Conduct all interviews privately to safeguard confidentiality. Establish systems to gather and record evidence. Treat all parties with dignity and respect. During the investigation, consider issuing a gag order prohibiting anyone from discussing the alleged harassment.
4. *Enforce your policy:* If your investigation confirms sexual harassment, notify the involved parties and decide on disciplinary action. Depending on the harasser's work record and the gravity of the charge, you may decide on an oral or written warning, a deferral of a raise or promotion, a demotion, suspension or discharge. Be fair in your judgment, and evenly apply your disciplinary actions. Make sure you have all the necessary documentation to back up any disciplinary action. Keep all records in one file so they will be easily accessible if the victim or harasser decides to sue.
5. *Conduct anti-harassment training:* Use these sessions to communicate your policy, answer questions and give employees detailed information about how to identify, respond to and prevent sexual harassment.

Violence against Women

Agencies Perpetuating Violence

The status of Indian women is, after a long history of discrimination and subjugation undergoing a change in India. Women are now passing through a phase between subjugation and emancipation and are now entering the outside world leaving behind the age-old tradition of domestic confinement. However, gender based discrimination still represents the ugly face of the society. Gender bias has widened the gap between women and men and put the women in disadvantageous treatment.

Violence against women vary with different economic, social and cultural contexts, there is no doubt that the phenomenon is universal and a major factor in the subordination of women worldwide. In the 1980s, when violence against women first became a major issue for women's movements in every region, the focus was on acts of overt physical and sexual violence. This include for example female infanticide, female foeticide, wife battering rape, wife burning in private sphere, sexual harassment, stoning and rape in public arenas.

By the 1990s the definition of violence had been expanded to include more structural forms of gender based violence. Certain cultural practices, like son preference, dowry custom, virginity tests etc., were highlighted as demeaning to women and fostering conditions that normalize and tolerate abuse of women's rights. In this way, violence against women increasingly has been understood as encompassing an environment in which such abuses can be perpetrated with impunity and sometimes even with social sanction. Violence against women, regardless of the nature of the perpetrator an individual group, institution, the state or society is a human rights violation and is treated as such whether it happens in the home, within the family or outside of it.

Definition of Violence

The term 'Violence against Women' means any act of gender based violence that results in or is likely to result in physical, sexual or psychological harm or suffering to women including threats of such acts, coercion or arbitrary deprivation of liberty whether occurring in public or private life.

In other words, we can say that, violence is defined as the intentional use of physical force or power, threatened or actual, against oneself, another person, or against a group or community that either results in or has a high likelihood of resulting in injury, death, psychological harm, mal-development or deprivation.

According to United Nations Declaration of Elimination of Violence against Women in the book 'Women in the Third World (1998)', Violence is defined as any act of gender based violence that results in, or is likely to result in physical, sexual or psychological harm or suffering to women, including threats of such acts, coercion or arbitrary deprivations of liberty whether occurring in public or private life.

Gender violence includes rape, sexual assault; relationship violence in heterosexual and same sex partnerships, sexual harassment, stalking, prostitution and sex trafficking. The term *'gender violence'* reflects the idea that violence often serves to maintain structural gender inequalities, and includes all types of violence against men, women, children, adolescents, gay, transgender people and gender non-conforming. This type of violence in some way influences or is influenced by gender relations. To adequately address this violence, we have to address cultural issues that encourage violence as part of masculinity.

Forms of Gender Violence

Various forms of gender violence are as follows:

1. *Physical violence*—leading to injury
2. *Sexual violence*—robbing women of their dignity not only by indecent behaviour but also raping

3. *Verbal violence*—use of abusive and derogatory language, against a women or her dignity
4. *Social violence*—demeaning, disparaging and humiliating a woman
5. *Emotional violence*—deprivation of love and affection, concern, sympathy and care
6. *Intellectual violence*—denial of rights to take part in decision making
7. *Other forms of violence*—include not providing women educational opportunities, denial of reproductive rights, denial of access to health facilities or committing atrocities like forcing women to enter into professions like trafficking and prostitution.

Domestic Violence

Domestic violence or Family violence is when someone uses abusive behaviour to control and/or harm a member of their family, or someone with whom they have an intimate relationship. Family violence includes many different forms of physical and emotional abuse, as well as neglect carried out by family members or intimate partners. It may include a single act of violence, or a number of acts that form a pattern of abuse. Family violence can have serious and sometimes fatal consequences for victims and for those who see or hear the violence.

Family violence is the willful intimidation, physical assault, battery, sexual assault, and/or other abusive behaviour as part of a systematic pattern of power and control perpetrated by one intimate partner against another. It includes physical violence, sexual violence, psychological violence, and emotional abuse. The frequency and severity of family violence can vary dramatically; however, the one constant component of family violence is one partner's consistent efforts to maintain power and control over the other. Family violence is an epidemic affecting individuals in every community, regardless of age, economic status, sexual orientation, gender, race, religion, or nationality. It is often accompanied by emotionally abusive and controlling behaviour that is only a fraction of a systematic pattern of dominance and control. Family violence can result in physical injury, psychological trauma, and in severe cases, even death. The devastating physical, emotional, and psychological consequences of domestic violence can cross generations and last a lifetime.

Family violence is not just physical violence. A person can be the victim of one or more forms of violence or abuse including:

- Physical abuse
- Sexual abuse
- Emotional abuse
- Financial abuse
- Neglect

School Violence

School violence is a subset of youth violence. Violence is the intentional use of physical force or power, against another person, group, or community, with the behaviour likely to cause physical or psychological harm. School violence is any activity that can create a disturbance in an educational system. It's not just school shootings. It includes verbal and physical altercations. It is also bullying through electronic means or social media, threats, weapon use, or gang activity. School violence can also be defined as a physical or verbal altercation on the way to school, on the way home from school, or at a school-sponsored event that can cause physical or psychological harm to another individual, school, or community. School violence has occurred at the grade school and high school level.

Examples of violent behaviour include:

- Bullying
- Fighting (e.g., punching, slapping, kicking)
- Weapon use
- Electronic aggression
- Gang violence

Workplace Violence

Workplace violence is violence or the threat of violence against workers. It can occur at or outside the workplace and can range from threats and verbal abuse to physical assaults and homicide, one of the leading causes of job-related deaths. However it manifests itself, workplace violence is a growing concern for employers and employees nationwide. The best protection employers can offer is to establish a zero-tolerance policy toward workplace violence against or by their employees. The employer should establish a workplace violence prevention program or incorporate the information into an existing accident prevention program, employee handbook, or manual of standard operating procedures. It is critical to ensure that all employees know the policy and understand that all claims of workplace violence will be investigated and remedied promptly. In addition, employers can offer additional protections such as the following:

1. Provide safety education for employees so they know what conduct is not acceptable, what to do if they witness or are subjected to workplace violence, and how to protect them.
2. Secure the workplace. Where appropriate to the business, install video surveillance, extra lighting, and alarm systems and minimize access by outsiders through identification badges, electronic keys, and guards.

3. Providing drop safes to limit the amount of cash on hand. Keep a minimal amount of cash in registers during evenings and late-night hours.
4. Equipping field staff with cellular phones and hand-held alarms or noise devices, and require them to prepare a daily work plan and keep a contact person informed of their location throughout the day. Keep employer-provided vehicles properly maintained.
5. Instructing employees not to enter any location where they feel unsafe. If possible providing an escort service or police assistance in potentially dangerous situations or at night

Media Violence

Media violence is defined as visual portrayals of acts of physical aggression by one human or human-like character against another. This definition has evolved as theories about the effects of media violence have evolved and represents an attempt to describe the kind of violent media presentation that is most likely to teach the viewer to be more violent.

The print as well as the electronic media has taken an active role against violence in different forms. The media often exposes and defines social issues such as sexual harassment in different forms etc. This also draws public attention leading to a public opinion. The electronic as well as the print media plays a very important role in the society to eradicate violence in various forms.

Institutions Redressing Sexual Harassment and Abuse

The institutions redressing sexual harassment and abuse mention must be made of the following institutions:

United Nations International Children's Emergency Fund (UNICEF)

UNICEF has played a very important role is redressing sexual harassment and abuse. UNICEF has encouraged taking all appropriate measures to create a proper harmonious work environment and to protect women from exposure to any form of discrimination, harassment, sexual harassment or abuse of authority. UNICEF conducts mandatory awareness programmes to raise awareness of its zero tolerance of discrimination, harassment, sexual harassment and abuse of authority to provide guidance on the relevant policy and procedures and to foster the creation of a harmonious working environment. Heads of office/division are responsible for ensuring that their staff undertake and complete the mandatory training programme on prevention of discrimination, harassment, sexual harassment and abuse of authority in the workplace.

Indian Law to Protect Women against Sexual Harassment at Workplace

No woman shall be subjected to sexual harassment at any workplace, mandates a new law in India. Now a reasonable law is in place in India to deal with sexual harassment at workplace to a great extent but its implementation is a difficult task in a women unfriendly environment. The first thing to do to make the law work is to make its legal provisions known to the stakeholders of the law.

Law covers unorganized sector: The law covers women in organized and unorganized sector including the private sector. It covers domestic worker who is employed to do domestic work in any household for remuneration whether in cash or kind, either directly or through any agency or temporary, part time or full time basis, but does not include any member of the family of the employer. However, the law does not cover members of the armed forces.

Employer to Institute a No-harassment Policy: The law mandates the employers to provide a safe work environment devoid of sexual harassment to their women employees. Employers have to take preventive and remedial measures to make the work environment safe for women, failing which they will be punished. Employer is liable for not taking reasonable precautionary measures to prevent sexual harassment.

The employers are mandated to formulate a policy which prohibits sexual harassment as part of institution's service regulations as a precautionary measure to provide a healthy workplace environment. The officer responsible for implementing the law is the head of the institution or any person responsible for the management, supervision and control of the workplace. As well the officers under the central and state governments have been assigned certain responsibilities to make the law work

University Grants Commission (UGC)

The University Grants Commission has also notified the *'prevention, prohibition and redressal of sexual harassment of women employees in higher education institutions'*. This also ensures that UGC has laid down strict rules against any types of violence or sexual harassment in higher educational institutions. In this context it must be mentioned that in the school level *"Protection of Children's Right Act"* and *"Right to Education"* is very much prevalent nowadays.

The Legal Aid Cell of West Bengal which is also an NGO has played an important role in cases of violence as well as sexual harassment.

18

Schemes for Girls Education and Development

Government schemes and programmes for women and child can be grouped into two parts:

1. Women Welfare and Empowerment Schemes of Government of India
2. Central Government Sponsored Schemes for Child Protection and Welfare

1. Women Welfare and Empowerment Schemes of Government of India

The Central Government Sponsored Schemes for Women Empowerment Schemes are listed below:

Beti Bachao Beti Padhao Scheme

Beti Bachao, Beti Padhao (Save girl child, educate girl child) is Central Government Sponsored Scheme by Government of India. The prime goal of this scheme is to generate awareness and improving the efficiency of welfare services meant for women. Also, it aims to celebrate the Girl Child and Enable her Education.

The Beti Bachao, Beti Padhao (BBBP) Scheme has been introduced to address the issue declining Child Sex Ratio (CSR). This scheme is being implemented through a national campaign and focused multi-sectoral action in 100 selected districts low in CSR, covering all States and UTs. This scheme is implemented by the joint initiative of Ministry of Women and Child Development, Ministry of Health and Family Welfare and Ministry of Human Resource Development.

Prime Minister Modi launched the programme on 22 January 2015 from Panipat, Haryana on the occasion of International Day of the Girl Child, and called for the eradication of female foeticide

Objectives of Beti Bachao Beti Padhao Scheme

The objectives of this scheme are as follows:

1. To prevent gender biased sex selective elimination.
2. To ensure survival & protection of the girl child.
3. To ensure education of the girl child.

Benefits of Beti Bachao Beti Padhao Scheme

The benefits of this scheme are summarized as below:

1. Improvement of the Nutrition status of girls by reducing number of underweight and anaemic girls under 5 years of age
2. Ensuring girls' attendance and equal care monitored, using joint ICDS NRHM Mother Child Protection Cards.
3. Increasing the girl's enrolment in secondary education
4. This scheme provides girl's toilet in every school.
5. It aims to promote a protective environment for Girl Children through implementation of Protection of Children from Sexual Offences
6. Train Elected Representatives/ Grass root functionaries as Community Champions to mobilize communities to improve CSR & promote Girl's education.
7. Reduction of Gender differentials and child mortality
8. To improve the Sex Ratio at Birth (SRB)
9. Evolving a sustained Social Mobilization and Communication Campaign to change societal norms, to create equal value for the girl child.
10. Mobilizing and empowering frontline worker teams as catalysts for social change, in partnership with local community/women's/youth groups
11. Developing capacity of Panchayati Raj Institutions/Urban local bodies - especially women panchayat /urban local body members, to create community and peer support for making panchayats / urban wards girl child friendly.

Indira Gandhi Matritva Sahyog Yojana (IGMSY)

The Indira Gandhi Matritva Sahyog Yojana (IGMSY) is a maternity benefits scheme implemented by the Ministry of Women and Child Development, Government of India. This scheme is for the pregnant and lactating women of 19 years of age or above for first two live births to contribute to a better enabling environment by providing conditional cash transfer for improved health and nutrition and to also promote health and nutrition seeking behaviour in them. It provides partial wage compensation to women for wage-loss during childbirth and childcare and to provide conditions for safe delivery and good nutrition and feeding practices. It provides cash maternity benefit to the women. The pregnant women of 19 years of age and above is entitled to a cash incentive of Rs. 4000 in three installments for first two live births.

Objectives of Indira Gandhi Matritva Sahyog Yojana (IGMSY)

The objectives of this scheme are summarized as below:

1. To promoting appropriate practice, care and institutional service utilization during pregnancy, safe delivery and lactation
2. To encouraging the women to follow (optimal) nutrition and Young Child feeding practices, including early and Exclusive breastfeeding for the first six months; and
3. To providing cash incentives for improved health and nutrition to pregnant and lactating mothers in order to contribute to better enabling environment.

Benefits of IGMSY

The conditional cash transfer benefits of Rs. 6,000 to be paid in two instalments of Rs. 3,000

1. The first transfer (at the end of second birth / pregnancy trimester) of Rs. 3,000 to the mother
2. The second transfer (three months after delivery) of Rs. 3,000 to the mother.

One Stop Centre Scheme for Women

One Stop Centres (OSC) are meant to support women affected by violence, in private and public spaces, within the family, community and at the workplace. Women facing physical, sexual, emotional, psychological and economic abuse, irrespective of age, class, caste, education status, marital status, race, and culture will be facilitated with support and redressal. Aggrieved women facing any kind of violence due to attempted sexual harassment, sexual assault, domestic violence, trafficking, honour-related crimes, acid attacks or witch-hunting who have reached out or been referred to the OSC will be provided with specialized services. OSC are set up in each State/UT. This scheme facilitates access to an integrated range of services including medical, legal, and psychological support. The OSC will be integrated with Helpline No. 181 and other existing helplines. Women affected by violence and in need of redressal, services could be referred to OSC through these helplines.

Objective of One Stop Centre Scheme for Women

The objectives of this scheme are as below:

1. To provide integrated support and assistance to women affected by violence, both in private and public spaces under one roof.
2. To facilitate immediate, emergency and non-emergency access to a range of services including medical, legal, psychological and counseling support under one roof to fight against any forms of violence against women.

Benefits of One Stop Centre Scheme for Women

The overall benefits under this scheme are summarized as below:

1. *Emergency Response and Rescue Services*: OSC will provide rescue and referral services
2. *Medical Assistance*: Women affected by violence would be referred to the nearest Hospital for medical aid/examination
3. *Assistance to Women in lodging FIR/NCR/DIR*: The OSC will facilitate the lodging of FIR/NCR/DIR.
4. *Psycho-Social Support/ Counselling*: A skilled counsellor providing psycho-social counselling services would be available on call. This counselling the process will give women confidence and support to address violence or to seek justice for the violence perpetuated. Counselors shall follow a prescribed code of ethics, guidelines and protocols for providing counseling services.
5. *Legal Aid and Counselling*: To facilitate access to justice for women affected by violence, legal aid, and counseling would be provided at OSC through empanelled Lawyers or National/State/District Legal Service Authority.
6. *Shelter*: The OSC will provide temporary shelter facility to aggrieved women. For long term shelter requirements, arrangements will be made with Swadhar Greh/Short Stay Homes (managed/affiliated with government/NGO). Women affected by violence along with their children (girls of all ages and boys up till 8 years of age) can avail a temporary shelter at the OSC for a maximum period of 5 days. The admissibility of any woman to the temporary the shelter would be at the discretion of Centre Administrator.
7. *Video Conferencing Facility*: To facilitate speedily and hassle free police and court proceedings the OSC will provide video conferencing facility (through Skype, Google Conferencing etc.). Through this facility, if the aggrieved woman wants, she can record her statement for police/ courts from OSC itself using audio-video electronic

Rajiv Gandhi National Creche Scheme for Children of Working Mothers

With rising employment opportunities for women and the growing need to supplement household income, more and more women are entering the job market. With the breaking up of joint family system and the increasing number of nuclear families, working women need help in terms of quality, substitute care for their young children while they are at work. Creche and Day Care Services are not only required by working mothers but also women belonging to poor families, who require support and relief for childcare as they struggle to cope with the burden of activities, within and outside the home.

Therefore women need a safe place for their children in their absence. It has become necessary to provide support to the young children in terms of quality, substitute care and other services while the mothers are at work.

A creche is a facility which supports/ make able to parents to leave their children while they are at work and where children are provided the stimulating environment for their holistic development. Creches are developed in such a way that they provide group care to children, usually up to 6 years of age, who need care, guidance and supervision away from their home during the day.

Objective of Rajiv Gandhi National Creche Scheme for children of Working Mothers

The objectives of this scheme are as follows:

1. To provide day-care facilities for children (6 months to 6 years) of working mothers in the community.
2. To improve nutrition and health status of children.
3. To promote physical, cognitive, social and emotional development (Holistic Development) of children.
4. To educate and empower parents /caregivers for better childcare.

Benefits of Rajiv Gandhi National Creche Scheme for children of Working Mothers

The scheme will provide the following services:

1. Daycare Facilities including Sleeping Facilities.
2. Early Stimulation for children below 3 years and Pre-school Education for 3 to 6 years old children.
3. Supplementary Nutrition (to be locally sourced)
4. Growth Monitoring.
5. Health Check-up and Immunization.
6. Other services provided under this scheme are as Drinking water and Sanitary Facilities, Food and Cooking Facilities, Growth Monitoring, Health Check-up, Medicine & First Aid Kit, Equipment, and Play Material

Support to Training and Employment Programme for Women (STEP)

The STEP Programme is a 100% Central Sector Scheme. Under this scheme, Training is provided to poor and marginalized women in traditional trades which are largely in the informal sector. The Programme of STEP advocates the objective of extending training for up-gradation of skills and employment for women through a variety of action-oriented projects.

STEP Program has been introduced to address occupational aspirations of poor women who do not have the opportunity of formal skill training. This scheme emphasis on Skill Development for self or wage employment because Skills and knowledge are the driving forces of economic growth and social development of a country.

Objective of Support to Training and Employment Programme for Women (STEP)

The objectives of this scheme are as below:

1. To provide skills that give employability to women.
2. To provide competencies and skills that enable women to become self-employed/entrepreneurs.
3. To upgrade the skills of poor and marginalized women.
4. To provide employment to them on a sustainable basis.

Benefits of Support to Training and Employment Programme for Women (STEP)

Under this scheme, Assistance is given in any sector i.e Agriculture, Horticulture, Food Processing, Handlooms, Tailoring, Stitching, Embroidery, Zari etc Handicrafts, Computer and IT enabled services along with soft skills and skills for the workplace such as spoken English, Gems and Jewellery, Travel & Tourism and Hospitality for imparting skills related to employability and entrepreneurship.

Provision of for support services (Health, Childcare, Education, sanitation etc.), access to credit and imparting nutrition education

Swadhar Greh

A Scheme that caters to primary needs of women in difficult circumstances

This scheme, initiated by the Department of Women and Child Development, provides temporary accommodation, maintenance and rehabilitative services to women and girls rendered homeless due to family discord, crime, violence, mental stress, social ostracism or are being forced into prostitution and are in moral danger. The scheme provides shelter, food, clothing, counseling, training, clinical and legal aid aims to rehabilitate women in difficult circumstance.

Objective of the Scheme of Swadhar Greh

Under the scheme, Swadhar Greh aims to achieve the following objectives:

1. To provide to the basic need of shelter, food, clothing, medical treatment and care of the women in distress and who are lacking social and economic support.
2. To enable them to recover their emotional strength that gets hampered due to their encounter with unfortunate circumstances.
3. To provide them with legal aid and guidance to enable them to take steps for their re-adjustment in family/society.
4. To rehabilitate them economically and emotionally.
5. To act as a support system that understands and meets various requirements of women in distress.
6. To empower/encourage them to start their life afresh with dignity and conviction.

Benefits of the Scheme of Swadhar Greh

The benefits of this scheme are as follows:

1. Temporary residential accommodation with the provision of food, clothing, medical facilities etc. are provided to the beneficiaries.
2. Provision of Vocational Training and skill up gradation training for economic rehabilitation of such women to the eligible women.
3. Counseling, awareness generation, and behavioral training are given.
4. Legal aid and Guidance, Medical Facilities are provided
5. Also Counseling through telephone facility is given.

Women Helpline Scheme: A Single National Help Line Number for Women

Scheme for Universalisation of Women Helpline is meant to provide 24 hours immediate and emergency response to women affected by violence. This scheme is being implemented since from first April 2015 by the Union Ministry of Women and Child Development.

The scheme meant to provide 24 hours immediate and emergency response to affected women through referral (linking with appropriate authority such as police, One Stop Centre, hospital) and information about women related government schemes programmes across the country through a single uniform number. Department of Telecommunication, Government of India has allocated short code 181 to all States/UTs as Women Helpline (WHL).

Women Helpline (WHL) is working with the One Stop Centre Scheme (OSC) under which one OSC will be set up in every State/UT to provide integrated support and assistance to women affected by violence, both in private and public spaces under one roof.

Objective of Women Helpline Scheme

The objectives of the Scheme are:

1. To provide toll-free 24-hours telecom service to women affected by violence seeking support and information
2. To help crisis and non-crisis intervention through referral to the appropriate agencies such as police/Hospitals/Ambulance services/ District Legal Service Authority (DLSA)/Protection Officer (PO)/ OSC.
3. To provide information about the appropriate support services, government schemes and programmes available to the woman affected by violence, in her particular situation within the local area in which she resides or is employed.

Benefits of Women Helpline Scheme

The benefits are summarized as below:

1. *Violence against Women (VAW) Prevention:* As soon as an aggrieved woman (AG) or somebody on her behalf will contact WHL, she will be immediately assisted by the call responder appointed there. The responder will refer her to relevant support services like medical aid, police assistance or connect her to OSC for professional counselling, shelter, legal aid etc;
2. *Information of Women Empowerment Schemes and programmes:* The information about the laws, existing schemes and government programmes related to women empowerment and protection are provided. It will help to women about processes to be adopted for accessing benefits of these schemes and programmes.

Scheme for Working Women Hostel

The many more women are leaving their homes in search of employment in big cities as well as urban and rural industrial clusters. One of the main difficulties faced by such women is lack of safe and conveniently located accommodation. Hence this scheme has been initiated by the Government of India.

This scheme aims to promote availability of safe and conveniently located accommodation for working women who need to live away from their families due to professional commitments.

Objective of Scheme for Working Women Hostel

The objectives of this scheme are as below:

1. To promote availability of safe and conveniently located accommodation for working women, with day care facility for their children, wherever possible, in urban, semi urban, or even rural areas where employment opportunity for women exist.

Benefits of Scheme for Working Women Hostel

Hostel, Day Care Centre and Medical first aid are benefitted to the beneficiaries.

2. Central Government Sponsored Schemes for Child Protection and Welfare

The Central Government Sponsored Schemes for Child Protection and Welfare Schemes are listed below:

- Integrated Child Protection Scheme (ICPS)
- Kishori Shakti Yojana (KSY)
- Sabla or Rajiv Gandhi Scheme for Empowerment of Adolescent Girls

Integrated Child Protection Scheme (ICPS)

Objective of Integrated Child Protection Scheme (ICPS)

The objectives of this scheme are summarized as below:

1. To institutionalize essential services and strengthen structures for emergency outreach, institutional care, family and community based care, counselling and support services at the national, regional, state and district levels;
2. To enhance capacities at all levels, of all functionaries including, administrators and service providers, members of allied systems including, local bodies, police, judiciary and other concerned departments of State Governments to undertake responsibilities under the ICPS;
3. To create database and knowledge base for child protection services, including MIS and child tracking system in the country for effective implementation and monitoring of child protection services;
4. Undertake research and documentation;
5. To strengthen child protection at family and community level, create and promote preventive measures to protect children from situations of vulnerability, risk and abuse;

6. To ensure appropriate inter-sectoral response at all levels, coordinate and network with all allied systems;
7. To raise public awareness, educate public on child rights and protection on situation and vulnerabilities of children and families, on available child protection services, schemes and structures at all levels

Benefits of Integrated Child Protection Scheme (ICPS)

ICPS brings several existing child protection programmes under one umbrella and initiates new interventions with focus on:

1. Mapping needs and services for children and families at risk;
2. Preparing child protection plans at district and state levels; the plan would be gradually extended to block and community levels;
3. Strengthening service delivery mechanisms and programmes including preventive, statutory, care and rehabilitation services;
4. Improving access to and quality of services provided;
5. Promoting and strengthening non-institutional family based care options for children deprived of parental care, including sponsorship to vulnerable families, kinship-care, in-country adoption, foster care and inter-country adoption, in order of preference;
6. Developing capacity of service providers;
7. Strengthening knowledge base, awareness and advocacy;
8. Establishing an integrated, live, web based data base (on children in difficult circumstance, children in care, service providers and services provided), for evidence based monitoring and evaluation and service planning decision making;
9. Monitoring and evaluation;
10. Building partnerships and alliances for child protection at all levels, particularly at the grass-root community and district levels.
11. Strengthening linkages with other bodies and institutions such as the National/State Human Rights Commissions and National/State Commissions for Protection of Rights of the Child, etc.
12. Details of the exclusive service delivery structures provided for under ICPS may be seen in the subsequent chapters.

Kishori Shakti Yojana (KSY) for Adolescent Girls

Kishori Shakti Yojana (KSY) has been introduced to by Ministry of Women and child Development. This scheme aims to empower adolescent girls (Age) of 11–18 years with focus on out-of-school girls. It emphasis on their nutritional and health status and upgrading various skills like home skills, life skills and vocational skills. This scheme provides nutritional and health education including sanitation and personal hygiene aspects.

Also, it focuses on education with particular attention on school dropouts and functional literacy among illiterate adolescent girls. Educational activities should be conducted through non-formal education pattern. Non-formal education is provided to adolescent girls. It gives physical, developmental and sex education. Also, it gives free vocational training activities for adolescent girls for their economic empowerment.

Objective of Kishori Shakti Yojana (KSY)

The objectives of this scheme are as follows:

1. To improve the nutritional and health status of girls in the age group of 11-18 years.
2. To provide the required literacy and numeracy skills through the non-formal stream of education
3. To encourage a desire for more social exposure and knowledge and to support them improve their decision making capabilities
4. To train and equip the adolescent girls to improve/ upgrade home-based and vocational skills
5. To promote awareness of health, hygiene, nutrition and family welfare, home management and child care, and to take all measure as to facilitate their marrying only after attaining the age of 18 years and if possible, even later
6. To gain a better understanding of their social environment related issues and the impact on their lives and take initiatives to become productive members of the society.
7. To encourage adolescent girls to initiate various activities to be productive and useful members of the society
8. To improve the nutritional, health and development status of adolescent girls, promote awareness on health, hygiene, nutrition and family care
9. To link them to opportunities for learning life skills, to train and equip the adolescent girls to improve/upgrade home based and vocational skills.

Benefits

Under this scheme following benefits are provided:

1. This scheme provides nutritional and health education including sanitation and personal hygiene aspects to adolescent girls.
2. It gives vocational training to the girls.
3. It provides physical, developmental and sex education. And also focuses on education through non-formal education.

Sabla or Rajiv Gandhi Scheme for Empowerment of Adolescent Girls Nutrition and Health

This scheme is popularly known as SABLA Scheme. This scheme is Centrally Sponsored Scheme for benefitting Adolescent Girls (AGs). Empowering adolescent girls (Age) of 11–18 years with focus on out-of-school girls by improvement in their nutritional and health status and upgrading various skills like home skills, life skills and vocational skills. Also It emphasis on Out of School Adolescent girls who are provided life skill education and vocational training along with supplementary nutrition.

Objective of Sabla

The objectives of this scheme are summarized as below:

1. To enable the Adolescent Girls for self-development and empowerment
2. To improve their nutrition and health status of adolescent girls.
3. To promote awareness about health, hygiene, nutrition, Adolescent Reproductive and Sexual Health (ARSH) and family and child care.
4. To upgrade their home-based skills, life skills and tie up with National Skill Development Program (NSDP) for vocational skills
5. To Mainstream out of school Adolescent Girls into formal/non formal education
6. To provide information/guidance about existing public services such as PHC, CHC, Post Office, Bank, Police Station, etc.
7. To make awareness among them about health, hygiene, nutrition, Adolescent Reproductive and Sexual Health (ARSH), and family and child care
8. To upgrade home based skills, life skills and vocational skills

Benefits of the Scheme

Under this scheme, following services are provided:

1. Nutrition provision: Healthy nutrition is supplied to AGs
2. Iron and Folic Acid (IFA) supplementation
3. Health check-up and Referral services
4. Nutrition & Health Education (NHE)
5. Counseling/Guidance on family welfare, ARSH, child care practices and home management
6. Life Skill Education and accessing public services
7. Vocational training for girls aged 16 and above under National Skill Development Program (NSDP)

19

Gender and Society

History and Current Scenario of Indian Women

Medieval India was considered the "Dark Ages" for Indian women. Medieval India saw many foreign conquests, which resulted in the decline in women's status. When foreign conquerors like the Mughals and the British invaded India they brought with them their own culture, which in some cases adversely affected the condition of women and in some cases emancipated them. Over the ages in India women have been treated as the sole property of her father, brother or husband, not been given any choice or freedom of her own. All this gave rise to some new evils such as Child Marriage, Sati, Jauhar and restriction on girl education.

Sati: The ritual of dying on the funeral pyre of the husband is known as "Sati" or "Sahagaman". According to some of the Hindu scriptures women dying on the funeral pyre of her husband go straight to heaven so it's good to practice this ritual. Initially it was not obligatory for the women but if she practiced such a custom she was highly respected by the society.

Jauhar: It is also more or less similar to Sati but it is a mass suicide. Jauhar was prevalent in ancient Rajput societies. In this custom wives immolated themselves while their husbands went to perform Saka, i.e face the larger army of the enemy knowing that they will be killed since they are outnumbered. When people of the Rajput clan became sure that they were going to die at the hands of their enemy then all the women arrange a large pyre and set themselves afire, while their husband used to fight the last decisive battle with the enemy. Thus, protecting the honour of the women and the whole clan.

Child Marriage: It was a norm in medieval India to get girls married at the age of 8-10. They were not allowed access to education and were trained in house work instead. Child marriage had its own share of problems such as increased birth rate, poor health of women due to repeated child bearing and high mortality rate of women and children.

Restriction on Widow Remarriage: The condition of widows in medieval India was very poor. They were not treated as equals and were subjected to a lot of restrictions. They were supposed to live pious life after their husband died and were not allowed entry in any celebration. Their presence in any good work was considered to be a bad omen. Many widows also had to have their hair shaved off as a mark of mourning. They were not allowed to remarry.

Purdah System: The veil or the 'Purdah' system was widely prevalent in medieval Indian society. It was used to protect the women folk from the eyes of foreign rulers who invaded India in medieval period. But this system curtailed the freedom of women.

Female Education: The girls of medieval India and especially Hindu society were not given formal education. They were given education related to household chores.

Devadasis: It was a custom prevalent in Southern India. In this system girls were dedicated to temples in the name of gods and goddesses. The girls were then onwards known as 'Devadasis' meaning servant of god. These Devadasis were supposed to live the life of celibacy. All the requirements of Devadasis were fulfilled by the grants given to the temples. In temple they used to spend their time in worship of god and by singing and dancing for the god.

Modern Indian Women's Problems

The status of women in modern India is a sort of a paradox. If on one hand she is at the peak of ladder of success, on the other hand she is mutely suffering the violence afflicted on her by her own family members. As compared with past women in modern times have achieved a lot but in reality they have to still travel a long way. Women have left the secured domain of their home and are now in the battle field of life, fully armored with their talent. They had proven themselves. But in India they are yet to get their dues. The sex ratio of India shows that the Indian society is still prejudiced against female. There are 917 females per thousand males in India according to the census of 2011, which is much below the world average of 990 females. There are many problems which women in India have to go through daily, some of which are:

Malnutrition: One of the major causes of mal nutrition among Indian women is gender inequality. In many parts of India, especially rural India, women are the ones who eat last and least in the whole family. This means they eat whatever is left after the men folk are satiated. As a result most of the times their food intake does not contain the nutritional value required in maintaining the healthy body. In villages, sometimes women do not get to eat a whole meal due to poverty.

Poor Health: Malnutrition results in poor health of women. The women of India are prejudiced from birth itself. They are not breast fed for long. In the want of a son get pregnant as soon as possible which decreases the caring period to the girl child, where as male members get adequate care and nutrition. Women are not given the right to free movement that means that they cannot go anywhere on their own if they want and they have to take the permission of male member of family or have to take them along. This means that women miss visiting doctors even when they should, which adds to their poor health.

Maternal Mortality: The maternal mortality rate in India is among highest in the world. As females are not given proper attention, which results in the malnutrition and then they are married at an early age which leads to pregnancies at younger age when the body is not ready to bear the burden of a child. All this results in complications, which may lead to gynecological problems, which may become serious with time and may ultimately, lead to death.

Lack of Education: In India women's education never got its due share of attention. From medieval India women were debarred from the educational field. According to medieval perception women need just household education and this perception of medieval India still persists in villages of India even today. Girls are supposed to fulfill domestic duties and education becomes secondary for them whereas it is considered to be important for boys. Although scenario in urban areas has changed a lot and women are opting for higher education but majority of Indian population residing in villages still live in medieval times. The people of villages consider girls to be curse and they do not want to waste money and time on them as they think that women should be wedded off as soon as possible.

The main reason for not sending girls to school is the poor economic condition. Another reason is far off location of schools. In Indian society virginity and purity is given utmost importance during marriage and people are afraid to send their girl child to far off schools where male teachers teach them along with boys. The lack of education is the root cause for many other problems.

Mistreatment: In India violence against women is a common evil. Not just in remote parts but even in cities women bear the brunt. They are subjected to physical and mental violence. They are the one who work most but are not given their due. Every hour a woman is raped in India and every 93 minutes a woman is burnt to death due to dowry problem.

Overworked: Indian women work more than men in India but their work is hardly recognized as they mainly do unskilled work. Their household chores is never counted as a work, if a woman is working in a field to help her husband it will also be not counted as a work.

Lack of Power: In India a large percentage of women do not have power. They cannot take decisions independently not even related to their own life. They have to take permission of male members for each and every issue. They don't have any say in important household matters and not in matter of their own marriage.

Marriage: The family mainly fixes the marriages in India. The scenario in villages is bad. The girl is not consulted but is told to marry a groom whom her family has chosen for him. They are taught to abide by the whims and fancies of their husbands. Going against the wishes of husband is considered to be a sin. In marriage husband always has the upper hand. The groom and his parents show as if they are obliging the girl by marrying her and in return they demand hefty dowry.

Dowry: This is the another serious issue in modern India, courts are flooded with cases related to death due to dowry harassment by husband and in laws. Now-a-days, parents have to give hefty amount in dowry, the in laws of their girl are not concerned whether they can afford it or not. If a girl brings large amount of dowry, she is given respect and is treated well in her new home and vice versa. Due to this evil practice many newly wed women of India have to lose their lives.

Female Infanticide/Foeticide: Today with the help of technology the sex of the unborn baby is determined and if it is a girl child then it is aborted. In all this procedure women do not have any say they have to do according to the wish of their husbands even if she does not want an abortion, she has no choice.

Divorce: The divorce rate in India is not so high compared to western countries but that does not mean that marriages are more successful here.

Though, there are problems in the lives of Indian women but they are always ready to fight all the odds and enjoy their life to the full they have their own talent, hobbies, and they socialize according to Indian customs.

Issues Related to Indian Women

There are various issues and problems which women generally face in the society in India. Some of the problems are mentioned and described below:

Selective Abortion and Female Infanticide: It is the most common practice for years in India in which abortion of female fetus is performed in the womb of mother after the fetal sex determination and sex selective abortion by the medical professionals.

Sexual Harassment: It is the form of sexual exploitation of a girl child at home, streets, public places, transports, offices, etc by the family members, neighbors, friends or relatives.

Dowry and Bride Burning: It is another problem generally faced by women of low or middle class family during or after the marriage. Parents of boys demand a lot of money from the bride's family to be rich in one time. Groom's family perform bride burning in case of lack of fulfilled dowry demand.

Disparity in Education: The level of women education is less than men still in the modern age. Female illiteracy is higher in the rural areas, where over 63 per cent or more women remain unlettered.

Domestic Violence: It is like endemic and wide spread disease affects almost 70 per cent of Indian women according to the women and child development official. It is performed by the husband, relative or other family member.

No Property Rights: Girls have no property rights like boys forever.

Child Marriages: It means early marriage of the girls by heir parents in order to be escaped from dowry. It is highly practiced in the rural India.

Inadequate Nutrition: Inadequate nutrition in the childhood affects women in their later life especially women belonging to the lower middle class and poor families.

Domestic Violence and Status in the Family: It is the abuse or violence against women.

No Military Service: Women are considered as inferior to men so they are not allowed to join military services.

Status of Widows: Widows are considered as worthless in the Indian society. They are treated poorly and forced to wear white clothes.

Gender Roles in Society through Variety of Institutions

The behaviors of men and women that are considered socially appropriate are called gender roles. A gender role is a set of societal norms dictating the types of behaviors which are generally considered acceptable, appropriate, or desirable for people based on their actual or perceived sex or sexuality. Gender roles are usually centered on conceptions of femininity and masculinity, although there are exceptions and variations. The specifics regarding these gendered expectations may vary substantially among cultures, while other characteristics may be common throughout a range of cultures.

In the early and mid-20th century, men were considered responsible for taking care of the family financially. They took their jobs as sole providers very seriously. They also had the responsibility for guiding the family. While they may listen to what their wives had to say, they made the final decisions. Men did not do household duties or child care. They felt the need to be strong and refrained from showing too much emotion or sharing too many personal feelings, especially with those outside of the family.

Women were expected to be in charge of running the household. Mothers did the laundry, cooked the meals, and cleaned the rooms. They also took care of the children, giving them the care and attention that was required. The wealthier families might hire a nanny, and child care became more widely used in the later 20th century. But the women were often in charge of directing the nannies and dropping off or picking up from day care. Women were seen as more emotional than men, more likely and more encouraged to open up about their feelings. While there are many differences today, these patterns of behavior have left an indelible impact on society and our thoughts about men and women.

Family

Gender roles are defined by the socio-cultural norms of any society. In most of the societies the family systems are based on the gender roles and it is the predesigned gender roles that help members of the family to run the family with bound responsibilities. Even when parents set gender equality as a goal, there may be under lying indications of inequality. For example, when dividing up household chores, boys may be asked to take out the garbage or perform other tasks that require strength or toughness, while girls may be asked to fold laundry or perform duties that require neatness and care. It has been found that fathers are firmer in their expectations for gender conformity than are mothers, and their expectations are stronger for sons than they are for daughters. This is true in many types of activities, including preference of toys, play styles, discipline, chores, and personal achievements. As a result, boys tend to be particularly attuned to their father's disapproval when engaging in an activity that might be considered feminine, like dancing or singing.

Caste

Caste refers to a traditional Hindu model of social stratification, which defines people by descent and occupation. A suffocating patriarchal shadow hangs over the lives of women throughout India. From all sections, castes and classes of society, women are victim of its repressive, controlling effects. Those subjected to the heaviest burden of discrimination are from the Dalit or "Scheduled Castes", known in less liberal democratic times as the "Untouchables". The name may have been banned but pervasive negative attitudes of mind remain, as do the extreme levels of abuse and servitude experienced by women. They experience multiple levels of discrimination and exploitation, much of which is barbaric, degrading, appallingly violent and totally inhumane.

Religion

The main religions of the world all contain certain ideas about the appropriate roles for men and women in society, and traditionally, this has placed women in the home and men in the 'outside' world. This holds true even now-a-days, where much change is occurring in societies with increasing female labour market participation and changes in attitudes accompanying this. Religions differ to some extent in this regard, but similar normative claims about men's and women's roles are present across all denominations. The cultural and religious activities that negatively impacted against the education of the girl child were most found.

Culture

Expectations about attributes and behaviours appropriate to women or men and about the relations between women and men – in other words, gender – are shaped by culture. Gender (like race or ethnicity) functions as an organizing principle for society because of the cultural meanings given to being male or female. Culturally determined gender ideologies define rights and responsibilities and what is 'appropriate' behaviour for women and men. They also influence access to and control over resources, and participation in decision-making. These gender ideologies often reinforce male power and the idea of women's inferiority. Culture is sometimes interpreted narrowly as 'custom' or 'tradition', and assumed to be natural and unchangeable. Despite these assumptions, culture is fluid and enduring. Dominant cultures reinforce the position of those with economic, political and social power, and therefore tend to reinforce male power. Globalization also has implications for the diffusion of culture, particularly of western culture.

Media

The main aim of mass media is to be universal and suitable for everyone, in order to gather the largest possible audience. Thus television, responsible for providing the central social discourse, is supposed to be "a mirror of the society". However, because of stereo typical way of explaining the reality, some groups are underre presented or ignored, and therefore the society image is incomplete. For instance, the way in which male and female roles are presented in commercials reflects the traditional notions of gender, where women are dominated by men. The attempts to break down the stereo types are emancipation of women, growing role of individualism, globalization and revaluation of patterns and social roles. Mass media not only gives people information and entertainment, but it also affects people's lives by shaping their opinions, attitudes and beliefs. Now-a-days the differences between male and female roles are smaller, however mass media still perpetuates traditional gender stereo types. Moreover, due to their great influence on people's attitudes, they can depict certain social groups in negative and unrealistic manner.

They can be a very useful tool for those remaining power. By manipulating the message, media can create a certain image of reality, which is consistent with the policy of the dominant group. As a result, the reflection of a real world is incomplete and distorted. Although people are aware of the unequal representation of certain social groups in mass media, it is hard to remain objective and in sensitive to its influence.

Advertisement

Women are more often presented in commercials, because they are seen as responsible for making every day purchases. Men generally advertise cars, cigarettes, business products or investments, whereas women are shown rather in the commercials with cosmetics and domestic products. They are also more likely portrayed in the home environment, unlike men, who are shown outdoors. Another important distinction is the face-ism phenomenon in the commercials, which consists in showing the entire figure in case of women and close-up shots in case of men. In advertisements, man plays as athletic, successful, professional, seducer with a beautiful woman by his side. He also has a branded car and a smartphone. The other type is less popular and presents men devoted to their families who can save enough time for them. Men are very rarely presented during house-cleaning. And if they are, it is rather a satirical imager they appear as the experts and they advise women, for instance, how to do laundry properly. Advertising specialists also use the stereo type of male friendship, which can be called "buddy narratives"; men are presented as acting together, for instance by going to a football match or to the pub.

Films

Most people would be surprised to learn that gender segregation plays out at different levels of the film industry, where behind-the-scenes and on screen inequality runs rampant. The bollywood films have well portrayed the changes happening in the society the films have always been criticized for its almost ignoring the issues of gender. In most of the films, women are given a second tier status; they are characterized as inferior and weaker parts of the society always seeking help from their male counterpart. The only importance they are given is as an item girl or a one-dimensional catalyst for the hero's journey. The heroines are harassed and embarrassed in the name of courtship and issues like sexual assault and rape have been shown regularly in films. The treatment of women in films are either as domestic dolls pandering to the whims and fancies of the dominating husband and in-laws is another cliché that we come across. Women are generally shown as mere adornments to the house. Most mainstream movies portray the man-woman relationship in the mould of one social activity, namely, falling in love and either getting married of jilted for money or family prestige bestowed by birth.

Law and State

"The state sets the framework within which couples lives in a legal relationship called marriage, it determines the age of consent to sexual intercourse, it makes certain kinds of intercourse criminal acts, it forbids or regulates the grounds on which abortions can be undertaken legally. The courts set precedents and rules which determine what happens when a marriage breaks up. All of these functions profoundly affect the quality of people's lives and are part of social policy". Law is pervasive and affects many aspects of people's lives, women and men alike. Inequalities in endowments, access to resources and rights, social (and household) status, voice and agency are perpetuated, codified, contested and redressed through norms and the institutions established or resulting from such norms, be they social or legal. Although these inequalities can affect both women and men, women are lagging behind men in many fields.

20

Gender, Power and Education

Individual gender identity is formed by the family or by society. The gender identity of men and women are framed psychologically by family and society that are historically and culturally framed and the nit leads to gender inequalities. According to Ann Oakley, 'Gender' is a matter of culture; it refers to the social classification of men and women into 'masculine' and 'feminine'. One gender identity is the name given to the way in which a person acts in relation to their sex and societies expectations.

A child when born is not only classified by sex but also assigned a gender. This is followed by the difference with which s/he are addressed, handled, treated and clothed and this regulation taught how s/he should behave to be a part of society, s/he is born in to. This is called socialization. Socialization is the process in which we learn the norms and values of the society we live in. The specific process of socialization which teaches children their gender roles is also called gendering and gender indoctrination.

In most societies women are expected to have qualities such as gentleness, caring, nurturing and obedience, men are expected to be strong, self-confident, competitive and rational. Men are considered to be the head of households, bread-winners, owners and manager of property, and active in politics, religion, business and women on the other hand are expected and trained to bear and look after children, to nurse the infirm and old, do all household work etc. So, this is society that turns males and females into masculine and feminine. Socialization takes place through four processes namely manipulation, canalization, verbal appellation and activity exposure. All four processes are normally differentiated by sex and all are features of the child's socialization from birth on.

Gender Identities and Socialization Practices

Gender Identity

Gender identity refers to the deeply felt sense of being a man, woman, neither or other. Gender identity interacts and is often expressed in relation to both gender roles and gender expressions (modes of dress, gestures and behaviour) as well as sex (the physical appearance of the body, hormone balance etc).

Components of Gender Identity

Stoller identified three components in the formation of core gender identity. They are as follows:

1. Biological and hormonal influences
2. Sex assignment at birth
3. Environmental and psychological influences with effects similar to imprinting

Types of Gender Identity

Femininity and masculinity or one's gender identity refers to the degree to which persons see themselves as masculine or feminine given what it means to be a man or woman in society. Femininity and masculinity are rooted in the social (one's gender) rather than the biological (one's sex) system. The types of a person's gender identity are given below:

Table 20.1: Types of Gender Identity

Masculinity	Identifying oneself of male gender and acting accordingly is known as masculinity.
Femininity	Identifying oneself of female gender and acting accordingly is known as femininity,
Androgyny	Having both the characteristics of masculinity and femininity at high level is called androgyny.
Undifferentiated	Being low on both the basic dimensions of gender identity i.e., masculinity and femininity, is labeled as undifferentiated

Development of Gender Identity

The formation of a gender identity is a complex process that starts with conception but which involves the growth processes during gestation and learning experiences after birth. There are differences log the way, but the language and tradition in many societies ms1st that every individual should be categorized as either a man or a woman. The first thing, most adults ask about a baby (their own or anyone else's) is whether it is a boy or a girl. The birth announcement begins with that information, a male or female-sounding name is selected, pink or blue clothing is bought, the baby's room is decorated in either a feminine or a masculine style, and *"gender appropriate"* toys and clothing are provided. Developmental aspects of Gender Identity are given below:

Table 20.2: Developmental Aspects of Gender Identity

Adolescence and Adult	Gender identity is well established and gender stereotypes are well understood. The individual mayor may not identify with the gender stereotypes associated with his or her sex. That is, a person may adopt these sex-linked stereotypes or those of the opposite sex or those of both sexes or those of neither sex.
Later Childhood	Sex identity becomes very clear, and gender identity (I am a male or I am a female) develops as part of the self-concept. Child also is learning culturally designated 'appropriate' and 'inappropriate' characteristics associated with gender. By age 5, gender stereotypes begin to be acquired.
Ages 2 To 4	Child learns social categories of male and female and labels self and others as boy or girl, though with a somewhat limited understanding of precisely what this means.
Conception	Genes on the sex chromosomes determine whether a biological male or a biological female has been conceived.

Socialization

Socialization is the process of internalizing society's values in order to adapt to one's culture. It influences how people behave as males and females in society. The social learning process that imbibes people into understanding the various aspects of culture includes the process of gender socialization. Gender socialization encompasses the process of learning society's gender roles and their advantages and limitations.

The main agents of gender socialization are parents, peer, siblings, school, society and religion. For very young children parents and family play the central role in shaping gender socialization. They determine how the family interacts with a boy as well as the types of toys and clothes that the baby is given.

According to A M Colman the meaning of socialization is,

> "The process beginning in infancy, whereby one acquires the attitudes, values, beliefs, habits, behaviours, patterns and accumulated knowledge of one's society through child-rearing, education and modification of one's behaviour to conform with the demands of the society or group to which one belongs."

In brief socialization is defined as a learning process, one that involves development or changes in the individual's sense of self.

Socialization is a process that starts at birth and continues through the lifespan. Each person learns values, beliefs and social norms through socialization. This process also influences a person's identity and role within society. Socialization is a learning process where one develops a 'sense of self' as we are socialized, but socialization is much more than that. If socialization was just a learning process, we could call it education and be done with it. If socialization was only about our "sense of self" we could leave with psychologists and not be bothered ourselves. But, socialization is more than just education and it impacts more than just your sense of self.

The socialization process one goes through is significant and sophisticated and any definition of it should capture that significance. In order to understand the significance of the socialization process, the first thing one has to understand is that socialization is not a political, socially, or even spiritually neutral process. That is, the things a child is taught from childhood and the ways he/she isto behave are not random. As stated earlier the socialization process begins with the birth, it is not just about the child and the family, it is about the social and political order within which he/she is born into. In other words, socialization teaches one the social order. When the socialization process begins, one does not have a choice. Whatever society one is born into, whatever the sex of the body one happens to inhabit, one is given no choice about what s/he will learn. Immediately after one is born, and long before one has the intellectual capacity to understand what it is that is happening to her/him, the process of imposing the social order begins.

Gender Socialization

Gender socialization is the process by which individuals are taught how to socially behave in accordance with their assigned gender, which is assigned at birth based on their biological sex. Gender socialization is a more focused form of socialization, it is how children of different sexes are socialized into their gender roles and taught what it means to be male or female.

According to UNICEF, Gender socialization is the process by which people learn to behave in a certain way, as dictated by societal beliefs, values, attitudes and examples. Gender socialization begins as early as when a woman becomes pregnant and people start making judgments about the value of males over females. These stereotypes are perpetuated by family members, teachers and others by having different expectations for males and females.

Family and Gender Socialization

The child's first world is that of his family. It is a world in itself, in which the child learns to live, to move and to have his being. Within it, not only the biological tasks of birth, protection and feeding take place, but also develop those first and intimate associations with persons of different ages and sexes which form the basis of the child's personality development.

The family is the primary agency of socialization. It is here that the child develops an initial sense of self and habit-training eating, sleeping etc. To a very large extent, the indoctrination of the child, whether in primitive or modem complex society, occurs within the circle of the primary family group. The child's first human relationships are with the immediate members of his family mother or nurse, siblings, father and other close relatives.

Here, he experiences love, cooperation, authority, direction and protection is also learnt from family in childhood. People's perceptions of behaviour appropriate of their sex are the result of socialization and major part of this is learnt in the family.

As the primary agents of childhood socialization, parents play a critical role in guiding children into their gender roles deemed appropriate in a society. They continue to teach gender role behaviour either consciously or unconsciously, throughout childhood. Families also teach children values they will hold throughout life. They frequently adopt their parents' attitudes not only about work but also about the importance of education, patriotism and religion. As family plays a very important role in guiding children and such are highlighted below:

- Parents' Role as Teacher
- Parents' Role as a Model
- Child Abuse
- Space in the Family
- Sibling Relations
- Home Environment

Family socialization begins a process through which humans learn and develop to be the adult persons they become. For some, the effects of family socialization are very evident and long lasting; for others, there is not much obvious effect; and for still others, it looks like there's no relationship at all. If you look closely, you'll see that some adults choose to adopt behaviours and values that are completely opposite from those of their families. For those individuals it can be said that the socialization is just as strong, but it has a different effect. For some adults, their interactions with family continue in such a close relationship that the family maintains a dominant role in their ongoing socialization. Family plays a very important role in the gender identity of a child. In this context Lawrence Kohlberg's (1966, 1969) Cognitive-Development theory needs to be mentioned. He suggested that children had made a cognitive judgement about their gender identity before them selected same sex models for sex typed behaviours.

Stages of Kohlberg's Cognitive-Developmental Theory

Basic gender identity: The child knows that he or she is a male or a female, but the child fails to realize that gender is a constant attribute. Most three year olds had reached this stage.

Gender stability: The child knows that their gender is stable over time. A child in this stage knows that boys will grow up to be men and that girls will grow up to be women.

Gender consistency: The child knows a person gender stay the same regardless of changes in the person's activities or appearance. For example, a 6 or 7 year old who had reached this stage knows a person gender stay the same when a person dress up like a member of the other sex or when a person does cross-sex activities.

Importance of Family in Gender Socialization

The family is considered as the institution that has the greatest impact on gender socialization. It is in the family that a child first learns what it is to be 'male' or 'female'. There are a number of ways in which parents and other family members guide their children and teach them to conform to the norms that prevail in society with regard to the appropriate behaviours, attitudes and roles of members of each sex. We shall look at how gender socialization takes place in the family

The parents usually hold a number of gender stereotypes, which are ideas about how a girl and a boy should ideally act and think. Therefore, they tend to treat children of different sex differently. For example, mothers will tend to hold a baby girl delicately while she may bounce her baby boy on her knees. Boys and girls are handled and spoken to and dressed differently. Oakley (1974) refers to this difference in treatment as 'manipulation'.

Children are also given different toys to play with. Boys are usually given guns, trucks, footballs, bricks and a variety of other active and mechanical toys with which they can play inside or outside the home. Girls are more usually given dolls, tea sets, miniature cooking appliances, sewing machines and other toys that are usually linked to the home. Thus, the choice of toys for the children seem to an image of what is expected of them in their future life as men and women. Parents also tend to apply different rules to their children. Boys, for example, are more likely to be granted permission to play on the street or to come late at home than girls. They are usually given more liberty.

School and Gender Socialization

Schooling is one of the most important socialization processes that a child goes through outside her family. It shapes the child's understanding of self in relation to others. The schools and the teachers play a very important role in a child's formative years. The child starts to understand her/his identity beyond the family, role that each one in the society assumes, through friends, teachers in school and most importantly books that they read in class room. A child's understanding of gender specific role gets almost fixed when schooling starts and get re-enforced every day by the behaviours towards them by the teachers, staff, member of the school.

They start being actor of the patriarchal system and carry it along much after they have left school.

After family the educational institutions take over the charge of socialization. In some societies (simple non-literate societies), socialization takes place almost entirely within the family but in highly complex societies children are also socialized by the educational system. Schools not only teach reading, writing and other basic skills, they also teach students to develop themselves, to discipline themselves, to cooperate with others, to obey rules and to test their achievements through competition. Schools teach sets of expectations about the work, profession or occupations they will follow when they mature. Schools have the formal responsibility of imparting knowledge in those disciplines which are most central to adult functioning in our society. It has been said that learning at home is on a personal, emotional level, where as learning at school is basically intellectual. The role of a school in the socialization process is given below:

- Acquisition of New Social Behaviour
- Restraint
- Use of Formal Language
- Group Cohesion
- Social Awareness
- Gender Identity

Importance of School in Gender Socialization

Schools are major contexts for gender socialization, in part because children spend large amounts of time engaged with peers in such setting. For nearly all psychological traits on which young boys and girls differ (e.g., reading ability, play preferences), the distribution of the two groups is overlapping. Schools can magnify or diminish gender differences by providing environments that promote within-gender similarity and between-gender differences, or the inverse (within-gender variability and between group similarity). Schools are important contexts for the socialization of young children's gender attitudes and behaviour. Teachers and classmates shape children's gender attitudes and, in turn, gender differences in cognition and behaviour. Unfortunately, teachers receive relatively little training in recognizing and combating gender stereotypes and prejudices - their own and others - and, as a consequence, teachers often model, expect, reinforce, and lay the foundation for gender differentiation among their pupils. Thus, most schools create and maintain - rather than counter act - traditional gender stereotypes, biases, and differences. However, educators who adopt a commitment to gender egalitarianism and thus promote cross-gender interaction, expose pupils to counter-stereotypic models, and discuss and teach challenges to gender stereotyping and harassment optimize their pupils' developmental outcomes.

Other Formal and Informal Organizations and Gender Socialization

Peer Group

Besides the world of family and school fellows, the peer group (the people of their own age and similar social status) and playmates highly influence the process of socialization. In the peer group, the young child learns to confirm to the accepted ways of a group and to appreciate the fact that social life is based on rules. Peer group socialization has been increasing day by day these days. Young people today spend considerable time with one another outside home and family. Young people living in cities or suburbs and who have access to automobiles spend a great deal of time together away from their families. Studies show that they create their own unique sub-cultures-the college campus culture, the drug culture, motorcycle cults, athletic group culture etc. Peer groups serve a valuable function by assisting the transition to adult responsibilities. Teenagers imitate their friends in part because the peer group maintains a meaningful system of rewards and punishments. The group may encourage a young person to follow pursuit s that society considers admirable.

Mass Media

From early forms of print technology to electronic communication (radio, TV, etc.), the media is playing a central role in shaping the personality of the individuals. Since the last century, technological innovations such as radio, motion pictures, recorded music and television have become important agents of socialization. Television, in particular, is a critical force in the socialization of children almost all over the new world. According to a study conducted in America, the average young person (between the ages of 6 and 18) spends more time watching the 'tube' (15,000 to 16,000 hours) than studying in school. Apart from sleeping, watching television is the most time-consuming activity of young people. Relative to other agents of socialization discussed above, such as family, peer group and school, TV has certain distinctive characteristics. It permits imitation and role playing but does not encourage more complex forms of learning. Watching TV is a passive experience.

Importance of Formal as well as Informal organizations in Gender Socialization

The media has a very powerful effect on culture, shaping societal structures and operations. Dominant media forms have heavily assisted in constructing gender and generalized norms. Advertising and mass media forms display codes that are associated with representing male and female attributes. These gender codes shape the way in which society views gender and assists in determining what acceptable gender performance is. It is through media's reinforcement of gender stereotypes, codes and gender displays that shape the way in which society perceives and constructs genders.

The self-identification of being male or female is shaped through cultural, and social conditions. Media forms often present these social and cultural aspects and set these as ideals for gender performance. Mass media forms a set of societal standards for men and women. These forms shape the way in which society views and identifies male and female characteristics. Often these gender assumptions cast negative representations that place barriers on women to develop and reach their true potential within society. These gender codes become heavily assimilated within mass media and marketing, as many advertisers display men and women to portray stereotypical gender norms and roles. Often these advertisements illustrate men and women differently, altering the way in which society views the sexes. Women within advertisements are often displayed in a sexualized nature that exposes females as vulnerable defenseless figures. Men within advertisements are often seen in stances that embrace power and status. Male advertisements conform to gender stereotypes and use body language to convey men as powerful, aggressive beings. Body language within advertisements allows companies to construct gender identity and reinforce generalized norms. Creating advertisements that construct to gender enables these companies to effectively market, as they are able to evoke identity through these products.

Advertisements marketed toward children expose gender identities and roles. These advertisements assist children in constructing gender identity, by displaying ads of children conforming to gender roles. For instance, famous toy company Hasbro Inc. created a product called the "Easy Bake Oven", which targeted young girls between the ages of 4-10 years old. The company created and marketed a product that was associated with feminine domestic roles and practises. The "Easy Bake Oven" advertisements featured young girls participating in feminine domestic practises (gender role), and deemed these domestic activities of baking as a fun hobby for girls.

Children at a very young age have a strong desire to fit in and feel accepted amongst their peers. Media images and mass messages in advertisements aid children in constructing identity by presenting gender roles as the 'norm'. Masculine and feminine functions become assimilated into modern culture, and are rendered to society as the common ideal for men and women. It becomes apparent that gender is socially and culturally constructed through media outlets. These media forms are extremely influential and can alter the way in which society perceives gender.

21

Gender and School

Gender Bias

Gender bias is a preference or prejudice toward one gender over the other. Bias can be conscious or unconscious, and may manifest in many ways, both subtle and obvious. It is the unequal treatment in employment opportunity such as promotion, pay, benefits and privileges and expectations due to attitudes based on the sex of an employee or group of employees. Gender bias can be subtle or overt, and can result in small or large consequences. Most countries have laws eliminating gender bias in work places. Gender bias can be a legitimate basis for a law suit under anti-discrimination statutes. Gender bias is behavior that shows favoritism toward one gender over another. Most often, gender bias is the act of favoring men and/or boys over women and/or girls. Gender bias occurs when people make assumptions regarding behaviors, abilities or preferences of others based upon their gender. Because there are strong gender role stereotypes for masculinity and femininity, students who do not match them can encounter problems with teachers and with their peers.

Gender Bias in Education

While the past few decades have seen an improvement in the treatment of females in classroom methods and curricular materials, it would be premature to declare victory and dismiss issues of gender bias. Today, our girls and boys remain the victims of gender stereotypes in text and resource materials. They are also victims of unintended or sexist behaviours by educators. Often teachers reflect varied expectations for children, based on a student's gender, class, race and ethnicity. Most teachers care deeply about the youngsters in their rooms. They are confident that they treat all their students the same. However, many teachers who analyze their own attitudes and behaviours discover the subtle and pervasive nature of gender inequity in the classroom.

1. Some biased behaviours in the classroom:
2. Usually males receive more teacher questions than females.
3. Minimal wait time for females' answers
4. More frequent follow-up questions with males
5. Uneven ratio of student/teacher interactions: # of responses male to female = 7:3
6. Males are also more likely to call out or act out, demanding and receiving teacher attention.
7. Segregated seating patterns reinforce unequal teacher attention. Classrooms are characterized by gender segregated classrooms
8. Boys are more likely to be called up to the front of the room to do demonstrations (for example a science demonstration)
9. Boys are more likely to be disciplined than girls, even when the misbehavior is identical
10. Girls are more likely to be praised for the appearance and neatness of their work
11. Females often stereotyped into clerical role because of neat notes
12. Teachers are more likely to offer boys specific feedback on their work – including praise, criticism and remediation
13. Boys are more likely to receive attributions to effort and ability, teacher comments giving them confidence that success and competence is simply a matter of applying themselves
14. Girls are often told, "It's okay, as long as you try."
15. Make sure there aren't 'girls' jobs and 'boys' job.

Gender Bias in School Enrollments

Discrimination based on gender is one of the primary impediments to education. And it affects boys and girls. In some regions, boys' educational opportunities are limited by gender roles that force them to work rather than attend school. These financial responsibilities are often increased in boys' adolescent years, making it difficult for them to complete secondary school in some regions. However, in many parts of the world, girls are most often the victims of gender discrimination as they pursue an education. Education is the only key to bring gender equality. Increase in literacy rate should bring equality based on gender but in Indian society gender equality is not yet achieved up to the expected level. Because the roles of gender are taken from the society that plays a root cause for inequality though women are educated.

While the past few decades have seen an improvement in the treatment of females in classroom methods and curricular materials, it would be premature to declare victory and dismiss issues of gender bias. Today, our girls and boys remain the victims of gender stereotypes in text and resource materials. They are also victims of unintended or sexist behaviors by educators. Often teachers reflect varied expectations for children, based on a student's gender, class, race and ethnicity. Most teachers care deeply about the youngsters in their rooms. They are confident that they treat all their students the same. However, many teachers who analyze their own attitudes and behaviors discover the subtle and pervasive nature of gender inequity in the classroom.

A common response from teachers when asked about gender inequity in class rooms is that they treat all their students the same. There are two problems with this statement. First, students are diverse and have different learning issues, thus treating all students in the same way means that some students will have a better learning experience than their peers. Second, teachers may be ignoring their unconscious gender biases towards their students, their schools and themselves. If ignored, these gender biases, which may have developed from cultural norms, may lead to bias in the classroom.

Gender Bias in Dropouts

There is a gap in enrolment in schools of girl students when compared to boys. Parents seeing limited (economic) benefits in educating daughters, lack of women teachers and separate schools for girls, supportive facilities (like adequate and clean toilets in schools) and transport facilities to travel to school and back, all these inhibit parents from getting their girls enrolled. Girls have to stay at home once they attain puberty and must be protected till they are married. And they become part of another family, leaving the parental home. Add to this, the commonly held belief that marriage is the be-all and end-all for girls, leading to early marriage and pregnancy. So naturally the son is sent to the school, not the daughter which we call it as gender bias in school enrollment. The school alone cannot be blamed for this pity condition of enrolment.

The above reasons also result in high dropout rates at (upper) primary stage. So, there is a gap in retention of girls in schools, even if they enroll at the primary stage. In many places in the rural areas where there are primary schools, there is no scope for studying further as there are no schools having upper primary and secondary sections and girls are not sent to far away schools because of this. Fear of the girl child and vulnerability is often the only reason given. The other factor to be taken into account is that are there enough opportunities for girls to achieve their full potential in the way boys do in the education system. Often there are unrecognized, unintended and unknown biases in the minds of the teachers, administrators and peers in schools, which inhibit girls. For girls in rural areas and from deprived castes, communities and tribes and for handicapped girls, all the above problems are accentuated much more than in the case of boys because of dual or multiple disadvantages. It is well-known that two thirds or more of our women are illiterate and less than half of them are educated up to the primary level.

Gender Bias in Household Responsibilities

The gender discrimination in schools is an extension of what we think in the family, in society and in the community in which we live. Unless there is camaraderie, dignity and partnership among the members of and within the family, it is difficult to expect the school to create it artificially in the school environment, and to pursue it without reference to what is happening in society. There has to be a democratic environment in the home for the child to be democratic in his/her lifestyle. Any programme of gender discrimination elimination in educational institutions must take into confidence, the parents and guardians and undoubtedly the teachers (both men and women), for whom there must be continuous programmes orienting them to equality in thought and deed. Persons in the community and the media have to be involved, for the programme touches the lives of children outside of schools. It cannot succeed if pursued in the school alone. Male and female are two wings of the society. Development of the society is not possible without balance (equal growth, equal development, equal opportunity etc.) between them. Continuous neglect of one is the silent killer of another. Most of the parents do not give equal opportunity to their female child. Though, equal opportunity to all is one of the fundamental rights in India. However, till now females are not getting equal opportunity within the family. Therefore, there is a reason behind intra household gender discrimination. The reason is, purely, "selfishness" of the parents.

Social Attitudes towards Girl's Education

The social barriers and social attitudes standing in the way of girls attending schools—poverty, compulsions of older girls in families having to look after the home and siblings, the conception or misconception that girls do not need education and/or that what is taught in schools is irrelevant to them. Marriage is the be-all and end-all for girls. So, naturally the son is sent to the school, not the daughter.

There are two extreme types of parental and social attitude / behavior—perfect altruistic and perfect capitalistic (or selfishness). If parents are perfectly altruistic about their child then both the types of child are equally welcome in the family. The share of the family cake will be identically equal for both male and female child. Investment for human capital accumulation will be same for both the types of child. If parents are altruistic then social norm has no influence on behavior of the parents towards their child. On the other hand, if parents are perfectly capitalistic then they try to get what can give maximum returns. Then they always try to invest on that very project from where they can get maximum returns. In India social norm sets male child remain with the parents when female child goes to second home (husband home) after marriage. Therefore, parents (when child matures) can get the returns from male child but not from the female child, due to social norm. Therefore, as a rational capitalist, parents welcome only male child. As human capital is the potential of earning, parents invest only on the male child for human capital accumulation. They do not spend anything on their girl child rather they assign some duties so she herself covers spending on her food. Therefore, such parents welcome only male child in the family. However sex of the new born child is determined by the invisible hand. Therefore ex-post outcome is girl child labour and education to male.

Value accorded to Women's Education

Women of present are much liberated than the past. The status of woman has undergone a great change today. They are making sincere efforts to rise in all spheres of life. Women have proved to be more responsible and work with greater dedication. No country can achieve development without educating her women. An educated woman can perform her duties with better efficiency. She can run her family in a better manner and can help her children in their studies also. Moreover, if a woman is educated she is treated with respect. She has not to lead a life of dependence on men, Education fills her with confidence and she is able to win her due place in society.

Today, government has become aware that female education is as important as that of men. A Sanskrit shaloka says that *"a woman is under the guardianship of her father before marriage, dependent on her husband after her marriage and on her son after the death of her husband."* But, this attitude of treating a woman as a ward or a dependent has been in existence for centuries. But now all these have been changing rapidly. With the spread of education women have now begun to claim equality with men.

Women education has given a number of opportunities. Today, more and more woman is taking up jobs. The time has come when they are working for their enlistment. They are making sincere efforts to raise themselves in all spheres of life. Many male bastions have been broken by women who are now pilots, scientists, engineers, astronauts and so on.

Today, they are able to raise their voice for reservation of seats not only in colleges and offices, but also in the parliament.

Issues related to Gender in School

The socialization of gender within our schools to some extent ensures that girls are made aware that they are unequal to boys. There is some evidence that girls are becoming academically more successful than boys, however examination of the classroom shows that girls and boys continue to be socialized in ways that work against gender equity. Teachers socialize girls towards a feminine ideal. Girls are praised for being neat, quiet, and calm, whereas boys are encouraged to think independently, be active and speak up. Girls are socialized in schools to recognize popularity as being important and learn that educational performance and ability are not as important. In this way, lot of issue creating a gender bias in schools. Some of the issues related to gender in schools are discussed below:

Sexual Abuse: Abuse is defined as "to ill-use, to misuse, or to insult." Adults use children to meet their own sexual needs and gratification.

Table 21.1: Indicators of Sexual Abuse

Sexual Abuse	
Physical Indicators	**Behavioral Indicators**
Itching or pain in the genital area	Eating disorders
Vaginal discharge	Fear of someone
Infection	Changes in attitude
Anal bleeding	Self-harm or suicide attempts
Pregnancy	Becomes aggressive

Child sexual abuse is a form of child abuse in which a child is abused for the sexual gratification of an adult or older adolescent. It includes direct sexual contact, the adult or otherwise older person engaging indecent exposure (of the genitals, female nipples, etc.) to a child with intent to gratify their own sexual desires or to intimidate or groom the child, asking or pressuring a child to engage in sexual activities, displaying pornography to a child, or using a child to produce child pornography. Effects of child sexual abuse include shame and self-blame, depression, anxiety, post-traumatic stress disorder, self-esteem issues, sexual dysfunction, chronic pelvic pain, addiction, self-injury, suicidal ideation, borderline personality disorder, and propensity to re-victimization in adulthood. Child sexual abuse is a risk factor for attempting suicide. Much of the harm caused to victims becomes apparent years after the abuse happens. Sexual abuse by a family member is a form of incest, and results in more serious and long-term psychological trauma, especially in the case of parental incest.

Sexual Harassment: Harassment is conduct, gestures or comments which are insulting, intimidating, humiliating, hurtful, malicious, degrading or otherwise offensive to an individual or group of individuals, and which create a hostile or intimidating environment for work or sports activities, or which negatively affect performance or work conditions.

Sexual harassment is a form of prohibited harassment. It is defined as unwelcome sexual advances, requests for sexual favors and other verbal or physical conduct of a sexual nature. The definition also encompasses unwelcome display or communication of sexually offensive materials.

Examples of Sexual Harassment

- Verbal comments
- Obscene or sexually explicit media contact
- Non-verbal actions
- Physical touching
- Unwanted requests to perform sexual acts or sexual favors

Forms of Harassment Relationships: Sexual harassment may occur in a variety of circumstances in workplaces as varied as factories, school and academia. Often, but not always, the perpetrator is in a position of power or authority over the victim (due to differences in age, or social, political, educational or employment relationships) or expecting to receive such power or authority inform of promotion. Forms of harassment relationships include:

1. The perpetrator can be anyone, such as a client, a co-worker, a parent or legal guardian, relative, a teacher or professor, a student, a friend, or a stranger.
2. The victim does not have to be the person directly harassed but can be a witness of such behavior who finds the behavior offensive and is affected by it.
3. The place of harassment occurrence may vary from school, university, workplace and other.
4. There may or may not be other witnesses or attendances.
5. The perpetrator may be completely unaware that his or her behavior is offensive or constitutes sexual harassment or may be completely unaware that his or her actions could be unlawful.
6. The incident can take place in situations in which the harassed person may not be aware of or understand what is happening.
7. The incident may be one time occurrence but more often it has a type of repetitiveness.
8. Adverse effects on the target are common in the form of stress and social withdrawal, sleep and eating difficulties, overall health impairment, etc.

9. The victim and perpetrator can be any gender.
10. The perpetrator does not have to be of the opposite sex.

Perception of Safety at School, Home and Community Schools

Schools are at the frontline of child protection since they have the potential to both teach protective behaviors effectively and to a greater number of children than any other system, including parental instructions. This is because a large part of the truly "awake" time of a child is spent at school. Besides, educators have a special role in combating child sexual abuse, as they possess the knowledge, training and opportunity to observe and respond to children's behaviour and physical conditions over a period of time. Moreover, due to daily close contact they are in a unique position to identify these children who need help and protection.

Strategy of Schools to Prevent Child Abuse or Preventive Safety Steps at Schools

The following way schools should prevent the child abuse in their circumstances.

1. Ensure teachers, volunteers and anyone else with access to children is properly screened and trained.
2. Implement and enforce a policy for reporting child sexual abuse and handling disclosures from children.
3. Establish protocols and screening for school computer use. Provide training to students and teachers on acceptable use of computers.
4. Assess your environmental structure and take every possible step to make it safer for children.
5. Make certain campus security is in place so that all visitors are screened through the office and the unusual incidents/visitors are handled.
6. Provide programmes and roles for parents to make them a part of their children's safety and security at school and while going to and from school.
7. Choose or develop child-safety programmes that are based on accepted educational theories, appropriate for the child's age and levels of education and development. And these are designed to offer concepts that will help children in building self-confidence in order to handle better and protect themselves in all types of situations. Use multiple program components that are repeated several years and use qualified presenters who include role-playing, behavioral rehearsal, feedback and active participation in presentations.
8. Safety planning and design for women and girls is important because it creates public spaces where women and all users have equal

opportunity to be healthy, secure and happy. This kind of planning is based on the fact that the physical design of urban spaces affects women's use and enjoyment of the public realm.

9. Safety planning and design for girls around the world, exercising their right to education can be full of risk. They are at risk from violence on the journey to and from school and in the classroom itself. This violence may take the form of aggressive sexual behaviour, intimidation and physical assault by boys, sexual advances by male students and teachers, corporal punishment and verbal abuse.

Home

Parents are the most important adult in child's life and to whom child looks up. We understand that parents do care for their children and whil econcerned about their safety, unfortunately cannot ensure it always. But they can equip themselves with information and skills to build self-protective behavior among their wards. The most important factor for children's protection is a strong self-esteem. Let them know how important they are toyou. Be available when they need to talk. Be honest and open with them when they ask difficult questions. And always believe what your child tells you, no matter how unbelievable or difficult to believe it is. Talking about child sexual abuse with your child may seem difficult, but the possible consequences of not talking with your child are even worse - that they might be sexually abused and do not know where to turn for help.

Strategy to Prevent Child Abuse or Preventive Safety Steps

At Home

The following are some of the preventive safety in our children life.

Encourage Kids to talk about their Day: Children cannot be expected to understand when it is okay to say "no" to or run away from an adult. This would be too confusing. Instead, build trust by regularly talking to them about their day. Make them feel comfortable raising any topic. Then, if your kids report any unacceptable behavior by others to you, it is your responsibility to take action.

Become Educated on Sexual Abuse: Get familiar with the facts. It is vital for you to educate yourself about sexual abuse.

Look for "Red Flags.": Sex offenders often "groom" parents and children to gain their trust. They can be very slick and fool you into thinking they are trustworthy, but there is always a "red flag" that is just a little bit unusual. For instance, if an adult has many toys and video games in his house and several local kids go there every day, this is a possible red flag. If he doesn't seem to have any adult friends or activities, this is a bigger red flag. Check this person out. Have a conversation with him, if possible. If he is on the sex offender registry, report him to the authorities.

Know Where Your Children Are and Who They are With at All Times: Know your children's friends and their parents. Make sure they are reliable before you allow your child to spend time at their house.

Teach Children that the Danger May come From Someone they Trust: Tell your kids, "Bad touch is bad touch and no one gets to do it to our bodies. If anyone does bad touch, you go to a grown up for help. When you are not sure about whether something a grown up is doing is okay, ask another grown up to help you."

In Community

Community also influences lot the development of surrounding children's growth. The following are some of roles of community to prevent the child abuse:

Know: Learning more about child rights and child sexual abuse can help you ensure the safety of children in your family, your neighborhood and your community

Talk: Talk to your colleagues, friends, relatives and family about the problem. Help break the silence around child sexual abuse.

Observe: Be alert to the behavioral and physical indicators of sexual abuse in children. Don't just hear children's voices, listen to them.

Help: If you suspect a child of being abused, assist the child.

Advocate: Ask your child's school to incorporate personal safety curriculum and to implement a school child protection policy.

Involve: Volunteer your time and resources to organizations working against child sexual abuse.

Adult and Non-Formal Education for Women's Development

Adult education is a practice in which adults engage in systematic and sustained self-educating activities in order to gain new forms of knowledge, skills, attitudes, or values. It can mean any form of learning adults engage in beyond traditional schooling, encompassing basic literacy to personal fulfillment as a lifelong learner. In particular, adult education reflects a specific philosophy about learning and teaching based on the assumption that adults can and want to learn, that they are able and willing to take responsibility for that learning, and that the learning itself should respond to their needs.

Driven by what one needs or wants to learn, the available opportunities, and the manner in which one learns, adult learning is affected by demographics, globalization and technology. The learning happens in many ways and in many contexts just as all adults' lives differ.

Importance of Vocational Training and Income Generation for Women

Education and training are essential components of any strategy to improve agricultural and non-farm productivity and rural incomes. Learning about improved production technologies and methods, new products and markets, business skills, as well as life skills (such as health management, decision-making, self-confidence, or conflict management) can make a big difference for many of the rural poor, particularly the women folk. Women often have different training needs than men since they are more likely to work as contributing family workers, subsistence farmers, home-based micro-entrepreneurs, or low-paid seasonal labourers, in addition to handling their domestic work and care responsibilities.

Skills developmentis a key to improving household productivity, employability and income-earning opportunities for women and also for enhancing food security and promoting environmentally sustainable rural development and livelihoods. Vocational Education and Training (VET) is important as it enriches a person for life and it provides the competencies which are necessary in a democratic society. Rural women are more benefitted if they can make use of the available opportunities in vocational education and training.

Gender Equality

Gender equality, also known as sex equality, gender egalitarianism, sexual equality, or equality of the genders, is the view that everyone should receive equal treatment and not be discriminated against based on their gender. Gender equality is achieved when women and men enjoy the same rights and opportunities across all sectors of society, including economic participation and decision making, and when the different behaviours, aspirations and needs of women and men are equally valued and favoured. The following sections deals about the roles of various stakeholders in reinforcing gender equality in the school environment.

Role of Schools in Reinforcing Gender Equality

The gender inequities pervading society are carried into the school environment. This is evidenced in school processes such as teaching, teacher–student interaction, school management, and the plan and design of the physical infrastructure. Teaching and learning materials, for example, may contain gender stereotypes. Teachers are not always aware of the gender specific needs of both girls and boys. School management systems may not sufficiently address gender constraints such as sexual harassment, and many schools do not have adequate or separate toilets for girls and boys. As a result, the schools do not provide a gender responsive environment for effective teaching and learning to take place. In order to arrive at such a school, a holistic approach involving various interventions is required. The holistic intervention package can include the following elements:

1. Undertaking gender sensitization of parents, community leaders and members, teachers, girls and boys in order to raise their awareness and understanding of the need to support girls' education.
2. Training teachers in the skills for making teaching and learning processes responsive to the specific needs of girls and boys.
3. Empowering girls with skills for self-confidence, assertiveness, speaking out, decision making and negotiation in order for them to overcome gender-based constraints to their education.
4. Empowering boys with skills to de-link from gender oppressive attitudes and practices such as macho-ism, bullying and sexual affronts and to develop the self-confidence needed to accept gender equality positively.
5. Training the school community to manage sexual maturation issues of both girls and boys with particular emphasis on menstruation management.
6. Training teachers and students in guidance and counselling skills.
7. Establishing guidance and counselling desks in order to provide services for the social and psychological development of girls and boys.

Ideas to Promoting Gender Equity in Schools

The following are some of ideas to promoting gender equity in schools:

1. Establish an award to recognize children who promote equity
2. Do a play about gender equity in school
3. Write an equity column or article in the paper
4. Organize a walk, race, or athletic event for equity
5. Honor people who foster gender equity in their work and life spirit
6. Develop posters that promote equity
7. Create a videotape on gender equity
8. Reformulate or construct an equitable workplace
9. Monitor a school or district for equity
10. Award a gender equity scholarship
11. Present an equity workshop at a conference
12. Observe classrooms to detect bias in interactions
13. Manage an equity booth at a toy, computer, or grocery store

Role of Peers in Reinforcing Gender Equality

Like teachers, peers contribute to the socialization of gender difference via multiple Pathways. Upon entering school, children encounter large numbers of peers, many of whom model traditional gender behaviour, producing and reinforcing the content of gender stereotypes. In addition, schools are characterized by gender segregation. When many peersare available, children tend to select same-sex playmates. Children's gender segregation, in turn, affects their play experiences, leading them to spend more time in stereotypic play. Furthermore, gender segregation predicts children's future conformity to gender stereotypes. Peers also contribute to gender differentiation by teaching their classmates stereotypes (e.g. "Short hair is for boys not girls") and punishing them for failing to conform to stereotypes via verbal harassment and physical aggression. Importantly, intervention programmes can teach young children to recognize and challenge their peers's exist remarks (e.g., "You can't say girls can't play!"). Peer group influence begins in pre-school and continues as children progress through school and expand their social world. This influence reinforces activities involved in play, academic success, popularity, body image, and dress and continues through out the life cycle.

Role of Teachers in Reinforcing Gender Equality

Teachers play a crucial role in every classroom. They are the actors who shape the success or failure of their students. Their interpretation of the curriculum, interaction with learners, and way they assign duties and homework, are important factors in a child's schooling. The following are some of the role of teachers to reinforcing gender equality.

1. Teachers and teacher-educators should examine their syllabuses with the view of incorporating a gender dimension by: including the introductory themes on gender; and by exploring gender issues within some of the topics of existing syllabus.
2. Teacher educators themselves be gender sensitive through gender awareness and sensitization programmes.
3. Teacher educators and teachers should employ engendered patterns of classroom organization and interaction,
4. Teacher educators and teachers should engendered teaching approaches be employed.
5. Capacity building centres should be established in all educational regions intended to train teachers and teacher educators in gender-laden education.
6. Teachers and teacher educators should be:

- conducting workshops,
- introducing gendered classroom organization and interaction;
- introductory lessons on gender;
- focus on gender issues within the existing syllabus topics;

- introducing gender issues career guidance;
- analyzing gender issues in instructional materials and
- conducting research projects on gender issues.

Role of Curriculum and Textbooks in Reinforcing Gender Equality

In schools and colleges, the curriculum is usually full, which means it is not easy to integrate a gender equity perspective in the design, content and teaching approaches of the many subjects that teachers may have to cope with. Moreover, curricula are often developed by experts and owned' by the state, so it is difficult to lobby for change where this might be seen to challenge governmental control. But, where diversity is recognized and participatory processes are employed, women and girls from different backgrounds can participate in discussions about curricula decisions and how they are represented — considering that they are diverse groups. When considering how teaching and the curriculum can be made gender-equitable, the following areas need attention:

Curriculum Content: There is need to consider what girls from poor, and marginalized environments, are offered by their schooling, and to provide, for example, literacy learning in a way that enhances their confidence, so that they can begin to transform their lives.

Learning Methods: Often, images in text-books are simply 'check-listed for their portrayal of gender images. Children do not necessarily have simplistic, preconditioned responses to images in text-books, and need a more sophisticated understanding of and response to how children learn about gender text-books.

Language of Instruction and Literacy: Children who are geographically or culturally marginalized from mainstream education may find themselves being taught in a language that they do not use. Girls and women often have less access to, and use of national "prestige" language than men.

Methods of Evaluation and Assessment: Examinations tend to dominate assessment, but other methods should be used, such as continuous assessment. In addition, "girls could have more equal opportunities in school if teachers talk to them more and encourage them, for instance by giving them more prizes for participating in different classroom activities". For teaching and the curricula to be gender equitable in schools, it is important to properly educate teachers on gender quality teaching through the courses and practical materials that are provided.

The curriculum, and ways of teaching and learning, can reproduce ideas and practices marked by gender inequality. Gender inequalities and wider social, political and economic inequalities, can influence the access that girls and boys have to different parts of the curriculum. Teachers' awareness of, and approaches to gender issues in teaching and learning, are crucial if gender-equitable education is to be achieved. Curriculum content, the relationship between teachers and students, and teacher-education, require special attention and policy development if gender-equitable education is to be achieved. Government and other relevant stakeholders:

1. Ensure that curriculum development involves consultation at all levels of society about gender equality, and what decisions mean for women and girls, especially those who may be marginalized because of language, social practice or environmental degradation.
2. Develop and implement government-agreed standards for quality and equality in education.
3. Ensure that there are strong legal measures to outlaw sexual violence and harassment in schools, with clear procedures for dealing with abuse, winch are widely communicated.
4. Ensure that training in gender equality is included in the teacher-education programme, both in pre-service training and in-service school-based, college-based training or university-based training.
5. Develop capacity and role of the inspectorate and gender units to support gender equality in the classroom at all levels of educational institutions.
6. Assess the planning and budgeting processes and ensure that officials at all levels of education have the capacity to implement them. Put in place any necessary training enquired to achieve this.

22
Gender Issues in Curriculum

Education is an integral part of the arrangements that govern children's lives. Thus, in order to achieve substantive and equal citizenship, special curricular and pedagogic strategies have to be developed to empower children, specially girls, to overcome disadvantages and develop their capabilities to exercise their rights and choices. The aim is to achieve a substantive equality of outcome, not merely a formal equality of treatment. In fact, we may even require inequality of treatment, i.e. special treatment for the socially disadvantaged learners, to enable them to achieve equality of outcome.

The ultimate aim of a progressive gendered project of education is to propel the learner from individual to collective transformation, towards achieving substantive citizenship. Thus, the objective is to enable girls to graduate from individual empowerment to becoming autonomous and equal citizens who play an active role in transforming the collective life of a democracy; so while developing the individual capabilities of girls to claim their rights, education should also foster in the young a deepened understanding of, commitment to, and capability to uphold the constitutional values of justice, equality, citizenship and freedom at the collective level.

Knowledge, as it has been shaped in every discipline, and through language itself, normalizes, and establishes as "natural", the inequalities of gender. The critical challenge is of deconstructing such paradigms, and of redressing the iniquities in the very construction of knowledge. Contemporary scholarship in virtually every discipline is now marked by significant research on gender issues. This has had deep implications for what is seen as knowledge, and how learning is viewed. School education should be updated in keeping with such research, and incorporate the critically gendered dimensions of knowledge in each discipline to transform the ways in which all subjects are approached and taught in schools.

Commitment to a critical reassessment of the hierarchical constructions of knowledge would logically translate into more analytical, participatory and pro-active pedagogical strategies in the classroom. Learner centered, experiential knowledge and reading against the grain become critical aspects of this approach, as do curricular and pedagogic practices, that equally reflect the life worlds of both girls and women, make visible the invisible, and carry within them the seeds of a just social transformation.

Such a pedagogical approach would be greatly enhanced by a teachers' needs too being viewed in relation to those of learners'. Critical reassessment of their own socialization would be an integral part of developing their own abilities as teachers if they are to be sensitive to the life-worlds of learners coming from diverse contexts. Innovative pedagogies have to be grounded not just in learning new games, songs and activities but developing in the teacher a conceptual and lived understanding of all that experiential knowledge and learning has to offer. In the final run it is not in monitoring teachers, but in enhancing training, and encouraging them to contribute to the shaping of critical, imaginative and innovative curricular and pedagogic process, that the real hope for transformation lies.

Curriculum and the Gender Question

The linkages between gender and curriculum are complex and challenging. School textbooks are a crucial component in the acquisition of knowledge and unless syllabi are revised to incorporate a gendered perspective–along with other marginalized perspectives–schooling will reproduce the narrow biases–and the narrow basis of mainstream social science knowledge. It is important to recognize that regardless of all the work produced by feminist scholars unless a gender perspective is incorporated in the syllabi each generation of children will absorb the biases of existing ways of understanding society and reproduce these ways of thinking into the future.

In context of the above, it is stated that gender inequality should be removed in various issues of gender relating to the aims of education, construction of knowledge, identify learning and pedagogy, curriculum, teacher education, science and mathematics, health, habitat and work education.

Curriculum

A gender-just and empowering curriculum should have the potential to enable students to critically engage with and challenge received knowledge about fixed gender identities. Insights from women's studies and the women's movement both in this country and in other parts of the world over the past twenty years have enriched our understanding of how education can form a part of this project of possibility. Experiences of literacy activists and those engaged in teaching women's studies at the university level show that it is possible to integrate gender into the curriculum, not as marginal or incidental but as critical to the content of different subject areas. The content itself can then be made to take on wider dimensions, involving various subject areas in the school curriculum.

Feminist critiques of knowledge also have the potential to influence more just and inclusive pedagogical practices and facilitate creation of "child-friendly" classrooms that empower students as well as teachers. They open up possibilities for gender inclusion in an integrated approach within and across different core academic areas of the school curriculum. Assuming that the evolutionary approach to education involves building upon experiences and thought structures that are familiar, the curriculum will have to be designed such that it helps the child critically understand her surroundings before recognizing and negotiating other contexts. The themes that become important in such a context will have to relate to work, body, sexuality, marriage, parenthood, family, caste, community, state, modernity, economy, violence, conflict, heterogeneity and hierarchy. These cross cut into language, social science and science As against the surfeit of information that is sought to be passed on to the student, the emphasis should be on introducing these issues and developing critical thinking through them. These themes could be taken up in each of the subjects that are taught at school at every stage. Complexity in thinking can be introduced as the stages advance. Higher stage here would therefore indicate strengthening of critical tools rather than accumulation of information.

Learning and Pedagogy

Teacher and student engagement is critical in the classroom because it has the power to define whose knowledge will become a part of school-related knowledge and whose voices will shape it. Students are not just young people for whom adults should devise solutions. They are critical observers of their own condition and needs and should be participants in discussions and problem solving related to their education and future opportunities. Hence, children need to be aware that their experiences and perceptions are important and be encouraged to develop their mental skills needed to think and reason independently. What children learn out of school – their capacities, learning abilities, and knowledge base – and bring to school is important to further enhance the learning process. This is all the more critical for children from underprivileged backgrounds, especially girls, as the worlds they inhabit and their realities are underrepresented.

If children's social experiences are to be brought into classrooms, it is inevitable that issues of conflict must be addressed. Conflict is an inescapable part of children's lives. They constantly encounter situations which call for moral assessment and action, whether in relation to subjective experiences of conflict involving the self, family and society, or in dealing with exposure to violent conflict in the contemporary world. Yet the official curriculum tends to legitimize a certain vision of society and its knowledge, a vision that is related to dominant discourses.

Learning about alternate ways of being – or ways of being that are usually made invisible or delegitimized – involves 'unlearning' gender, both at the individual and collective levels. To enable children to do this, the curriculum has to accommodate pedagogic strategies that deal with the idea of conflict, between what is observed and valued in contemporary society, in the social worlds that children inhabit, and what can be in a gender-just and less violent world. To use conflict as a pedagogic strategy is to enable children to deal with conflict and facilitate awareness of its nature and role in their lives.

Impact of Gender Question Related to Curriculum

Though there are many recommendations and committees set up on women education and curriculum set up for the purpose yet there are lot of dropout rates in schools relating to girls. There are many factors related to the above but the prime cause is the reason for gender inequality and poor thinking. To enhance this, the following measure should be taken such as--(a) Quality Education for girls and (b) Inclusive Education for girls. According to Sarva Siksha Abhiyan (SSA) education should be equal and for all but we are yet to observe how much it is still practiced.

The curriculum's presentation of gender relations is frequently based upon popular assumptions or upon ideas perpetuated by dominant groups. And it normally posits the male as the normative epistemic subject. It rarely takes into account the differentiated contributions, capacities and perspectives of women. We need to envisage a process of education that teaches the young to question such gender issues. It is imperative that we design creative interventions at the level of textbooks, curriculum and pedagogy, that moves towards a critique of all forms of gender control.

Role of Curriculum in Reinforcing Gender Issues

In schools and colleges, the curriculum is usually full, which means it is not easy to integrate a gender equity perspective in the design, content and teaching approaches of the many subjects that teachers may have to cope with. Moreover, curricula are often developed by experts and owned' by the state, so it is difficult to lobby for change where this might be seen to challenge governmental control. But, where diversity is recognized and participatory processes are employed, women and girls from different backgrounds can participate in discussions about curricula decisions and how they are represented — considering that they are diverse groups. When considering how teaching and the curriculum can be made gender-equitable, the following areas need attention.

Curriculum Content: There is need to consider what girls from poor, and marginalized environments, are offered by their schooling, and to provide, for example, literacy learning in a way that enhances their confidence, so that they can begin to transform theft lives.

Learning Methods: Often, images in textbooks are simply check-listed for their portrayal of gender images. Children do not necessarily have simplistic, preconditioned responses to images in textbooks, and need a more sophisticated understanding of and response to how children learn about gender textbooks.

Language of Instruction and Literacy: Children who are geographically or culturally marginalized from mainstream education may find themselves being taught in a language that they do not use. Girls and women often have less access to, and use of national "prestige" language than men.

Methods of Evaluation and Assessment: Examinations tend to dominate assessment, but other methods should be used, such as continuous assessment. In addition, "girls could have more equal opportunities in school if teachers talk to them more and encourage them, for instance by giving them more prizes for participating in different classroom activities". For teaching and the curricula to be gender equitable in schools, it is important to properly educate teachers on gender quality teaching through the courses and practical materials that are provided.

Make Curricula and Teaching More Gender Equitable: The curriculum, and ways of teaching and learning, can reproduce ideas and practices marked by gender inequality. Gender inequalities and wider social, political and economic inequalities, can influence the access that girls and boys have to different parts of the curriculum. Teachers' awareness of, and approaches to gender issues in teaching and learning, are crucial if gender-equitable education is to be achieved. Curriculum content, the relationship between teachers and students, and teacher-education, require special attention and policy development if gender-equitable education is to be achieved. Government and other relevant stakeholders:

1. Ensure that curriculum development involves consultation at all levels of society about gender equality, and what decisions mean for women and girls, especially those who may be marginalized because of language, social practice or environmental degradation.
2. Develop and implement government-agreed standards for quality and equality in education.
3. Ensure that there are strong legal measures to outlaw sexual violence and harassment in schools, with clear procedures for dealing with abuse, winch are widely communicated.

4. Ensure that training in gender equality is included in the teacher-education programme, both in pieservice training and in-service school-based, college-based training or university-based training.
5. Develop capacity and role of the inspectorate and gender units to support gender equality in the classroom at all levels of educational institutions.
6. Assess the planning and budgeting processes, and ensure that officials at all levels of education have the capacity to implement them. Put in place any necessary training required to achieve this.

Gender and the Hidden Curriculum

Gender is a social construct that impacts attitudes, roles, responsibilities and behavior patterns of boys and girls, men and women in all societies. Gender relations vary from society to society. It is a women's and people's issues shaped by power relations in multicultural societies like India. It deals with human concerns encompassing diversities and differences. It has been the most endemic form of discrimination operating across cultures in developed and developing societies. When one analyses the present context of gender discourses, the prime concern is how gender functions as a determinant of politics of knowledge production. Education has the inbuilt potential of initiating social change in the context of gender relations. Therefore, conscious and pluralistic interventions have been put forward by the Government of India to address gender equality in education at the centre and state level. A landmark initiative was undertaken in 1986, with the enactment of the National Policy on Education (NPE) and its revised POA 1992. This philosophy has also been reflected in the National Policy on Empowerment of Women 2001. The policy focuses on promoting gender sensitive curriculum for addressing gender discrimination at all levels of education. The new draft of National Policy lays emphasizes on "Encourage, Educate and Employ", all irrespective of their socio-economic background.

Gender concerns in education have also been reflected in curriculum frameworks developed by apex national organization like National Council of Educational Research and Training (NCERT). In this regard curriculum frameworks of 1975, 1988, 2000 and 2005 have made specific efforts to focus attention on gender disparities in education. The journey has been from concern to substantial inclusion.

While a lot of efforts have been made on integrating gender concerns in education; globalization, liberalization and expansion in information technology have once again made it mandatory for revisiting gender concerns in education in a proactive manner as an important developmental agenda.

There is now an emerging need to reflect and focus in a proactive manner on transforming attitudes, beliefs and behavioral patterns that impact gender relation in family, community, school and work place and so on. Gender debates and discourses have to be operationalised within the overarching concern for democratizing education. In this context, constitutional commitments, policy initiatives, schemes and programmes have been conceptualized by Centre and State Governments at different points of time to address gender barriers in education.

Hidden Curriculum

Hidden curriculum is an important component of diverse schooling process operating across our country. It is an integral part of all activities that take place within and outside classrooms that are learned but not openly intended. Hidden curriculum is related to the transmission of norms, values, beliefs and behavior that either reinforces existing social and cultural ethos of the society or attempts to question and critique them. In the context of gender, it either perpetuate unequal power relations operating among gender, or help in evolving methods of questioning it and thereby becoming an important equalizing agency for addressing paradoxes between policies on gender equality in education and practices. Different aspects of learning that contribute to the success of hidden curriculum are practices, procedures, rules, relationship and structure operating in different types of schools. Unintended learning can result from interactions with educational administrators, teachers, peers and other functionaries that play a crucial role in overall personality development. The important visible sites that reflect hidden curriculum are pedagogical processes, classroom management and all curricular activities that take place in schools.

According to NCERT, "curriculum encompasses the essential and appropriate knowledge taught in schools. It involves the praxis of policy as well as the syllabi used in the teaching-learning process. Teaching and learning materials, classroom practices, evaluation and assessment procedures and language policy are all components of curriculum are 'learned' in school. It demands investigation of the contexts within which the children make meaning of, or responds to, these notions, through the filter of her/ his subjective experience while growing up as female/ male in society. While it is important to understand the ideologies underlying the presentation of gender in school textbooks, it is equally pertinent to examine how these ideologies are expressed at the level of everyday school practices and experiences, through what is often termed the 'hidden' curriculum."

Hidden Curriculum of Gender in Schools

1. Organizational arrangements (including the division of physical spaces within the classroom and the school a long lines of gender).
2. Differential task assignment and sexual division of labour in school (boys allowed to go out of school, girls sweep and clean).

3. Routines, rituals and practices in everyday school life (like segregated seating separate lines for girls and boys, or having them form separate teams).
4. Systems of rewards and punishments, disciplining of boys and girls through different strategies, teacher's labelling patterns, teacher-student and student-student interactions

Aspects of Hidden Curriculum

Some aspects of hidden curriculum are given below:

Language

Over a period of time, language has coded in its texture a large number of elements that perpetuate gender stereotypes. It is not just that many scholars, including some distinguished linguists, have described female speech as 'trivial' and 'a string of pearls' signifying nothing, but a substantial part of the lexicon and syntactic expressions encode gender-bias. Detailed analysis of male-female conversation has also revealed how men use a variety of conversational strategies to assert their point of view. The received notions of what it means to be 'masculine' or 'feminine' are constantly reconstructed in our behaviour and are, sometimes unwittingly perhaps, transmitted through our textbooks. In fact, the damage done by the 'gender construction of knowledge' is becoming Syllabus for Secondary and Higher Secondary Levels 146 increasingly obvious.

Language, including illustrations and other visual aids, plays a central role in the formation of such knowledge and we need to pay immediate attention to this aspect of language. It is extremely important that textbook writers and teachers begin to appreciate that the passive and deferential roles generally assigned to women are socio-culturally constructed and need to be destroyed as quickly as possible. Voices of women in all their glory need to find a prominent place in our textbooks and teaching strategies.

A teacher plays a critical and crucial role in promoting gender fair language. Language influences both thought and behaviour directly and indirectly. Teachers need to pay attention when engaged in communication with their learners. This comprises addressing learners, developing activities and materials for reference and using language in general while interacting with parents and the community.

Classroom Organization and Management

In India school and classrooms vary in many contexts. There are large and small size classrooms in the urban, semi-urban, and rural contexts. The classroom organization and management goes a long way in shaping gender relations. Several research studies over the years have clearly shown how the classroom environment can facilitate students learning and remove gender bias and stereotype. In fact, a gender friendly environment can easily be created by a teacher in any context. It just requires sensitivity and positive intent. A gender friendly classroom environment and its overall management can build harmonious relations between boys and girls at different stages of education. This can be done by adopting some of the suggestive measures:

1. To begin with teachers must define their roles as mentors and facilitators and not as instructors and knowledge experts aiming to disseminate information.
2. As a facilitator, the teacher should ensure that physical and social environment of the classroom promotes healthy relationships between boys and girls. Sitting arrangements and all activities should as far as possible be done in mix group in co-educational schools and in single sex, it should cut across class, caste, region and faith.
3. Equal participation of boys and girls in teaching learning process must be ensured.
4. For ensuring greater participation of girls, participatory activities like—role play, problem solving, and quiz etc must be adopted in the teaching of languages, social science and science.
5. Allocation of classroom duties should reflect gender neutrality. Boys and girls should participate equally in maintaining cleanliness, observing classroom decorum, decorating the class and conducting routine classroom chores.
6. The teacher must also entrust the responsibility of organizing classroom activities equally to both the sexes.
7. To develop effective oral communications skills, reading and recitation should be jointly assigned to boys and girls with correct pronunciation, voice modulation and expressions.
8. The teacher should be able to identify slow learners and organize appropriate remedial classes for them.
9. In the teaching learning process, special emphasis must be given to sharing of examples of women achievers who have contributed to different fields. This will help in attitudinal reconstruction.
10. The use of visual aids like pictures and puppets, depicting women working in fields along with men, in hospitals as doctors and nurses, sharing household chores with men etc. can also help to create gender inclusion and parity.
11. In the transaction of subjects like mathematics, sciences, social science and languages, care should be taken to include examples of both boys and girls, men and women drawn from different walks of life so that the message of equal capability gets highlighted.

12. The classroom culture should be built in a manner that interactions between boys and girls reflect mutual respect. The classroom ethos should be made open and supportive, so that both boys and girls feel free to share their personal experiences without apprehensions.
13. The concept of equality of sexes may be explained by elaborating on the intelligence and capabilities of girls and women. The teacher must also ensure equal participation of boys and girls in activities like drawing, painting, music and dance.

Gender in Text and Context

The National Curriculum Frame work (2005) document recognized that: "we must use text books as one of the primary instruments for equality, since for a great majority of school going children, as also for teachers, it is the only accessible and affordable resource for education".

The textual material that is developed for the school-going children is of paramount importance in education. It is the text book that they are exposed to in the class room, and the teacher conveys its meaning and interpretation, while embossing his / her own ideas on the minds of children, who are yet in the formative stage. This is one of the earliest and most important influences on the young, growing minds.

It is necessary and relevant to study and understand how gender is depicted in primary school text-books, because by age seven, and perhaps as early as age four, children begin to understand about the basic concept of self. Gender Schema Theory suggests that youngsters develop a sense of femaleness and maleness based on gender stereotypes and organize their behaviour around them.

Textbooks and Gender

In the Indian context textbooks are important repository of knowledge. It is an important teaching and learning material that teachers and students rely upon across the country. Implicit and explicit knowledge woven in textual materials pertain to the domain of social science, science, mathematics, languages and other emerging and applied fields of knowledge. The content of all disciplines are determined by experts, who de-limit it as per age, ability and level of understanding of children. In addition, books are part of the social milieu and they attempt to mirror social realities.

Therefore, some very crucial questions that arise in minds of all stakeholders are:

1. Do textbooks reflect social realties?
2. How do they address issues and concerns of different segments of society?

3. How are Gender relations portrayed in the content, visuals and exercises?
4. Are Human values woven in textbooks?
5. Do textbooks depict sensitivity towards the habitat?
6. Do they inculcate reading habits among children?

Since textual materials are pivotal sources of knowledge it is important that they include issues of equity and equality, as children both boys and girls from all segments of society access them. Therefore, portrayal of Gender relation and there contributions are important in the thematic selection pertaining to all disciplines and their portrayal in the visual depiction. Textual materials world over and in the Indian context have been analyzed from different perspectives including gender. A gender audit of textual material would help in knowing:

1. Whether textual materials relates to all disciplines address contributions and achievement of men and women in an adequate manner.
2. Whether textbooks reflect heterogeneous identities of all groups in an inclusive manner.
3. Whether textbooks bridge all segments of society related to gender, caste, class and religion and location.
4. Whether they assist in initiating transformatory attitudinal changes among learners.
5. Whether they help in addressing different forms of conflicts.
6. Whether they sensitize on promoting critical thinking among children for questioning stereotypes, myths and misconceptions and customary practices derogatory to the status of women.

Role of UNESCO in Promoting Gender Equality through Textbooks

In 2009, UNESCO prepared a guide manual titled *"Promoting Gender Equality through Textbooks: A Methodological Guide"*. The main aim for preparing this manual is to eradicate gender bias from the textbooks and to provide guidelines to prepare gender bias free curriculum throughout the world. Besides this, Department of Women's Study of NCERT also published two reports named "Text Books: an Important Variable in Girls' Education and Gender Equality (2006)" and "Gender Analysis of NCERT Primary Textbooks of Classes I to V: Overall Analysis (2013-14)".

Necessity of Textbooks

Textbooks allow access to all sorts of information. Not only do they develop the ability to read and write but they also encourage critical thinking, independence and creativity. For many pupils and their families, textbooks are the only introduction to the written word in homes where there are no books, whatever the reason: the culture, distribution or supply problems, cost, etc. Because the poorest children do not have access to teaching aids, they often face the greatest difficulties in learning. Thus access to textbooks is usually one of the first recommendations made by policy-makers.

For teachers, textbooks have been the basic – and sometimes only – teaching resource, extending their means of instruction, since textbooks contain the general components of the curriculum, structure the teaching sequence and form the basis of assessment. In fact, they may play a part in self-education and compensate for lack of teacher qualifications. In this respect, the teacher's handbook is a valuable contribution which strengthens the textbook's impact on pupils.

Textbooks: An Important Variable in Girls' Education and Gender Equality

Despite progress in the last decade, there is still much to be done to "eliminate gender disparities" and, even more, to achieve equality, especially in education. The crucial problem is girls' underachievement, measured by access to schools, academic performance and "survival" within the education system. Many factors hold back girls' education: the economic situation and low income, a family and social environment with traditional patriarchal structures, and operational failures in the education system (shortages of schools, teaching materials and teachers, sexual abuse of girls, and so on).

There is also a link between girls' underachievement and textbooks, to the degree that gender inequality and discrimination are reinforced by textbooks, whose power of legitimation is all the greater because they are a rare commodity:

1. Girls have fewer books than boys, since textbooks are expensive and in short supply;
2. The representations of both genders in textbooks, reinforced through teacher/pupil interaction with the teacher, continue to put girls at a disadvantage.

For these reasons, girls must have equal access to textbooks and gender representations must be changed. Teachers must also be trained to avoid contributing to the transmission of representations that convey inequality, whatever textbook is used.

Textbook: Intersectionality with other Disciplines

This concept is thought to have first emerged during the 1960s in relation to the development of a radical and multiracial feminist movement. It can be defined as the study or concept of discriminative or oppressive institution on minorities and the way these groups are interconnected. Theory of intersectionality is based on the concept that oppressive institution within society such as racism, casteism, sexism and homophobia do not act independently but instead inter-related and continuously shaped by one another.

Overall Gender Perception of Textbooks

The NCERT textbooks at the primary stage of Classes I to V are mostly gender inclusive. The content and the visuals in all textbooks depict a joyful learning experience. Visuals and themes in the textbooks can be broadly classified as gender inclusive, gender neutral and those that are specifically related to different character s drawn from established Classics in English language and literature, historical events and from contemporary times. The themes in all the textbooks encourage creativity, imagination and attempt to engage children in activities related to Mathematics, Languages and Environmental Studies. All the authors have tried to link the themes with the lived reality of the learner. Human values related to learning to live together, respecting diversities and differences, sharing and caring, valuing women's work, preservation and conservation of environment, religious tolerance and developing a critical perspective are all woven in the content portrayal and visual depiction. Inspirational stories of women role models are specially mentioned in Environmental Studies textbooks and few are also stated in language textbooks. A significant aspect of some of the textbooks is the questioning of customary practices such as child marriage, showing men/boys as emotional and boys/men sharing household chores, and in child rearing and caring practices. The visuals in nearly all the textbooks focus on continuity and change in terms of dresses, new and emerging roles of men and women and briefly also on use of communication technology. Culture and festivals as well as local games have also been referred to in the books related to Mathematics, Environmental Studies and Languages. The Teacher's Pages attempt to develop inclusive environment in the classroom by suggesting group work, project work, discussion and learning together.

While all the textbooks have attempted to highlight gender concerns there are elements of stereotypes in some textbooks. Men are shown mainly in a variety of professions whereas women are mainly shown as homemakers, teachers, nurses and doctors. In the English textbooks a large number of characters are men/ boys. Animals in the different themes of the textbooks are gendered. The language used promotes stereotypical qualities of femininity and masculinity. Men and women are shown in relational category in all textbooks

Teacher as an Agent of Change

Gender issues are prevailing in society in all areas of life. To minimize these gender issues we need to start changing the mindsets of the younger generation of society as they are those who can bring about further change in society, with their innovative ideas, thoughts and practices. To do this we need good educated teachers who have a sound knowledge regarding gender issues. It has been observed that teachers reinforce gender roles also in the different expectations that they have for boys and girls in their classes. We all grow up among the influence of our family and cultures, and as teachers, we may see ourselves, rightly, in the role of instilling cultural values in the children in our classes as in.

Teachers play a very important part in the early upbringing of the child and their ideas and beliefs can change the thought patterns of young students. A teacher must therefore constantly be aware of the fact that his or her actions/ attitude/ behavior/ perspective/ approach/ manner/ outlook/ mind-set will help to shape a child's gender role. He/ she may use multiple strategies and interventions to ensure that students have equal opportunities to both create and obtain their goals. Studies have shown gender differences to have a direct relationship to preferential treatment, classroom dynamics and academic success.

Qualities of a Gender Responsive Teacher

- Teachers are required to be serious about the gender issue.
- For the teachers to bring about a change in the society they should be given pre hand knowledge over the issue.
- Teachers need not only gender sensitive curricula and textbooks but also gender equality education.
- Teachers can serve as role models for the students.
- Teacher thus becomes a mere transactor of knowledge rather than a creator of knowledge.
- The school teacher need to plays an important role in maintaining, modifying and reshaping her understanding of location, in terms of her class, caste, gender, religion, sexuality and region.
- In the present scenario, where a significant number of children belonging to diverse groups bring with them a variety of cultural practices, knowledge systems and ways of seeing, an understanding of identity becomes critical for the teacher.

Teacher as Facilitator

The teacher's role is to provide a safe space for children to express themselves and simultaneously to build in certain forms of interactions. While consolidating and constructively pushing the limits of the learner's understanding he/she needs to be conscious of how differences are expressed. An atmosphere of trust would make the classroom a safe space where children can share experiences, where conflict can be acknowledged and constructively questioned, and where resolutions, however tentative, can be mutually worked out. A space where they can practice democratic ways of interacting with each other and build skills to negotiate with conflicts outside the school. For girls in particular, schools and classrooms should be spaces to discuss processes of decision making, to interrogate the basis of their decisions and to make informed choices.

The construction of the female learner as passive may act against her within participatory teaching and learning contexts. In our schools, where gender-based constructions under pin ideas of classroom discipline and strict divisions are maintained between girls and boys, a girl who is interactive is likely to be pulled up for transgressing the 'gender code'. Clearly, there needs to be a rethinking of the agency of the learner in the classroom context. This re-conceptualization has to become an organic part of the way we think of education today and find a prominent place in teacher training programmes.

What kinds of practical outcomes are likely to arise from such pedagogy? These will differ in different educational settings (by location, background of learners, and also different subjects). However, we are likely to see: changes to curriculum and to classroom organization which allow for increased participation of girls and women (and other under-represented groups of students); encouragement of questioning the curriculum and what counts as school knowledge; breaking down of hierarchies and power networks that exclude girls and women, whether as pupils or teachers; greater understanding of the conditions which lead to bullying, racism and sexism, and homophobic behaviour, and more successful forms of intervention; greater valuing of pupils' experience and knowledge, and closer involvement of students in planning and evaluating their educational work; increased critical consciousness among students and ability to challenge narrowed conceptions, prejudices and stereotypes; to make informed choices.

To be a proper teacher educator and as a change agent the following guidelines should be kept in mind:

1. Girls and boys should be encouraged to sit together.
2. Co-curricular activities should not be gender biased.
3. Games and sports should not be gender biased.
4. The subjects as well as the examples taught by the tea her should not be gender biased. For examples, subjects like Political Science, Economics etc. have examples of male but the teacher should also point out the examples of their female counterparts.
5. While questioning in a class the boys and the girls should get the equal opportunity

23
Gender and Mass Media

The mass media plays a vital role in social change in any society. The important types of mass media are newspaper, magazine, television, film, advertisement and internet. It is under the influence of the mass media that women restricted within the four walls of the house have come to know about the world. Also, they are working in diverse fields of mass media shoulder to shoulder with men in capacities like journalists, newsreaders, film directors, writers and media executives. This type of participation has led to bring about a change in the society. According to Dr. Anita Arya, women have always played a vital role in the traditional media which included puppetry, folk drama, folk song, folk tales and the like, and their topics have revolved around women and their problems. The conventional folk arts have always presented a strong woman personality; while on the other hand, women have been presented as a stereotype in the role of a mother, wife or daughter.

Women as Depicted in Mass Media

According to Jo Bryant, media can play both positive and negative roles in the presentation of women's condition and image. The media is a powerful tool of education and socialization. While on the one hand, the media has raised the women issues prominently; it has, on the other, also presented a negative image of the women, due to which violence against women has increased.

Such instances include pornography and vulgar presentation of the women's body shown in the media. When we look in detail, we find that the media possesses a narrow viewpoint so far as women are concerned. Its method of their presentation has been such that confirms the stereotyped gender roles, in which women are displayed as wife, mother or midwife, especially in advertisements. For example, a women office-goers is also shown feeling anxious what she has to cook at home after work.

Women in Cinema/Films

All cultural media, whether they are theatre, art or architecture, present the moral and approved structure of the society. The media is influenced by the social values on the one hand, and on the other, it also works to challenge the established social values and carve out a new image. Thus, it is a two-way process by which both society and media are affected. The viewers are profoundly influenced by what they see on the screen. There are only few films in which women are shown as an independent personality; mostly they are stereotyped as wife, mother and sister in their conventional roles.

Portrayal of Women on Television

Most of daily soaps and serials telecast on television are women-based, yet they appear to be treading the orthodox path. In all family soaps, women are shown renouncing, forgiving and forbearing who can go to any extent in order to defend the values of the family and society. Sometimes, there are villain women too who are bent upon destroying the family life because something bad has been done to them previously.

As against films, women are not depicted as sex objects on television; rather they are assigned important roles. The following characteristics can be observed in the roles assigned to women in television soaps:

1. Most women characters, whether married or single, are homely.
2. Working women work only because of some trouble, and they are often shown unhappy with the work.
3. For women, marriage is portrayed like a very natural and essential situation. If a character is unmarried, she is shown making an attempt to marry; and if she is a widow/divorced, she is shown to be unhappy, despite the fact of her success in the profession; yet they are shown gloomy owing to their single status.
4. Women are presented in an ideal form when shown in relation to men, they are dependent and cooperative, and it is not desirable for them to possess independent views.
5. The women who break family bonds in the society or family are not shown to be happy ultimately. Most serials portray women as dependent on men, in which good wives do not raise their voice against ill-treatment, and husbands often bring the second wife because the first wife is unrefined or impolite. The husband is worshipped, so is the sacred bond of Mangalsutra (the sacred thread/jewellery worn round the neck by a Hindu married woman), and those who put on jeans and skirts are against the Indian traditions and customs, and are immoral. The focus of the directors and producers of such films is the homely women, and they conveniently forget that what women view on the screen goes

on to form a public opinion. Women too appear to be following these soaps without using their reason or logic.

Portrayal of Women in Advertisements

After films and television, it is advertisements that influence the most, in which women are much propagated. The focus of most advertisements is women and children who form the chunk of consumers. Even those products which are meant for men, like truck tyres or auto, women models are used in abundance. There are a number of gender discriminative advertisements as of men's fairness creams or scent or deodorants by the smell/attraction of which women are spellbound and such a theme is common to almost all of them. There are also advertisements in which the mother is anxious to know how to bring up her children or how a young woman can control her husband; and girls are often shown making a bid to fascinate men who wear a particular suits, shoes and ties or drive a particular type of car. Women are shown to be attracted to such products in a bid to promote them among men, though they have little concern with women. Much emphasis is laid on gender identity of women, by which her image, role and status is down graded in the society.

Portrayal of Women in Print Media

At present, the issues and news concerning women are prominently published, but it was not so in the beginning. The front page seldom carried a heinous crime, rape, murder or dowry death. Some newspapers published the 'women edition or page' and there is little earnest or serious concern about women in these. Women magazines are often elitist and generally they promote such values in which women are presented as a consumer product meant for men or family. There is seldom an image in which she is shown earning livelihood or is a scholar. In addition, the advertisements carried in these newspapers and magazines present women as sex symbols and doing different types of anti-women activities.

A subtle change is there these days, in which women are shown as career women and self-supporting individual, while men are also shown taking part in domestic duties and carrying out children's responsibilities.

Portrayal of Women on Internet

The internet is being used in the modern times to share day-to-day information and expand knowledge. Of course, it is also contributing to present a negative image of women, some people blackmail women after having obtained information about them from the net. There are several online service providers that make their private information public, as e-mail, phone number, home address and the like, which affects both men and women; however, women are more intensely affected by this.

Impact of Mass Media on Women

Women are affected by the mass media in several ways, the important ones being as follows:

1. The mass media is an important part of the socialization process and it is used to present in a stereotyped image. Moreover, emphasis is laid on her sexual image which hurts her personality.
2. The women's role as a partner in the society or economic activities is simply overlooked. It appears that she has no economic role in the society. This type of inference is quite baseless; but the fact remains that women form 20 per cent of the total workforce in the country, but this figure does not include those women who work without salary or wages, like at home, rural women in dairy industry, women working in fields. Thus, the media presents women as consumers and dependent (especially through advertisements and cartoons)
3. The media often works according to the needs of the male viewers. Therefore, women are not given much representation on issues even concerning women, as a consequence of which, women start to adopt the men's viewpoint, and they grow habitual of accepting the men's view as they see the world's affairs.

Therefore, the media, especially films and advertisements, should avoid from portraying the following:

1. Sex stereotyping.
2. Children being portrayed as strengthening this stereotyping (in which girls are shown copying the mother, and boys behave themselves as men).
3. Promoting improper marriage ideas.
4. Concluding that marriage and motherhood are the ultimate goals.
5. Showing women as followers and backbenchers; and showing them as dependent on men.
6. Promoting the products which enhance women's self-confidence, and claims that they are inferior and they need reform and security.
7. The advertisements which propagate that woman need men's greater and better knowledge and their guidance for even common tasks.

Indecent Representation of Women (Prohibition) Act, 1987

In India, this act was enforced to upgrade and improve the level of media so far as representation of women in the media is concerned. This law can be relevant in the issues concerning sexual harassment under the following provisions:

1. If an individual shows books, photographs, paintings, films, pamphlets etc., which depict women in an indecent way, he will be sentenced to aminimum of two years' imprisonment.
2. Under section 7 of the act, if a woman is presented in the company complex indecently, there is a provision of legal action against the company.
3. The National Commission for Women and the Women and Children Welfare Department have suggested some amendments to this act, which are as follows:

The title of the act should be changed from *'Indecent Representation of Women (Prohibition) Act'* to *'Derogatory and Indecent Representations of Women'* in addition to the following amendments:

- To amend section 2(a) to include the word 'advertisement' as inclusive of electronic and other media.
- To include section 2(g) which expands the sense of the word 'publish' which should comprise web services too.
- To include section 4 (A) under which the competent officials should be empowered to complain against scheduled voluntary organizations.
- To modify section 6 under which the punishment under the act should be made stricter.

Recommendations

There is need to have social awareness in the country for offering a change in the attitude towards women and girls. Besides, there is need to give women a space for their expression and participation in the decision-making process and free expression. Women should come forward to make their presence felt in different modes of the media, as print and electronic. The government too should form a working group of women in print and electronic media that should formulate the role and image of women to be presented in the media and also review the policies and laws regarding the media. All types of media workers and officials should be motivated to be sensitive to women issues and present their positive image.

Research should be encouraged in construction of gender perspective in the media. All consultative and management committees should be motivated to appoint women and men in a fixed ratio. The rules and regulations of the censor board should review the rules regarding indecent representation of women, and there is need to pay attention to the distinction between pornography and obscenity. The women working in electronic and other media should be encouraged and given recognition. All such films and advertisements that weaken the women's status and encourage stereotyping should be discouraged. An effort should also be made to remove all those negative images and examples present in textbooks and other instructional training materials in formal and non-formal education. The causes for lower reach of women to the media should be ascertained so that it can be ascertained which modes of the media have access to women. The theater writers and directors should be motivated not to show women in stereotyped roles, rather they should be motivated to present women as farmers, producers, managers etc. Also, they should invite open discussions on these issues.

The government can undertake the following steps in the direction of presenting women in a balanced and un-stereotyped role:

1. Such methods should be encouraged and research implemented which present women and girls in a balanced image in the fields of education, information and communication, and they should be depicted in multi-dimensional roles.
2. Gender sensitive training programmes should be held for media professionals, managers and owners so that they present women in the media in an unstereotyped, balanced and multi-dimensional roles.
3. The media should be motivated to abstain from presenting such an image in which women are presented as inferior, sexual objects; it should be motivated to present women in constructive roles, main roles and carrier of development.
4. This concept should be encouraged that the sexual stereotypes give birth to gender discrimination as shown in the media, and such an attempt is disrespecting and outrageous and scandalous.
5. Proper laws should be enacted for the media preventing it from displaying pornography and violence against women and children.

24

Gender Sensitization

Gender sensitization refers to the modification of behavior by raising awareness of gender equality concerns. This can be achieved by conducting various sensitization campaigns, workshop, programmes etc. Sensitization in the domain of Humanities and Social Sciences is seen an awareness informed propensity or disposition which aims at changing behavior so that it is sensitive to certain issues. Gender sensitization may be seen as *"the awareness informed disposition or propensity to behave in a manner which is sensitive to gender justice and equality issues."*

It is interlinked with gender empowerment. Gender sensitization theories claim that modification of the behavior of teachers and parents (etc.) towards children can have a causal effect on gender equality. Gender sensitizing *"is about changing behavior and instilling empathy into the views that we hold about our own and the other genders."* It helps people in examining their personal attitudes and beliefs and questioning the 'realities' they thought they know.

Definitions of Gender Sensitization

1. Gender sensitization refers to theories which claim that modification of the behavior of teachers and parents (etc.) towards children can have a causal effect on gender equality.
2. Gender sensitizing "is about changing behavior and instilling empathy into the views that we hold about our own and the other sex." It helps people in "examining their personal attitudes and beliefs and questioning the 'realities' they thought they know.

Need for Gender Sensitization

The need for gender sensitization is given below:

1. Sensitization is by far the most effective and non-confrontationist approach of reforming the society.
2. Gender sensitization is the process of changing the stereotype mind set of men and women, a mindset that strongly believes that men and

women are 'unequal entities' and hence have to function in different socio- economic space.

3. Gender sensitization increases the sensitivity of people at large towards women and their problems.
4. Gender sensitization tends to change the perception that men and women have of each other.
5. It creates a mindset in men that no longer sees in women the stereotypical image.
6. The gender sensitization process enable the teacher to become instrument of change as far as status of women is concerned.

Process of Gender Sensitization

Gender sensitization programme are generally organized for group of people. The very aim of such programme is to bring a definite orientation in thinking, practices and approach of individual concerning gender. The process includes the following.

Change in Perception: Gender sensitization in first instance to change the perception then men and women has each other. It creates a mindset in men that no longer sees in women the stereotypical image. The impression that women are weak and unequal entity no more clouds the minds of common men. Rather they are seen as responsible and equal partners in socio-economic development. At this stage men realize the ill effects of prevailing biases against women on family and society. The general perception of men and women on rigid gender division of labour and other orthodox practices relating to gender begin to die down. Women also tends to develop the perception that they all subordinate to men and they have an equality important role to play in decision making at household or community and organization level.

Recognition: Persons exposed to gender sensitization also start behaving differently. They look at the positively endowed qualities of women. At this stage the male folk begin to recognize the virtues of women and their importance to the family and society. There is open and spontaneous appreciation for women's involvement in multifarious activities. The men who were reluctant to acknowledgement of women's contribution, come forward under the influence of sensitization to recognize their contribution. Asa result women's contribution becomes more and more visible.

Further women's talents and capabilities that were going unnoticed and unexpected become subject of attention. Women too become more conscious of their capabilities and contribution and take pride in the same.

The message that gender sensitization conveys is loud and clear. Women do possess wisdom and therefore they must be involved in decision making process. They have concerns and therefore they should be treated with dignity and given equal chance in sharing of social and economic benefits. Women cutting across socio-economic boundaries tend to see their problems in large perspective of women development and come forward to recognize the effort of fellow women. They even visualize the important role that men can play in their socio-economic development

Accommodation: The barrier between men and women starts crumbling down and the society slowly over the personal problem of adjustment between them. Men tend to rationalize behavior by shedding their egos as far as gender relations are concerned. Instead of complaining or reacting to the behavior of women, men learn to exercise patience and restraint and take the things in a positive way. The difference between men and women narrows down as men allows women to function in a comfortable environment in the available socio-economic space. Problem creates i.e. those who were discouraging and obstructing women in their socio-economic participation become supporters of women empowerment. In the family, women start gaining importance as their opinion and suggestions are counted for overall development and management of family. At community and organizational level too, women were encouraged to play their role in matters of management. It is also observed that women, on their part tend to underplay the problems with their counterpart and wish to solve their problems through dialogue.

Action: Gender sensitized person become instrument of change as far as status of women in the society is concerned. They become action oriented and alert to see that women are neither neglected nor discriminated against and they get their due status in the society. Conscious efforts are made to create a favorable climate that allows nurturing and flourishing of women's talent and provides more flexibility and freedom to women. Moreover sensitized person becomes more inclined to take such steps that would make the gender equation more even and balanced. A number of affirmative actions are initiated to bring improvement in conditions of women. Women also become open rotaries of

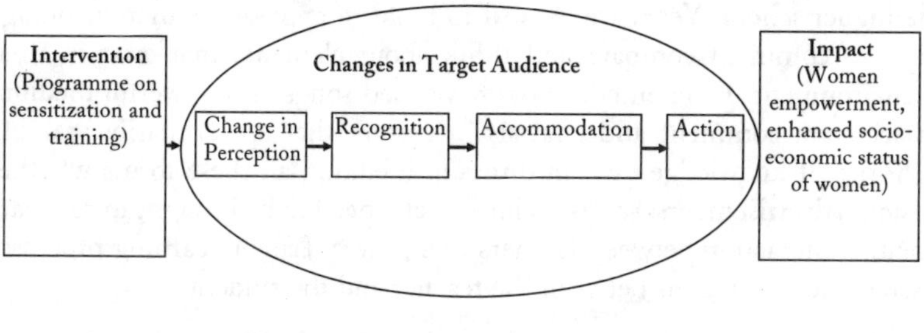

Figure 24.1: Gender Sensitization Process

women empowerment and organize themselves for collective action against different forms of bias and discriminatory practices. They tend to become pro-active to gain a respectable position in family and in the society.

Gender Sensitization Strategy

Pedagogic strategies to promote gender sensitization through education are as follows.

Participation: Most feminist educators understand that knowledge is not neutral, that teacher and students alike bring 'texts' of their own to the classroom which shape the transaction within it. Feminist pedagogy emphasizes participatory learning and teaching, within which subjectivity, emotions and experience have a definite and valued place. While participation is a powerful strategy, its pedagogic edge is blunted when it is ritualized. Participation, when seen as an instrument to achieve certain specified, predetermined objectives and where the teacher's own ideas dominate classroom discussion is not meaningful. It involves appreciation of importance of starting from experience of both students and teachers.

Recognizing Difference: Implicit in any effort at facilitating real participation is to work with the principle of recognizing difference. As children share reflect on their individual and collective experiences they simultaneously acknowledge and relate these to the experiences of others who may not form a part of their social reality. It is important that this difference not be marked by status but by diversity. Pedagogies that provide space for individual children to express themselves freely in the classroom, without fear of judgment and stereotyping are essential building blocks in working towards a future where they can have more critical engagements with what is being taught in the middle and higher classes.

Reading against the Grain: However it is possible and also necessary to be able to equip students to "read against the grain", to critically question received knowledge, whether it is biased text book or other literary sources in their own environment. Undoubtedly this is an objective that education would aspire for in the higher school. Yet there is need to build in approaches that encourage learners to comment compare and think about elements that exist in their own environment. Women educators have used songs as a powerful medium for discussion, comment and analysis in culture that are primarily oral. As repositories of knowledge exist in different medium, all these forms whether television, advertisements, songs, paintings etc. need to be brought in to create a dynamic interaction between learners themselves. Lateral learning processes necessitate new equations between the teacher and the student.

Acknowledging Power: A gender sensitive pedagogy is one that does not merely affirm different individual and collective experiences but it located these within larger structures of power. Question such as who is allowed to speak for whom? Whose knowledge is most valued? Inform engagements with learners. A Bachelor of Elementary Education teacher reflected on her course that the 'gender and schooling' paper has made her conscious of these realities. She said that she may not able to change everything but she will try and make difference where she can within the classroom. This translates into evolving different strategies for different learners. For example encouraging a child to speak in class may be important for some children and learning to listen to others may be of priority for others.

The Teacher as Facilitator

The teacher's role is to provide a safe space for children to express themselves and simultaneously to build in certain forms of interaction. While consolidating and constructively pushing the limits of learner's understanding, s/he needs to be conscious of how differences are expressed. An atmosphere of trust would make the classroom a safe space where children can share experiences, where conflict can be acknowledged and constructively questioned, where resolutions, however tentative, can be mutually worked out. A space where they can practice democratic ways of interacting with each other and build skills to negotiate with conflicts outside the school. For girls in particular, school and classrooms should be spaces to discuss processes of decision making, to interrogate the basis of their decisions and to make informed choices.

Need for Gender Sensitization in Schools

The school, classroom and teachers are all part and parcel of a society. In a society people may suffer from various problems such as poverty, gender discrimination, oppression, inequalities, gender biases and various other issues. Children in a school come from such various types of societies and in Indian societies we cannot chip away the reality of male domination. A father is the master of the house, irrespective of the fact that he may not be a bread winner. A male child is always given much freedom than his sister. When children come to school from such backgrounds, there are possibilities that there may be gender discrimination between peer groups or by teachers. Hence, there is a need for gender sensitization in schools so that children become aware of their roles in the society as future men and women.

Strategies/Measures of Schools to Sensitize Gender

Schools can take several measures to sensitize gender (equality) such as those given below:

1. Schools should employ staff who believe in and practice gender equality.

2. Schools should follow curriculum which is pro-girl child.
3. Moral Science education should be introduced as a regular subject at all levels and students should be examined in it like other graded subjects.
4. Female students should be encouraged to participate in activities which are similar to the activities in which the male students participate.
5. The course material should have the underlying theme of mutual respect between girls and boys and the same should be conveyed through the lessons.
6. Interactive sessions in the form of group discussions, debates and plays between boy and girl students should be conducted on the theme of gender equality under the supervision of teachers.
7. The school should fulfill its duty towards society by counselling parents and also other members of society to develop a healthy and positive attitude towards the female child (while not disregarding the male child).
8. Schools can felicitate female students publicly or during school assemblies for their extraordinary achievement in curricular and co-curricular areas. This would help girls to overcome the feelings of inferiority and help them to be confident.
9. Biographies and autobiographies of famous women should be included in the curriculum in order to inspire the female students to build their lives and career on similar lines.
10. Schools should encourage girls to be aware of their rights and duties, instill a sense of confidence in them, inspire them to be financially independent and impart training to them in self-defense.
11. Schools can definitely play a vital role to bring about a transformation in the mindset of the people towards the girl child and promote gender equality. A country can be called truly developed only if each male citizen treats each female citizen with respect, regard and equity. No other development is as important and crucial as the development of human values in society.

Role of Curriculum in Gender Sensitization

1. Graded concepts based on gender should be introduced through curriculum right from primary education.
2. The selection of texts and sketches should promote gender equality.
3. The "in-puts" given in texts need not project stereotyped roles for men and women. For example, look at the two sums given in a primary math text-book: Sum 1: Raman had Rs. 200 in his pocket. He spent Rs. 125 to fill petrol for his bike. How much money will be left with him? Sum 2: Kamala made 27 chapattis. Her children had eaten 13 chapattis. How many are left out? Why not Kamala ride the bike?

4. Upper Primary classes could have stories where women are protagonists.
5. Secondary and Senior Secondary sections could have lessons addressing the gender discrimination and class room activities could lead to discussions and debates on gender issues.

Role of Co-Curricular Activities in Gender Sensitization

Co-curricular activities would make a great impact in the minds of the young minds. Hence, the school and the educationists should explore the possible themes and related activities to promote gender sensitivity and complementing co-existence of men and women.

The themes may include:

1. mental agony and damage caused by violence against women,
2. unnoticed and unpaid excessive load of work thrust on women,
3. comforts and luxuries proffered to men and denied to women,
4. the yeomen service rendered by women at home,
5. great women achievers and the hardships they faced,
6. need for women empowerment,
7. exploration of opportunities for girls in this modern world,
8. need for equality and pleasant co-existence,
9. The activities may include: slogan writing, fancy dress competitions, elocution, debate, essay writing, story writing, poem writing etc.

Role of Community Based Activities in Gender Sensitization

Children from their opinions looking at the elders. Much depends on adults and the role model that they portray in front of the children. Hence, initiating community based activities involving the triangle of parents, teachers and media.

Role of Parents in Gender Sensitization

Parents' Meetings could be conducted with the themes of:

1. Needs & Rights of Girls
2. Issues connected with child abuse and protective measures to be taken
3. Stereotyping gender roles at home and how it affects attitude
4. Sensitizing boys at home positively.

Role of Media in Gender Sensitization

Media both print and visual media play an important role in forming opinions and spreading messages. Hence, the schools and Education departments should invite and involve the national as well as local media in sensitizing gender based issues. Seminars, workshops and campaigns could be worthy activities.

Bibliography

Annual Report (2008). Ministry of Human Resource Development, Department of Education, India.

Anumu, R. S. (2006). Women Education for Active Participation in the Next Millennium. A Seminar Paper Presented at the 3rd National Association of Colleges of Education at Lugard Hall, Kaduna.

Apeji, E. O. (2003). Women Education in Nigeria Challenges Facing It. A Seminar Paper Presented at Federation of Muslim Women Association Forum, Kano.

Athreye Viji. The Life of Transgender in India retrieved from www.mapsofindia.com/my-india/goverment/the-life-of-transgenders.

Belle, D. (1982). Ed. *Lives in Stress: Women and Depression*. New Delhi, Sage Distributors.

Bem, S. L. (1974). The Measurement of Psychological Androgyny. *Journal of Consulting and Clinical Psychology*, 42, 155-162.

Besser G. M, Thorner M. O. (1994). *Clinical Endocrinology*. Second Edition. Wolfe.

Bhasin Kamla (1993). *What is Patriarchy?* New Delhi, Raj Press.

Bhasin, K. (2000). *Understanding Gender*. New Delhi: Pauls Press.

Bhog, Dipta (2002). Gender and Curriculum. *Economic and Political Weekly*, 27th April, 37 (17). P.1638-1642.

Bottaro Jean, Visser Pippa, Dilley Liz, Cohen Sue (2006). *Social Sciences: Learner's Book, Grade 8*, Oxford University Press, South Africa.

Chappell, C. (2003). Researching Vocational Education and Training: Where to From Here? *Journal of Vocational Education and Training*, 55 (1), 21-32.

Chatterjee, J., & McCarrey, M. (1991). SexRole Attitudes, Values and Instrumental Expressive Traits of Women Trainees in Traditional vs NonTraditional Programmes. *Applied Psychology*, 40 (3), 281-297.

Christian Women Mirror (CWM) (2003). Celebrating the Girl-Child. A Seminar Paper presented at Deeper Life Association of Christian Women, Lagos.

Chung, Y. Y.-S. (2009). isdn.org. Retrieved June 30, 2014, from isdn.org/fileadmin/user_folder/pdf/: http://www.isdn.org.

D. Sadker & K. Zittleman (2003). *Teacher Education Textbooks: The Unfinished Gender Revolution*. Educational Leadership.

Desai N. and Krishnaraj M. (1980). *Women and Society in India* (2nd revised edition). Delhi, Ajanta Publication.

Dube, L. (2001). *Anthropological Explorations in Gender: Intersecting Fields*. New Delhi: Sage Publications Pvt. Limited.

Duffy, K. (1999). Education, Education and Citizenship. In C. Parsons. London: Routledge Publication.

E. Ohrn (1993). Gender, Influence and Resistance in School. *British Journal of Sociology of Education*. 147.

Euler-Ajayi, O. (2001). Training Women: A Reflection of the Nigerian Experience. *Education Today*. 2 (1), 5-11.

FAO (1997). Gender: The Key to Sustainability and Food Security. SD Dimensions, May 1997. http://www.fao.org/sd.

Faulkner, W. (2009). Doing Gender in Engineering Workplace Cultures: Part I — Observations from the Field. *Engineering Studies*, 1 (1) 3-18.

Fausto-Sterling, A. (2012). The Dynamic Development of Gender Variability. *Journal of Homosexuality*, 59, 398-421.

Fausto-Sterling, A. (2012). *Sex/Gender: Biology in a Social World*. New York: Routledge.

Feder, H. H., Phoenix, C. H., & Young, W. C. (1966). Suppression of Feminine Behaviour by Administration of Testosterone Propionate to Neonatal Rats. *Journal of Endocrinology*, 34(1), 131-132.

Fox Keller, Evelyn (1985). *Reflections on Gender and Science*. New Haven: Yale University Press.

Francis, B. (2000). Is Gender a Social Construct or a Biological Imperative? Family Futures: Issues in Research and Policy 7th Australian Institute of Family Studies Conference. http://www.aifs.gov.au/conferences/aifs7/francis.html

Freire, P. (2000). *Pedagogy of the Oppressed*. New York: Continuum.

G. S. Jaiswal, (March 2005). Foeticide: The Concept and the Law. *Social Welfare*, Vol.51, No.12.

G. Vijayeshwari Rao (2004), *Women and Society*. New Delhi, Himalaya Publishing House.

Gandhi N and Shah N. (1991). The Issue at State, Theory and Practice in the *Contemporary Women's Movement in India*. New Delhi; Kali for Women.

Gandhi Nandita and Shah Nandita (1992). *The Quota Question*, Akshara Mumbai.

Gender Identity Tobin, K., & Gallagher, J. J. (1987). The Role of Target Students in the Science Classroom. *Journal of Research in Science Teaching*, 24(1), 61–75.

Gerda Lerner, (1986). *The Creation of Patriarchy*, Oxford and New York: Oxford University Press.

Umrigar, Thrity. (2006). *The Space between us*. William Morrow and Company, Mumbai.

Girl's Power Initiative (GPI) (2002). Empower More Girls. A Paper Presented at Calabar Women Progress Association.

Government of India, M. O. (2001). Census of India-India at Glance: Scheduled Caste & Scheduled Tribes Population. New Delhi: Registrar General of India.

Gupta, Arun K. and K. Chander Zadoo (1999). 'Development of Women: Psychological Barriers', in *Association of Indian Universities* (ed.), Education and Women's Empowerment, AIU, New Delhi.

H. K. Dash; Krishna Srinath & B. N. Sadangi (2008). Gender Sensitization: Role in Reforming the Society. National Research Centre for Women in Agriculture.

Hacking, I. (1999). *The Social Construction of What?* Harvard University Press.

Hall, A. G. (2008). *Foundation Parents and Community Involvement in Early Childhood Education*. New York Harper and Row Press.

Henry, S. (2009). Social Construction of Crime. In J. Miller (Ed.), *21st Century Criminology: A Reference Handbook.* (pp. 296-306). Thousand Oaks: SAGE Publications, Inc. doi: 10.4135/9781412971997.n34

Hines, M. (1982). Prenatal Gonadal Hormones and Sex Differences in Human Behavior. *Psychological Bulletin*, 92(1), 56.

Howard, P. (2003). *Women and Plants, Gender Relations in Biodiversity Management and Conservation*. London, ZED Books.

Ibrahim, M. B. (1999). Social / Cultural Factors affecting Female Participation in Teaching Services at Post Primary Institutions in Zamfara State. Unpublished Master's thesis Faculty of Education, ABU Zaria.

Ijaduola U. (1996). *The Sisterhood, the Impact of Women Changing Roles in Social and Economic Life around the World*. New York: W. W. Marton and Company.

International Fund for Agricultural Development (IFAD) (2000). An IFAD Approach to Gender Mainstreaming: The Experience of the Latin America and the Caribbean Division. Rome, Italy: U. Quintily S.P.A.

Jane Pitcher and Whelahan (2005). *Fifty Key Concepts in Gender Studies*, New Delhi, Sage Publication.

Jones, K., Evans, C., Byrd, R., Campbell, K. (2000). Gender Equity Training and Teaching Behavior. *Journal of Instructional Psychology*, 27 (3), 173-178.

Julias, S. (1965). *Human Law and Human Justice*. U.S.A: Stanford University Press.

Kabeer, N. (2006). Social Exclusion and the MDGs: The challenges of durable inequalities' in *Asian Context*. University of Sussex: Institutes of Development Studies.

Kahle, J. B. (2004). Will Girls be Left Behind? Gender Differences and Accountability. *Journal of Research in Science Teaching*, 41(10), 961–969.

Kamala Bhasin (1993). *What is Patriarchy*, New Delhi, Kali for Women.

Kamala Bhasin (2000). *Understanding Gender*, New Delhi, Kali for Women.

Kanter, Rosabeth Moss (1977). *Men and Women of the Corporation*. New York: Basic Books.

Kapur, P. (1974). *Changing Status of the Working Women in India*. Delhi: Vikas Publishing House.

Kessler, S. (1990). The Medical Construction of Gender: Case Management of Intersexed Infants. Signs: *Journal of Women in Culture and Society*. 16 (1), 3-25.

Keval Kumar (2002). *Mass Communication in India*. Mumbai, Jaico Publishing House.

Khan, M. S. (1996). *Status of Women in Islam*. New Delhi: APH Publishing.

Khullar, M, (2005). *Writing the Women's Movement; A Leader*. New Delhi, Zubaan.

Kirk Jackie (2008). *Women Teaching in South Asia*. New Delhi SAGE.

Klein, S. (1985). *Handbook for Achieving Sex Equity through Education*. Baltimore, MD: The Johns Hopkins University Press.

Kolsky, E. (2010). The Body Evidencing the Crime': Rape on Trial in Colonial India, 1860–1947. *Gender & History*, 1.

Koopman, P., Gubbay, J., Vivian, N., Goodfellow, P., & Lovell-Badge, R. (1991). Male Development of Chromosomally Female Mice Transgenic for Sry. *Nature*, 351(6322), 117-121.

Kosambi, Meera (19954). Women's Oppression in the Public Gaze, RCWS SNDT Women's University, Mumbai.

Krishnamurthy, S. (1982). Impact of Social Legislations on the Criminal Law of India. Bangalore, R.R. Publisher.

Kumar, A. (2006). *Introduction to Sociology*. Jaipur: Rawat Publication.

Leopold, S., Beadling, L., Dobbs, M., Gebhardt, M., Lotke, P., Manner, P., Rimnac, C., & Wongworawat, M. (2014). Editorial: Fairness to All: Gender and Sex in Scientific Reporting. *Clin Orthop Relat Res*, 472, 391-392.

Lippa, R. A. (2005). *Gender, Nature, and Nurture*. Mahwah. NJ, Erlbaum.

Longman Dictionary of English language, Longman Group, Great Britain.

Macwan, M. (2006). *Dalits Rights, National Human Rights Commission*. New Delhi: Rajika Press Services Ltd.

Majumdar, M. (2004). *Social Status of Women in India*. New Delhi: Dominant Publishers.

Malti-Douglas, F. (2007). *Encyclopedia of Sex and Gender*. U.S.A: Thompson Gale.

Marshall, C.S. & Reihartz, J. (1997). *Gender Issues in the Classroom*. Clearinghouse, 70 (6), 333-338.

Mazumdar, Vina (1989). Gender Issues and.Educational Development: An Overview from *Asia, Occasional Paper*. New Delhi, Centre For Women's Development Studies.

Menon Nivedita (2004). *Recovering Subversion Feminist Politics beyond the Law*. New Delhi, Permanent Black.

Misra, Santosh Kumar (1999). 'Empowerment of Women through Extension Education' in *Association of Indian Universities* (ed): Education and Women's Empowerment, AIU, New Delhi

Money, J., & Ehrhardt, A. A. (1972). Man and Woman, Boy and Girl: Differentiation and Dimorphism of Gender Identity from *Conception to Maturity*.

Mueller R. F, Young I. D. (1996). *Emery's Elements of Medical Genetics*. Ninth Edition. Churchill Livingstone: New York.

Mukhopadhya and Singh W. (2007). *Gender Justice, Citizenship and development*. New Delhi, Zubaan.

N. Kabeer, & R. Subrahmanian (1996). Institutions, Relations and Outcomes: Framework and Tools for Gender- Aware Planning, in IDS Discussion Paper, No. 357, IDS, Brighton.

Narula, S. (2008). Equal by Law, Unequal by Caste: The 'Untouchable' condition in critical race perspective. New York: School of Law, New York University.

National Curriculum for Elementary and Secondary Education: A Framework, (1988), NCERT, New Delhi.

National Curriculum Framework for School Education, (2000), NCERT, New Delhi.

National Curriculum Framework for Teacher Education: Towards Preparing Professional and Human Teacher, (2009), National Council for Teacher Education, New Delhi,

National Curriculum Framework, (2005), NCERT, New Delhi.

National Policy for Empowerment of Women (2001). Department of Women and Child Development, Ministry of Human Resource Development, Government of India.

National Policy on Education (1986). Department of Education, MHRD, New Delhi

NCERT (2006). Gender Issues in Education.

NCERT (2006). National Focus Group on Gender Issues in Education (Position Paper), New Delhi

Nevid JS, Ficher-Rathus L, Rathus S. A. (1995). *Human Sexuality in a World of Diversity*. Second edition. Allyn and Bacon.

Newland, S. (2000). *Gender Equity*. London, Roberts Publishers.

Newspaper Indian Express (2014). Reserved Seats for Transgender Children in School retrieved from www.indianexpress.com/cities/Delhi

Nicholas Abercrombie, S. H. (2012). *Dictionary of Sociology*. New Delhi, Penguin Group.

Nigerian Kano. Monograph faculty of education. Kano.

Notwatski, N. & Grant, K. (2011). Sex is not Enough: The Need for Gender Based Analysis in Health Research. *Health Care for Women International*, 32 (4), 263-277.

Nozick, R. (1974). *Anarchy, State and Utopia*. U.S.A.: Harvard University Press.

Oakley, Ann. (1972). *Sex, Gender, and Society*. New York: Harper and Row.

Pant, M. (2006). Marginalised Citizenship of Nomades. In R. M. Tandon, *Participatory citizenship: Identity, Exclusion and Inclusion* (pp. 6-24). New Delhi: Sage Publication.

Partners for Law and Development (2004). *Cedaw: Restoring Rights to Women*. New Delhi: Partners for Law and Development & UNIFEM Publication.

Pillai, J.K. (1999). 'Empowering Women in India: New Roles for Education', in *Association of Indian Universities* (ed.): Education and Women's Empowerment, AIU, New Delhi.

Population Report (1994). Opportunities for Women. A *Journal of Health and Gender Equity*: U. S. A. 9-10.

Population Report (1999). Ending Violence against Women. A *Journal of Health and Gender Equity*: U. S. A. 9-13.

Position Paper National Focus Group on Gender Issues in Education (2006). NCERT, New Delhi

PRIA. (2013). Addressing Violence Against Dalit Women; Insights Based on Field Experiences in Haryana. New Delhi: PRIA.

Quadagno, D. M., Briscoe, R., & Quadagno, J. S. (1977). Effect of Perinatal Gonadal Hormones on Selected Nonsexual Behavior Patterns: A Critical Assessment of the Nonhuman and Human Literature. *Psychological Bulletin*, 84(1), 62.

Rajesh and MD Aslam Naved (2013). Approach Paper on Education and Employment opportunities & Challenges for Transgender, Ministry of Social Justice and Empowerment Government of India retrieved from www.socialjustice.nic.in/pdf/appendix5

Ramachandran, Vimala (2004). *Gender and Social Equity in Education: Hierarchies of Access*. New Delhi: Sage.

Rani, G. Vidya (1990). *Status of Women Employees in Government*. New Delhi, Mittal Publications.

Rao, A. (2003). *Gender and Caste*. New Delhi: Kali for Women.

Rawls, J. (1976). *A Theory of Justice*. Massachusetts: The Belknap Press of Harvard University Press Cambridge.

Regitz-Zagrosek, V. (2012). Sex and Gender Differences in Health. *European Molecular Biology Organization Reports*, 13 (7), 596-603.

Reinisch J. M, Beasley R. (1990). *The Kinsey Institute New Report on Sex*. Penguin Books.

Renold, R. (2006). Gendered Classroom Experiences. In C. Skelton, B. Francis, & L. Smulyan (Eds.), *The SAGE Handbook of Gender and Education* (pp. 439–452). Thousand Oaks, CA: Sage.

Report of the Central Advisory Board of Education (CABE). (2010). Ministry of Human Resource Development, Government of India, National Book Trust, New Delhi, India.

Rosemari Tong, Feminist Thought: A Comprehensive Introduction.

S. Stacki (2002). Women Teachers Empowered in India: Teacher Training Through A Gender Lens. Executive Summary.

Saigol, R. (2003). His Rights/Her Duties: Citizen and Mother in the Civics Discourse. Indian *Journal of Gender Studies*, 10:3, pp 379-403.

Sandhan Shodh Kendra (1996). *Gender Samvedanshilta va Shiksha*. Udaipur: Rajya Sthariya Karyashala.

Saramma Royce (2005). Stress Experienced by Homemakers with Young Children. Avinashilingam Deemed University, *Social Welfare*, Vol.: 51, No.12.

Sarkar Aanchal (2006). *Gender and Development*. Pragun Publication, New Delhi.

Satashivam. P (2012). Rights of Transgender People: Sensitising Officers to Provide Access to Justice.http://www.hcmadras.tn.nic.in/jacademy/Article/PSJ-CJO-SPEECH-Royappetah.pdf

Sen, A. (2004). *Social Exclusion: Concept Application and Security*. New Delhi: Critical Quest.

Sen, A. (2010). *Development as Freedom*. New Delhi: Oxford University Press.

Sharma R.K. (2004). *Demography and Population Problems*. Atlantic Publications & Distributors, New-Delhi -110027.

Sharma, A. (2002). *Women in Indian Religions*. New Delhi: Oxford University Press.

Shaywitz, B. A., Shaywltz, S. E., Pugh, K. R., Constable, R. T., Skudlarski, P., Fulbright, R. K., & Gore, J. C. (1995). Sex Differences in the Functional Organization of the Brain for Language.

Sinha K. (2011). Domestic Violence Linked to Deaths of 18 Lakh Girls, published in the *Times of India*, Pune.

Spence, J. T., & Helmreich, R. L. (1980). Masculine Instrumentality and Feminine Expressiveness: Their Relationship with Sex Role Attitudes and Behaviors. *Psychology of Women Quarterly*, 5, 147-163.

Springer, K., Stellman, J., & Jordan-Young, R. (2012). Beyond a Category of Differences: A Theoretical Frame and Good Practice Guidelines for Researching Sex/Gender in *Human Health. Social Science & Medicine*, 74, 1817-1824.

Srivastava Gouri (2012). *Gender and Peace in Textbooks and Schooling Processes*. New Delhi, Concept Publishing Company Pvt. Ltd.

Srivastava Gouri, Yadav Mona (2013). *Training Material for Teacher Educators on Gender Equality and Empowerment*, Vols. I, II and III, NCERT, New Delhi

Statistics of School Education (2006-11). MHRD, GOI, New Delhi.

Syllabus for Secondary and Higher Secondary Classes (2006). National Curriculum Framework 2005, NCERT, New Delhi

The Social Construction of Race. The Atlantic. http://www.theatlantic.com/national/ archive/2013/05/the-social-construction-of-race/275974/

Thorne, Barrie (1993). *Gender Play: Girls and Boys in School*. New Brunswick, NJ: Rutgers University Press.

Tong, Rosemanie (1998). *Feminist Thought: A comprehensive Introduction*. Rovtledge, London.

U.S. Food and Drug Administration (2014), Evaluation of Sex-Specific Data in Medical device Clinical Studies. Washington, D.C.

Veena Poonacha (2007). Different Voices, Divergent Struggles, Paper Presentation at Indian Academy of Social Science.

Wadekar S. (2010). War for Equality by Working Women, published in *Sakal* Daily Marathi News Paper, Kolhapur.

Wayne, K. W. (2000). *Citizenship in Diverse Societies*. New Delhi: Oxford University Press.

Westheimer R. K. (1994). *Dr. Ruths's Encyclopedia of Sex*. Continuum: New York.

What do we mean by Sex and Gender? (2015). World Health Organization.

Wikipedia, The free encyclopaedia retrieved from http://en.m.wikipedia.org/wiki/transgender

World Professional Association for Transgender Health (WPATH). (2011). Standards of Care for the Health of Transsexual, Transgender, and Gender-Nonconforming People. Minneapolis: WPATH. http://www.aifs.gov.au/conferences/aifs7/francis.html